CALIFORNIO VOICES

Soldado de cuera, reprinted by permission of Museo de América, Madrid

CALIFORNIO VOICES
The Oral Memoirs of José María Amador and Lorenzo Asisara

Number 3 in the Al Filo:
Mexican American Studies Series

Translated and Edited by
Gregorio Mora-Torres

University of North Texas Press
Denton, Texas

10 9 8 7 6 5 4 3 2
Permissions:
University of North Texas Press
1155 Union Circle #311336
Denton, TX 76203-5017

The paper used in this book meets the minimum requirements of the American National Standard for Permanence of Paper for Printed Library Materials, z39.48.1984. Binding materials have been chosen for durability.

Library of Congress Cataloging-in-Publication Data

Amador, José María, 1794–1883.
    Californio voices: the oral memoirs of José María Amador and Lorenzo
Asisara ; translated and edited by Gregorio Mora-Torres.
        p. cm.— (Al filo ; no. 3)
    Based on manuscripts originally recorded by Thomas Savage in 1877 for the
Bancroft Library.
    Includes bibliographical references and index.
    English and Spanish parallel text; study in English.
    ISBN 1-57441-191-8 (cloth : alk. paper)
    ISBN-13 978-1-57441-438-7 (paper : alk. paper)
        1. Amador, Jose Maria, 1794–1883—Interviews. 2. Asisara, Lorenzo,
    b. 1819—Interviews. 3. Mexicans—California—Interviews. 4. California—
    History—To 1846—Biography. 5. California—History—1846–1850—
    Biography. 6. Frontier and pioneer life—California. 7. California—Ethnic rela-
    tions. 8. Indians, Treatment of—California—History—19th century. 9. Indians
    of North America—Missions—California—History—19th century. I. Asisara,
    Lorenzo, b. 1819. II. Mora-Torres, Gregorio, 1954– III. Savage, Thomas,
    b. 1823. IV. Title. V. Series.
    F864.A525 2005
    979.4'03'092—dc22
    [B]   2004063717

Number 3 in Al Filo: Mexican American Studies Series

Illustrations reprinted by permission of The Bancroft Library,
Berkeley, California

Cover portrait of José María Amador, reprinted by permission
of the Amador County Archives

En Memoria de Magdaleno Mora Rojas (1919–2004)

Dedico esta obra a un historiador nato,
a mi padre, Don Magdaleno Mora Rojas.
Él vino de Michoacán a California a trabajar como bracero
y en algunos años se volvió traquero.

Como Don José María Amador, mi padre siempre admiró
la belleza del valle de Santa Clara
y siempre aprecío su capacidad para crear riqueza económica
y a la vez impulsar y fomentar riqueza cultural.
Y
en memoria de mi hermana
Magdalena Mora
(1952–1981)

* * *

In Memoriam

Magdaleno Mora Rojas (1919–2004)
I dedicate this book to a natural historian, my father,
Don Magdaleno Mora Rojas.
He came to California from Michoacán, México, to work as a
field worker and in a few years became a track laborer.

Like José María Amador, my father always admired the beauty
of the Santa Clara Valley and was always aware
of its capacity to create economic wealth and
to develop and promote cultural wealth.

Also, in memory of my sister
Magdalena Mora (1952–1981)

Contents

Illustrations, pp. 98–109

Frontispiece: Portrait of a soldado de cuera
Map of Northern Alta California, p. 26

Acknowledgments

This work is the product of collaboration by numerous people and institutions. I would like to thank The Bancroft Library at the University of California, Berkeley for giving me permission to publish José María Amador's *Memorias sobre la Historia de California.* I would like to express my appreciation to Larry Cenotto, archivist of the Amador County Archives and to the personnel at the San Jose History Museum for their assistance in locating materials on José María Amador. I also would like to recognize the University of Houston's Recovering the U.S. Hispanic Literary Heritage Project for a Grant-in-Aid that I received in 1996 to begin the process of transcribing and editing Amador's work.

I would like to thank Violeta Salinas for her dedication in transcribing and editing the entire original Spanish manuscript of the José María Amador *Memorias.* I would also like to thank Norbertha Torres for her help in revising the grammar in the Spanish version of the memoir so that it would conform to modern standards. I am very grateful to Karina Parra for providing much-needed assistance in helping to edit several versions of the entire manuscript and for her help in preparing the final Spanish and English drafts for publication; she supported this project from the beginning of the process to the end. Furthermore, I would like to recognize Phillip Tabera and Melody Knutson for reading and offering many helpful comments on several drafts of the memoir. I would like to express my gratitude to Erlinda Yañez and José C. Gonzales for providing me with much-needed technical assistance. I would like to thank Jeff Paul, Simón Domínguez, José Carrasco, Joel Franks, and Jesús Martínez-Saldaña for their encouragement to complete this work and other research on the Mexicans of Northern California. I would like to recognize Jaime E. Rodriguez, my mentor and friend, for inspiring me to research the history of México. Finally, I would like to thank my family for their steady emotional support. Las gracias van para mis padres Magdaleno y Esther; para mi hermanos: Ignacio, para Carmelo y su esposa Rosa, para Juan y su esposa Lorraine, para Hugo y su esposa Gloria; y también para mi

sobrina Magdalena y mis sobrinos, Juan Ignacio, Moctezuma, Salomón, Samuel, Hugo, y Xavier Omar.

I would like to extend my gratitude to the press readers whose insightful observations and valuable recommendations no doubt contributed immensely to the quality of this work. I would like to thank the director of University of North Texas Press, Ron Chrisman, for agreeing to publish this manuscript in a very unique format, as a truly bilingual historical work. Lastly, I would like to extend my heartfelt thanks to Roberto Calderón, editor of the Al Filo series, for having faith in this project from the time I first proposed it to him and for pushing it through the lengthy publication process.

Editor's Introduction

My connection with the memoirs of Don José María Amador was established quite unexpectedly. In the early 1990s, I started assisting a group of scholars from Stanford University who were working on a research project on the Chicano/Latino community of the Santa Clara Valley. The project researchers were studying various aspects of the Chicano/Latino community and one area that Professors Renato Rosaldo and Bill Flores—the research directors—thought needed to be examined was the valley's early Spanish and Mexican history. After first reading secondary sources, I visited The Bancroft Library to examine its well-known collection of early sources. While there I discovered a less-known collection of manuscripts that had been dictated by Californios, under the auspices of Hubert H. Bancroft, in the 1870s.

Since I was interested in the Mexican Californios of the Santa Clara Valley, I soon ran into the dictations of Juan Pablo Bernal, José Antonio Berreyessa, and José María Amador, a native of the Presidio of San Francisco. These memoirs had been transcribed by several individuals whom Hubert H. Bancroft had hired to assist him in his massive research project on the history of California. The best known of his research assistants were Thomas Savage and Henry Cerruti, who with their command of the Spanish language, traveled extensively throughout the state seeking out "sources." Chicana literary critic Rosaura Sánchez in *Telling Identities: The Californio Testimonios* argues that Bancroft saw himself as the "historian" and wanted to control both the "interviewers" and the "sources." Hence, Bancroft issued his employees scripted questions to direct them during the interviews. The interviewers initially had a difficult time getting access to the Californio sources. Even those Californios who did not understand English well were quite aware of the contempt that many Anglo-Americans, especially writers, had for them. They knew that for a long time Anglo-Americans had regarded them as lazy, backward, ignorant, and primitive. Californios were also aware that Anglo-American writers of California's past had written extensively

1

about the primitive conditions that existed in California prior to the United States' takeover of the region and about the great transformation that it had experienced since then. Mary Luise Pratt, who in her book *Imperial Eyes: Travel Writing and Tranculturation* critically analyzes works by European travelers to Africa and South America during the eighteenth and nineteenth centuries, would probably also consider these California writings colonial discourse. Obviously, the Californios were not pleased with the Anglo-American interpretation of their history.

The door to the Californio sources was opened when Henry Cerruti visited General Mariano Guadalupe Vallejo at his home in Sonoma in 1874. Vallejo, who at one time had been the wealthiest and largest landowner in the state and had figured prominently in California politics during the Mexican period, had already written a history of California prior to the U.S. annexation. To his dismay, the 900-page manuscript was destroyed during a house fire. Initially, Vallejo, who by now was very suspicious of Anglo-Americans, was hesitant to collaborate with Cerruti because he distrusted the Anglo-Americans' historiography of California. Nonetheless, Cerruti, born in Italy, was able to win Vallejo's trust and succeeded in convincing him of the need for the Californios' point of view to be included in the history of California. Apparently, Vallejo accepted Cerruti's arguments, and he soon began to collaborate with him and even allowed him to copy or borrow a vast collection of documents from the Mexican period that were in his possession. In addition, perhaps with the encouragement and assistance of Cerruti who called him a "man of literary taste," Vallejo began writing his memoirs again. He called them, "Recuerdos historicos y personales tocante la alta California." After they were completed in 1875, the reminisces consisted of five volumes and almost one thousand pages. Vallejo also aided Bancroft and his agents by writing letters to friends and relatives across California urging them to collaborate with the Bancroft history project and accompanied Cerruti to San Jose, Monterey, and Santa Cruz to personally call upon friends and acquaintances, making it clear that they had a duty to clarify the history of California. While it could be argued that Vallejo's actions were motivated by a selfish desire to ingratiate himself with Bancroft as well as because he wanted to be given a favorable place in history, his actions can also be interpreted as a form of opposition to the way that California's history was being written and as a way to ensure that the Californios would not be erased from their homeland's history.

After becoming aware of Vallejo's involvement in the Bancroft project, the Californios were more receptive to it. One problem that emerged from the method used to create these memoirs is that it required two individuals to produce them. For this reason, Sánchez believes that these dictations must be treated as "mediated narratives," that is, that they were collaborative works, products of Bancroft's transcribers and the Californio narrators. Clearly, she maintains that the memoirs were not independent works of Californios and undoubtedly were controlled and directed by Bancroft and his agents.

Sánchez is correct in arguing that the Anglo-American transcribers had some control over the interview process, yet this does not mean that Californio narrators were completely powerless to influence it. Indeed, the Californios had the power to refuse to be interviewed or even to control the interview. Often, it was the Californios' perception of the interviewer that would determine how they would respond to him. Henry Cerruti, for instance, had a difficult time trying to gain the trust of the Californios even while he was carrying with him letters of introduction from Mariano Guadalupe Vallejo. In his own memoirs edited by Margaret Mollins and Virginia E. Thickens, *Ramblings in California*, Cerruti writes that when he went to the Santa Clara Valley, he had a hard time convincing the local Californios to narrate their recollections to him because they were suspicious of his intentions. At times, that distrust was merited. For example, when Cerruti rode to the Bernal Ranch, he encountered a person who called himself Francisco Peralta; Cerruti doubted that that was his real name. After reading the Vallejo letter several times, Peralta took out an old, dusty English translation of the "Diary of Father Font," the priest who had accompanied Captain Juan Bautista de Anza during his long trek across the Arizona desert, which brought civilian settlers to California from Sonora. When Peralta saw Cerruti put the diary inside his overcoat, he quickly informed Cerruti, "General Vallejo requested that I should allow you to copy it. That, I am willing to do, but as to giving to you, my Font, that is out of the question." As was his practice, Cerruti, then took out a bottle of liquor and proceeded to offer a drink to Peralta to get him to open up. Peralta offered his views on how John C. Frémont and his small band of followers had abused the Mexican population of the Santa Clara Valley but refused to say anything about his own life. When he left the Bernal Ranch, Cerruti took with him the Font diary. A few days later Peralta wrote Vallejo claiming that Cerruti had stolen his beloved copy of "Father Font." Vallejo apparently informed Bancroft of Cerruti's action and the historian had the diary sent back to Peralta.

Peralta and the other Californios had reason to distrust Cerruti. Although Cerruti considered himself a true friend of Vallejo and the Californios and he often wrote in his memoirs that the Bear Flaggers were a band of lawless individuals and that the Anglo squatters were a bunch of thieves, he often acted very dishonestly. He offered only liquor to his sources and refused to discuss a monetary compensation for them, perhaps acting under orders from Bancroft. Moreover, he also deceived his friend Vallejo. After Vallejo allowed Cerruti to take his manuscripts to Cerruti's hotel room in Sonoma, the latter broke his pledge and secretly sent them to San Francisco, where Bancroft's band of clerks could copy them. Moreover, wherever he traveled, Cerruti always asked Californios to allow their historical documents to be copied or encouraged them to donate them to the historian Hubert H. Bancroft.

Cerruti was able to use Vallejo's letters of introduction to gain access to the Californios, but they did not necessarily allow him to interview them or only offered small interviews. Sometimes they refused to talk to him and denied that they had any historical documents. When Cerruti was in the Santa Clara Valley, for example, he went to visit the family of California's first Mexican governor, Luis Argüello. The person who met him was one of the dead governor's sons who told him that he did not know much about history and that the family had burned whatever historical documents they had possessed. Realizing that he needed help, Cerruti telegraphed Vallejo in San Francisco asking him to rush to Santa Clara. When Vallejo arrived, both Cerruti and Vallejo visited the Argüello home. The widow of Argüello received them and consented to talk to "Guadalupe" about her views on the American occupation of California. As a result of this strategy, a formula was developed in which Vallejo would interview the narrators and Cerruti would simply write down the narratives. This technique would be repeated several times as the two friends traveled to Monterey. They repeated it again when they returned to San Francisco by steamer. While at the Santa Cruz wharf, Vallejo ran into two old soldiers: Francisco Rodríguez and someone by the name of Pérez. Both of them recounted life experiences that they had shared with Vallejo in their youth. Yet, Rodríguez also narrated the tragic loss of his land after the U.S. occupation of California. He noted that even though his property had a perfect title, the Americans had still declared it illegal by using their courts. Throughout the interview, Cerruti merely listened and wrote down their interesting stories, preferring not to ask questions. He seemed to understand that the two Californios, like others, did not really trust him.

Rosaura Sánchez notes that as Bancroft's agents visited most of California, they managed to persuade a sizeable number of Californios to collaborate with them. Sánchez believes that eventually about sixty-two Californios—mostly men but including some women—agreed to narrate their memoirs. Some of these dictations were fairly extensive but a good number of them consisted of only a few short pages. These Californios agreed to speak through the "mediated narratives," but Sánchez points out that they allowed them to be controlled and used by Hubert H. Bancroft and other Anglo-American historians. Once the Californios gave their interviews, Bancroft's transcribers and Bancroft himself were free to interpret and use the information as they chose. Sánchez, however, believes that by narrating their remembrances the Californios also succeeded in countering the Anglo-American historiography of California. Mary Louise Pratt goes further by suggesting that in some cases the narrator shapes the perspectives of the transcribers. Although Bancroft and his research assistants were not travel writers, Pratt's observations can apply to them. She writes: "Every travel account has this heteroglossic dimension; its knowledge comes not just out of a traveler's sensibility and powers of observation, but out of interaction and experience usually directed and managed by the 'travelees,' who are working from their own understandings of their world and of what the Europeans are and ought to be doing" (135–36). Hence, even though Bancroft wanted to "invent" California according to his Anglo-American perspective he was prevented from doing so by his reliance on the Californios' views of their homeland.

Although Sánchez notes that the California memoirs are controlled texts, she also considers them authentic testimonials, or *testimonios*. She contends that there is a long tradition of *testimonios* in Latin America, which dates back to the chronicles of the Spanish conquistadors, explorers, and missionaries. Today, the *testimonio* tradition continues and is best exemplified by the dictations of Jesusa Palancares to writer Elena Poniatowska in México and those of Guatemala's Rigoberta Menchu and Peru's Domitila Barrios de Chungara. Sánchez asserts that despite their background as "mediated texts," the *testimonios* empowered the Californios, since they gave them a voice to denounce atrocities and injustices committed against them while at the same time allowing them to recount their lives and tell their own stories. Hence, while the collaborative method of the memoirs resulted in some loss of control by the Californios, they also won a voice to counter the hegemonic interpretation of history.

In *My History, Not Yours: The Formation of Mexican American Autobiography,* Genaro M. Padilla considers the Californio narratives to be autobiographical although they were products of a collaborative process. He notes that while the narratives were not self-composed by the narrators, through them, the narrators were able to recreate themselves and reproduce their past. For Padilla, these narratives reflected the very human desire of human beings to at least control their past if they were no longer capable of directing their present or shaping their future.

Both Sánchez and Padilla agree that the Californios who were interviewed by Bancroft's agents were guilty of being nostalgic. By the 1870s, most of them, including Vallejo, had been dispossessed of their land, reduced to abject poverty, and had become politically disempowered. Undoubtedly, the Californios harbored a deep resentment; some even expressed intense anger towards Anglo-Americans whom they blamed for their present dire condition. Hence, for Sánchez and Padilla, the Californio **testimonios** represent one last attempt to remember the past and in this act of not forgetting they were ensuring that they, too, would not be forgotten by history. Pratt also would concur with this observation.

While the Californios were able to reconstruct themselves and their past through their remembrances, Hubert H. Bancroft would have the last word on what to do with them. Bancroft, a self-centered cultural entrepreneur, believed that profit could be made by the writing of California's history. Thus, he chose to use the narratives merely as sources for his seven-volume *History of California* and another book, *California Pastoral.* Because Bancroft never considered the Californio narratives as anything but sources, he never intended to publish them. Bancroft even refused to publish Vallejo's own writings because he also regarded them only as source materials. Bancroft's refusal to publish his work profoundly hurt Vallejo, who interpreted his action as just another Anglo-American betrayal. It should be noted that Vallejo had come to see Bancroft as a genuine friend and had earlier donated the entire collection of historical documents that he owned to his library. Eventually all the Californio narratives, along with the Vallejo documents and thousands of other Californio, Spanish, and Mexican documents, were given to the University of California as part of The Bancroft Library Collection.

Sánchez and Padilla believe that it is essential to Chicano Studies scholarship, particularly to history, to bring back to life the testimonios of the old Californios. Sánchez writes that the "bones of 'our dead' have too long lain

cluttered in the mausoleum of 'the enemy,' and that without examining the Californios' contradictory countering of dominant regimes of representation embedded in these texts we will not be able to 'fan the spark of hope' in our construction of new politics of representation"(xi). Similarly, Padilla advises on the need to begin the "archaeological recovery" of perhaps hundreds of Californio memoirs, manuscripts and other documents that are hidden away at locations such as The Bancroft Library, The Huntington Library, state and regional historical societies, and even university special collections. To accomplish this, he urges that the narratives of the Californio *antepasados* must be rescued from "their lowercase status, chipping away the Bancroft text that encases them, brushing the dust off their covers, and, by publishing and reading them, restoring the presence of their voices"(26).

While Sánchez and Padilla do discuss the José María Amador memoir in their studies of the Californio narratives, they do not analyze it in any great length. Sánchez mostly focused on Mariano Guadalupe Vallejo's "Recuerdos historicos y personales tocante la alta california," Juan Bautista Alvarado's "Historia de California," and Antonio Coronel's "Cosas de California" while Padilla centers his analysis of the Californio works on the writings of Mariano Guadalupe Vallejo. Interestingly, Thomas Savage and Hubert Bancroft found the Amador narrative of immense value to the study of California history. When Thomas Savage went to the Santa Clara Valley he sought out Juan Pablo Bernal but was not too impressed with him. At the urging of Bernal, however, Savage went to visit the by-then aging José María Amador who was residing at the home of his youngest daughter, María Antonia Amador de Rodríguez, in the small hamlet of Whiskey Hill, just outside of Watsonville. Although he only stayed one week, Savage was astonished with the wealth of information that Amador gave him. At 229 handwritten pages, the Amador *Memorias* is clearly one of the lengthiest Californio works.

When Thomas Savage, the Havana-born son of New England parents, began his interviews with José María Amador, he undoubtedly was determined to follow the prescribed format that Hubert H. Bancroft had established for the Californio narratives. Yet, from the start of the interviews, it would be Amador, like many of his fellow Californios, who determined their direction. Often it was Amador who decided what the topics of discussion would be and what materials would be relevant for the narrative. For example, when Amador thought that it would be a good idea to include the views of indigenous people in the narrative, he invited his friend Lorenzo Asisara,

who had come to visit him, to comment on the Indian experience at the missions. It was through Asisara that Savage learned about the death of Father Andrés Quintana at Mission Santa Cruz. Amador also controlled what part of his life story was not to be told by again determining the direction of the narrative. This could be observed by examining the organizational structure of the memoir. Instead of commenting on his life after he returned from the gold fields during the Gold Rush, Amador regressed in time, preferring to talk about his younger years. Hence, unlike other Californios, he chose not to discuss his relations or encounters with Anglo-Americans during the crucial years of the 1850s and 1860s when Californios were facing very difficult times. Amador, moreover, decided not to discuss the loss of his Rancho San Ramón and the increasing impoverishment of himself and his family.

Although the Amador *Memorias* is a co-production by him and Thomas Savage, it is difficult not to see it both as autobiography and as a testimonio. The *Memorias* reveals a real, living person speaking through it. This person, who at times is given to exaggeration and the telling of tall tales, displays a wonderful sense of humor and marvelous wit. Furthermore, the **memorias** reveals a person whose voice vividly evokes sadness, anger, rancor, and resentment as well as charm, happiness, and joy. Lastly, this memorias presents an individual who keenly observed his homeland's political life and its misfortunes and who clearly struggled to make sense of the powerful changes that his *patria chica* experienced throughout his long lifetime.

Experts in the field of California history have long been familiar with the memoirs of Don José María Amador. Like Hubert H. Bancroft, many of them have used these memoirs in their writings to discuss California's Spanish and Mexican periods. Yet, in spite of the fact that the Amador *Memorias* has been a well-known historical source, it has been largely inaccessible to English language researchers and the general reader. To remedy this situation, I have taken the initiative to make this work available to the general public. My sole purpose in publishing this manuscript is to allow Don José María Amador to tell his story in his own words. Other scholars may decide to interpret the *Memorias*'s text for the modern readers.

To make the Amador memoirs available to the general reader, I have translated them from Spanish. Translation work is more an art than an exact science since it is often a subjective and interpretive process. My only hope is that I was able to accurately and fairly capture Amador's words, feelings, and thoughts although I realize I may not always have succeeded.

In terms of the methodology, I have re-organized Amador's *Memorias* into chapters to make them easier to read. Similarly, I have changed the punctuation to make the manuscript read and flow better. I have also strongly felt that any publication of the Amador *Memorias* must also include the Spanish original manuscript. Through it, the Spanish language readers will be able to capture the voice of Amador, which may have been altered in the English translation. To make the Spanish manuscript easier to read, I have also divided it into chapters. Moreover, the accents have been modified to conform to the modern standards of the Spanish language. Finally, at times, the punctuation has been changed to ensure greater clarity.

Throughout the English translation and this Introduction, Spanish terms will be put in boldface. These are terms that will be defined in the Glossary at the back of the book. Keeping them untranslated in the text maintains the unique flavor of Amador's *Memorias*.

* * *

Individuals have been writing about California since Spanish and other European navigators began to explore its coastline as early as the 1540s. Ever since California was first colonized by Spain in 1769, its government officials and Franciscan missionaries wrote their superiors in Mexico City countless letters and reports on the region's physical conditions, explorations that were undertaken, the local problems, or troubles with the indigenous peoples. Many of these documents are housed in the national archives of México and Spain; a good number of them now are a part of collections at The Bancroft Library, The Huntington Library, or local archives in California.

Since the late 1700s and early 1800s, foreign visitors also have published their accounts in several languages, including Spanish, English, French, and Russian. Individuals such as Bruno de Hezeta (1775), Juan Francisco de la Bodega y Quadra (1775 and 1792), Count La Pérouse (1785), Alejandro Malaspina (1791), George Vancouver (1792), José Longinos Martínez (1792), and Otto von Kotzebue (1825) explored and studied California. The accounts by Europeans provide descriptions about the vast natural wealth and the beauty of California while often portraying the local peoples as primitive "children of nature." In *Imperial Eyes: Travel Writing and Transculturation*, Pratt places these travelogues into three categories: sentimentalist, scientific, and commercial. She notes that sentimentalist writings depicted the writer as an individual who had to face epic trials, challenges, and encoun-

ters while exploring and "discovering" strange new lands. Other European travelers saw themselves as scientists who wanted to measure and map the geography as well as identify and catalogue "new" species of fauna and flora. They considered themselves scientific contributors to the just emerging scholarly field of natural history. Still other writers traveled the world to look for commercial and other types of economic opportunities. Pratt believes that all these writers used the colonial discourse in which they perceived themselves as "civilizers," and the people they came into contact as "natives," who possessed primitive cultures and lagged in human evolution.

Many of Pratt's observations on European travel writers can also be applied to the Euro-Americans writers who arrived in California before it was annexed by the United States. In the 1820s, visitors from the United States joined other travelers in writing their observations of California and its people. The accounts by Anglo-Americans, such as Henry Dana, Alfred Robinson, and Edwin Bryant, covered the same topics as their European counterparts but focused more on the negative attributes of Californios, both indigenous peoples and colonists. These writers tended to portray the natives of California as lazy, immoral, and primitive. Interestingly, Anglo-American male writers generally depicted Californio women in a more positive light than they did the men.

In 1877, Hubert H. Bancroft's researcher Thomas Savage, who was born in Havana, Cuba, and was the Spanish-speaking son of Anglo-American parents, traveled to San José to interview Juan Pablo Bernal on the Spanish/Mexican history of California. Bernal, who saw himself as a "capitalist," was a member of one of the town's most prominent Mexican families. Bernal told Savage about how he and some town residents pursued some Indian horse thieves until they killed all of them. He also told Savage about his role as a Mexican soldier defending his native homeland, California, from the American invaders during the Mexican War of 1846 and about the killing of some of his family members by "Bear Flaggers."[1] Savage wrote down Bernal's recollection but did not regard him a significant historical source. Because Savage thought of Bernal as a "giddy [and] rambling" person, he perceived him as a source that could not be taken very seriously. Savage, however, was thankful that Bernal recommended that he talk to his

---

[1] Juan Bernal, "Memorias de D. Juan Bernal," MS C-D 43, Bancroft Library, University of California, Berkeley.

brother-in-law, José María Amador. Savage found Amador living with his youngest daughter in the small village of Whiskey Hill, near the town of Watsonville. After spending seven to eight days with the eighty-three-year-old Amador, Savage realized that Amador had quite a story to tell about his life as a presidio soldier—*soldado de cuera*—and about the political events that he observed during his long lifetime. Amador dictated his rather extensive memoirs to Savage during that short span of time. It is through these recollections that Savage and other researchers are able to capture notable glimpses of Amador's rather amazing life, beginning with his experiences as a soldier, mostly at the Presidio of San Francisco under the Spanish and Mexican regimes. Had Savage stayed a longer period of time, who knows what other interesting stories Amador might have revealed to him? Much of the information that Amador gave Savage was used by Hubert H. Bancroft in his classic works, the seven-volume *History of California* and *California Pastoral*. It should be noted that while Bancroft used Amador as his principal source in examining presidio life, he rarely acknowledged him.[2]

Besides the information that José María Amador provides in his memoirs, little is known of his personal life. Savage notes that Amador was born in the Presidio of San Francisco on December 18, 1794. His father, Pedro Amador, was a soldier who attained the rank of sergeant and spent many years in Baja California before coming to the founding of the Presidio of San Francisco. It is difficult to accurately identify José María Amador's racial background. Although Jack Forbes lists his father as a Spaniard from Guadalajara, it is doubtful that he was a full-blooded Spaniard.[3] In his study of Hispano/Mexican pioneers of the San Francisco Bay Region, Forbes maintains that a great number of the soldiers and settlers had non-white ancestry. Many of these people were classified as *Mulatos, Mestizos, Coyotes, Moriscos*, and *Pardos*.

[2]H. H. Bancroft refused to acknowledge not only Amador but all of his Californio sources, including Mariano Guadalupe Vallejo. Hence, it should not be surprising when Bancroft also decided not to publicly credit the work of his research assistants, Henry Cerruti, Thomas Savage, and Henry L. Oak. In his article "Creation and Recreation of Californio Sociey," Douglas Monroy notes that Henry L. Oak, who did most of the writing of the seven-volume *History of California*, became very bitter when Bancroft simply did not acknowledge his work.
[3]Jack D. Forbes, "Hispano-Mexican Pioneers of the San Francisco Bay Region: An Analysis of Racial Origins," *Aztlan* 14, no. 1 (1983): 184. Forbes notes that the term "Español" does not necessarily indicate that a person had pure Spanish blood. An "Español" could also be a person of one-quarter or less Indian descent.

José María Amador does not appear to be a full-blooded Spaniard in the only surviving contemporary sketch of him, seen on the front jacket of this book. In fact, he looks more like an indigenous person or a *mestizo*, and possibly even a mulatto. The possibility that Amador was a multiracial person cannot be discounted. Other scholars support the contention that the first non-indigenous residents of California came from diverse racial backgrounds. In *Recovering History, Reconstructing Race: The Indian, Black, and White Roots of Mexican Americans*, Martha Menchaca notes the tremendous roles that Central Mexican Indians, especially Tlaxcalans, and "Afro-**Mestizos**" played in the colonization of New Spain's northern territories, including Alta California. Menchaca uses the term "Afro-Mestizo" to refer to various groups of mixed race people who had indigenous, African, or European blood. [4]

Like his father and some of his brothers, José María Amador also joined the army as a leather jacket soldier, a *soldado de cuera*.[5] He served a tour of duty of eight years beginning around 1809. By the time Amador enlisted as a soldier, he probably stood six feet tall and weighed 160 pounds; he also took to drinking brandy on a regular basis, enjoyed gambling, and like many Californios of his day, became a habitual smoker.[6] After completing his tour of duty, Amador reenlisted again for a second one at the Presidio of San Francisco in 1817, fearing that he was going to be drafted and forced to serve at the Presidio of Monterey. For the next decade, he served as a soldado de cuera, mostly under the command of Captain Luis Argüello. As a soldier, Amador participated in several expeditions to reconnoiter the Central Valley

---

[4]Martha Menchaca, *Recovering History, Constructing Race: The Indian, Black, and White Roots of Mexican Americans* (Austin: University of Texas Press, 2001). In their book, *The Forging of the Cosmic Race: A Reinterpretation of Colonial Mexico*, Colin MacLachlan and Jaime E. Rodriguez also discuss the extensive miscegenation that took place in colonial New Spain (Berkeley: University of California Press, 1980).

[5]Correspondence from José María Estudillo, Military Commander of the Presidio of Monterey, September 15, 1809, Pueblo Archives, San Jose Historical Museum. José María Amador entered the army fairly young, at age fifteen. He probably chose to become a soldier because he did not wish to live in the home of his father, Pedro Amador. José did not get along well with his stepmother. In a letter to the town commissioner of San José, dated October 2, 1809, José María Estudillo, the military commander of Monterey, asked him to investigate how Pedro Amador's wife treated her stepson. In another letter dated October 15, 1809, Estudillo writes that the San José town commissioner reported that José did not want to return to his father's home because his stepmother was "bad."

[6]Eloy Francisco Amador, "The Amador Family," Amador County Archives.

and the region north of the San Francisco Bay; in one expedition, his military company actually traveled all the way to the Columbia River in Oregon before turning back. In his narration, he provides detailed descriptions of the many places his company visited and the diverse Indian groups that it encountered. He notes that his military company fought Indians in Livermore, Stockton, Marysville, San Rafael, Santa Rosa, and Santa Barbara. In some Indian pursuits, they went deep into the Sacramento and San Joaquín valleys. Amador recounts several skirmishes in which soldiers and civilians fought together against Indians who raided ranchos for livestock. Amador made it clear that it was Indian "Auxiliaries" who often coerced the soldiers into attacking their own Indian enemies.[7] The cruelty displayed by the Moquelemne Auxiliaries during these military campaigns suggests that they had a deep hatred for their enemies that predated the arrival of the Spaniards to California. The Auxiliaries were adept at manipulating the Spaniards and Mexicans into fighting their battles.

In common with his fellow soldiers, Amador's perception and treatment of Indians was quite complex. Although he regarded them as inferior, he accepted some of them as friends. Yet, he felt no remorse for the mistreatment of Indians whom he considered enemies. His descriptions of battles are devoid of any compassion for the killings that soldiers committed or the imprisonment of Indians from the Central Valley *rancherías*. He did not question the justice of taking women and children away from their villages to place them in the missions. Finally, he did not find anything wrong with the mistreatment or punishment that Indians received from the missionaries and civilians.

Amador's story provides some insight into the lives of the presidio soldiers, but he does not give much information about the individuals who

---

[7]Virginia M. Bouvier, *Women in the Conquest of California: Code of Silence* (Tucson: University of Arizona Press, 2001). Although Bouvier should be commended for her extensive research and consultation of original and secondary sources, she is sometimes careless or misinterprets some of her sources. For example, in the case of the killing of the 200 people, she blames José María Amador (102). She claims that Amador was the brigadier general in command of the campaign (102). Bouvier makes two serious mistakes in her analysis. First, Amador never obtained a rank higher than *Alférez*, second lieutenant, and was already a retired soldier when he took part in this 1837 campaign. It should also be noted that most of the men involved in this campaign were actually civilian residents of San José, not regular soldiers. Second, the so-called "Indian allies" were not neophytes from Mission San José, but Moquelemnes from the Central Valley.

served in the presidios. Historians have noted that these soldiers were essential to preserving Spain's hold over California. Edna Deu Pree Nelson, a Eurocentric writer, for instance, sees the indigenous populations as "savages" who needed to be subdued by the "Dons" who came with Gaspar de Portolá and Juan Bautista de Anza to settle California. She maintains that these soldiers were "the ones who defended the presidios, missions, pueblos and ranchos against the savages; they planted crops, explored the interior, hunted wild beasts when provisions were low; they protected the Manila Galleon, and all the Spanish ships that came to California."[8]

Most professional historians view presidios less romantically and more realistically. Leon Campbell notes that the presidio soldiers were a "tough and hardy breed."[9] Most of the early soldiers were mixed bloods—*mestizos* and *mulatos*—recruited from the ranches or presidios of Northern México.[10] The first soldiers to arrive in California in the 1770s were middle-aged, averaging thirty-two years old, and most tended to be unmarried.[11] Campbell notes that this profile had changed by the 1790s. By this time, most presidio soldiers were older and married. José María Amador himself had thirty-seven children. His youngest child Eloy Francisco wrote in his memoirs about Amador's three marriages. Amador was first married on his twenty-eighth birthday to Magdalena Bernal, who bore him seven children. Then he wedded his second wife, María Josefa Sánchez Ortega, who gave birth to eight children, and lastly, he married Soledad Alviso who bore twenty-two chil-

---

[8]Edna Deu Pree Nelson, *The California Dons* (New York: Apple-Century-Crofts, 1962), 20.

[9]Leon Campbell, "The Spanish Presidio in Alta California during the Mission Period, 1769-1784," *Journal of the West* 16 (October 1977): 66.

[10]Bouvier tends to make helpless victims of all women, but in particular, indigenous women. She contends that Indian women were abused by their own men and by "Spanish soldiers." Moreover, she claims indigenous men used them for their sexual pleasure or would sometimes offer them as gifts to the Spanish soldiers, who would also satisfy themselves sexually with them (102). It is interesting to note that Bouvier utilizes the term "Spanish soldiers" as a euphemism for the colonial men of northern New Spain. Most of these soldiers, however, were *criollos, mestizos, mulatos*, and acculturated indigenous men. Jack D. Forbes, in his research on the Bay Area's Hispano Mexican pioneers, notes that two-thirds of soldiers at the Presidio of San Francisco in 1782 were of non-European or mixed ancestry. He further adds that at least half of the men were of Indian or part Indian background and almost seventeen percent had African blood (183).

[11]Leon Campbell, "The Spanish Presidio," 66.

dren.[12] The families of these soldiers often established houses in or in areas adjacent to the presidios. The vast majority of these soldiers could not read or write. José María Amador mentions that some of the soldiers from the presidio of San Francisco sought out his mother to teach them how to read because it was a necessary skill if they hoped to reach a higher rank.[13]

Impressively, Spain and later México were able to protect California with only a small number of soldiers. Both countries never provided sufficient resources to station a sizeable military force in the region. Until the 1790s, there were never more than 200 soldiers serving in Alta California. This remarkably small figure would remain unchanged even after México assumed control of California. Leon Campbell points out that in 1777, there was a sergeant, five corporals, and forty soldiers stationed at the presidio of Monterey, the largest of all the California presidios.[14] After it was designated the capital of the territory, the military force was doubled. San Francisco, the smallest of the presidios, had thirty-five soldiers, including a lieutenant, a sergeant, and four corporals.[15] The remaining two presidios, located in the south, had similar numbers of soldiers. Antonia Castañeda believes that the chronic lack of funding kept the California presidios woefully understaffed and unable to adequately recruit reinforcements.[16]

In view of the governments' general neglect, there is little doubt that the presidio soldiers experienced considerable hardships. Because of the failure to recruit replacements, soldiers had to serve long military terms. Common

---

[12]Some early Anglo-American researchers were awed with Amador's rather extensive family. They attributed his large family—or for that matter the large families of many Mexican males—to his exaggerated libido. These writers simply did not understand the high mortality rates among the people of the frontier. People could die from simple illnesses, long-term diseases, accidents, Indian attacks, childbirth, etc. It is interesting that Amador noted that he had outlived all of his siblings and most of his children.

[13]Often, in their efforts to show the victimization of women by the Californios, historians fail to examine how women skirted social restrictions. For example, Amador is very proud of the role played by his mother in teaching the children and the soldiers of the presidio. Bouvier, moreover, noted that Amador's sister, María Ignacia, who eventually settled in Southern California, established a reputation as a *curandera,* a folk healer. Even in those days, having positions as teachers and healers brought women much esteem and respect from community members.

[14]Campbell, 70.

[15]Ibid, 71.

[16]Antonia Castañeda, "Presidarias y Pobladoras: Spanish-Mexican Women in Frontier Monterey, Alta California, 1770–1821" (Ph.D. dissertation, Stanford, 1990), 199.

soldiers had to wait many years before they obtained permission to retire from the military. In addition to long military terms, soldiers suffered from low pay. At times, their pay failed to reach California because of civil wars in Central México. Although soldiers had food to feed themselves, they did not have money to purchase clothes or other necessities. Amador recounts that during the Mexican War of Independence when California became neglected by the Spanish Crown, some soldiers at the Presidio of San Francisco had to wrap themselves in blankets when performing guard duty because they did not have clothes to cover their naked bodies. Yet, despite the poverty and the dangers of military life, these soldiers continued to fulfill their duties because of their love for the profession and, at times, the loyalty and respect they held toward their superior officers.

Scholars have disagreed over how to view the relationship that presidio soldiers had with Indian women. Antonia Castañeda and Virginia M. Bouvier believe that these soldiers displayed a strong interest in the sexual conquest of Indian women. Both writers note that Father Junípero Serra, president of the California missions, and other priests repeatedly complained to authorities in Mexico City about sexual assaults committed by soldiers in almost every mission.[17] Apparently, the priests were driven to appeal to the vice-regal government because they felt that the territory's secular authorities, even the governor, were lax in restraining the soldiers' sexual predations. In spite of the priests' charges that the territorial government failed to punish these offenders, Castañeda does admit that, on occasions, these authorities did punish soldiers involved in illicit sexual acts. Yet, despite the potential for punishment, sexual attacks on Indian women continued.[18]

Leon Campbell does not reject the charge that sexual assaults did happen. Yet, he feels that the rate of rapes was much lower than some scholars believe. Campbell points out that only a few cases of rape reached the trial stage.[19] The Indian victims may have concluded that it would be useless to bring charges against people who sexually assaulted them so they chose not

---

[17]Castañeda, 79.

[18]Castañeda, 84. It should be noted that while the religious authorities continually criticized the presidio commanders and local authorities for not taking action against individuals who were involved in sexual attacks, they too were guilty of neglect in punishing them. Amador and Lorenzo Asisara, in this manuscript, make numerous references to priests who became sexually involved with Indian women. Some had a consensual relationship with these women but others forced themselves upon them.

[19]Campbell, 66.

to initiate legal proceedings against them. It should be noted that Amador, who at one time or another lived in the presidios and the missions, does not comment about the extent of these sexual occurrences. Campbell also observes that sexual assaults were not only rare but it was more common to see soldiers and Indian women living in concubinage.

Sexual liaisons also occurred between presidio soldiers and non-Indian women. During the governorship of Pedro Fages, Commander Luis Argüello of the presidio of San Francisco wrote him that he had punished the soldier Marcelo Pinto for having slept with the mother of Juan Francisco Bernal.[20] In 1809, Lieutenant José María Estudillo issued orders that the soldier Pedro García be flogged for causing a "scandal" with the wife of Juan Arroyo. Notably, Estudillo himself was accused of having an "illicit friendship" with Potenciana Ramiréz.[21]

Although presidio soldiers were poorly paid, some of them were successful in obtaining **ranchos** from the Crown and the Mexican government. Castañeda claims that the Spanish government gave twenty-seven concessions while the Mexican Government granted many more.[22] The biggest beneficiaries of these grants were former soldiers. For example, José María Amador received title to the Rancho San Ramón, which had been previously claimed by Mission San José. Amador was rarely critical of priests but when it came to the issue of land, he felt that they were trying to appropriate all of it for themselves. Land, in his opinion, was a source of constant conflict between civilians and priests.

Around 1827, José María Amador's request to retire from the army was accepted and he went to work as a foreman for Mission San Francisco de Solano. Later, he assumed the same function at Mission San José. After the mission was secularized, he was named its administrator, a post he kept until 1842. Perhaps because of his close association with mission priests, Amador believed that they were excellent, efficient caretakers of the missions. In addition to attending to their spiritual needs, he felt that the Fathers forged the neophytes into a productive labor force. Amador frequently praised them for transforming the missions into rather successful enterprises, the envy of the civilian population. He described the vast numbers of livestock (cattle, sheep, and horses) that

---

[20]Castañeda, 267.

[21]Apparently, Estudillo did not have a stable marital relationship. His wife had a long affair with Father Francisco José Viñals of Mission San José. Viñals was supposed to have fathered three of her children.

[22]Castañeda, 207.

were owned by the missions as well as the extensive fields and orchards that were worked by the neophytes. Finally, Indians also worked in the missions' carpentry and blacksmithing shops as well as the tanneries and textile shops.

As an employee of the missions, Amador also observed the missionaries' use of physical punishment on the neophytes. Amador notes that flogging was a daily occurrence. Reflecting the attitudes of his Californio contemporaries, Amador viewed punishment as necessary to correct the "natural" laziness, immaturity, and irresponsibility of Indians. Undoubtedly, he concurred with the missionaries that the Indians needed supervision, and some form of punishment on occasion to keep them on the straight path. Amador did not consider the punishment of Indians as necessarily cruel or inhumane. Most neophytes would not have shared Amador's views on mission life.

On one of the days that Thomas Savage conducted an interview with Amador, he met his Indian friend Lorenzo Asisara. Clearly reflecting his own people's experience, Asisara gave Savage a much different view of Indian life in the missions than the one provided by Amador.[23] Asisara described some of the priests as alcoholics who would ruthlessly beat the neophytes. To defend themselves against the Fathers' cruelty, the Indians occasionally resorted to violence. Asisara recounted how the Indians of Mission Santa Cruz murdered Father Andrés Quintana because they grew tired of the constant floggings he inflicted on them. What drove the Indians to commit this killing was that Quintana seemed obsessed with improving the quality of his whips and trying them out on them.[24] At another time, Indians from the same

---

[23]It is interesting to point out that despite the considerable amount of information that Asisara provided Savage regarding Indian life, Savage decided to title this manuscript "Memorias sobre la Historia de California" and only gives credit to José María Amador. In doing so, he affirmed the traditional belief that indigenous people did not have anything interesting to say.

[24]Virginia Bouvier notes that some historians believe that the neophyte conspirators actually cut off Father Andrés Quintana's testicles before burying him (136). This contention seems implausible, however. In Amador's memoirs, Lorenzo Asisara, the indigenous source consulted by Bouvier, says that when the conspirators planned Quintana's death, they were well aware that his death had to be made to appear a natural one. They knew that the slightest suspicion by the authorities that Quintana had been assassinated would lead to the immediate capture and severe punishment of the culprits. Hence, the conspirators chose to kill him by leaving no physical marks on his body and making his death look like a natural occurrence. They carefully suffocated him and to ensure his death they crushed his testicles. Apparently, they did not succeed completely because the military commander of Monterey, José María Estudillo, did not believe that Quintana had died a natural death and suspected foul play. Hubert H. Bancroft notes that Estudillo wrote Father Martínez requesting that a post mortem examination be made of Quintana's body (*California Pastoral*, 573). Yet, when the missionaries and military officials established the commission to investigate the cause of Quintana's death, it concluded that he had died from natural causes, probably from an illness of the testicles. For awhile, the conspirators were successful in hiding the true causes of Quintana's death. Several years passed before the authorities quite by accident discovered the way in which Quintana had been killed.

mission attacked Father Olbes with pieces of broken tile and stones when he tried to punish one of their own. Asisara did admit that some priests were kind and treated them well. Some of these popular priests engaged in consensual sex with Indian women.

Amador and Asisara also disagreed on other aspects of the missions. Believing that the missions reached their heyday during the Spanish period, Amador blames the civilian administrators who replaced the missionaries for their collapse. When secularization was implemented, California authorities named civilians to manage the missions. These individuals had the task of distributing the missions' assets to Indians, who they regarded as their rightful owners. Instead, the administrators sold off the properties and resources and pocketed the money. Asisara confirms Amador's views but added that priests bore some of the responsibility. He informed Savage that at Mission Santa Cruz, Father Antonio Suárez del Real conspired with some of his Indian friends to keep some of the most valuable assets, such as currency, bolts of cloth, and other items. In the end, the missions were reduced to complete poverty yet the Indians received very little of the wealth.

Although José María Amador generally held a favorable view of the mission priests, like other Californios he was critical of them for trying to claim much of the land. Amador noted that oftentimes, when civilians petitioned the government for a land grant, the missionaries would oppose these requests, claiming the missions needed the land. To Amador, the missionaries wanted to create a land-tenure system where the property of one mission started where the property of another ended. In spite of the resistance of priests, the Mexican government had committed itself to the secularization of California missions by the early 1830s. Hence, many Californios petitioned and received land grants in the 1830s and 1840s. This was a notable change from the policy of the Spanish Crown, which had issued only twenty-seven concessions in the entire period it controlled California. Like many fellow soldiers, Amador requested a land grant, which was apparently carved out from Mission San José. In 1834, Governor José Figueroa granted him title to his 16,517-acre Rancho San Ramón, where the present-day cities of Dublin and San Ramón are located.

After being ousted from his position as administrator of Mission San José in 1842, José María Amador—by then forty-eight years old—retired to his Rancho San Ramón. He chose to focus his energies on improving his ranch and raising livestock; his son, Francisco Eloy, notes that at one time he had

over 12,000 head of cattle and sold over 60,000 pesos of livestock.[25] He, moreover, also dabbled in trading hides. Around this time Amador became immersed in town life of San José. There are only a few records prior to 1840 that indicate that Amador was a resident of San José. This could be explained by the fact that Amador spent so many years serving at the presidio of San Francisco or residing in the missions where he was employed. Nonetheless, after the 1840s, records show that Amador was involved in several legal conflicts. For instance, in 1841 Francisco Pico sued him for the return of or payment for 132 *fanegas* of wheat.[26] Apparently, Amador claimed that this was a matter that Pico had to direct to Mission San José, not to him. Pico, however, maintained that it was Amador himself who had taken the wheat and hence it was his personal debt. Amador was most likely arrested in September over the Pico suit. One month later, the municipal judge decided to establish a commission, whose members would be chosen by Pico and Amador, to arbitrate the dispute.[27]

Amador became involved in several additional litigation cases. In May 1841, Ignacio Peralta filed a complaint against Amador for the false branding of cattle and stealing of hides.[28] In June 1845, Amador himself submitted a complaint against Lorenzo Pacheco for allowing his cattle and other livestock to graze on his Rancho San Ramón.[29] In July 1847, Eduardo Bale sued Amador but the source does not indicate the nature of the suit.[30]

While José María Amador refused to get involved in the political disputes of his homeland, he was a keen observer of the political events. Amador offered comments on the record of every California governor since Pablo Vicente de Solá. He also discussed the increasing animosity between Mexicans from the center of the Republic and the native-born Californios. Final-

---

[25]Amador himself boasted that he had established a reputation for being a breeder of fine horses. Other sources note that in addition to cattle, Amador kept 400 horses and 4,000 sheep.

[26]Correspondence from José F. Castro, Juez de Paz, May 27, 1841, Pueblo Archives, San José Historical Museum.

[27]Correspondence from José R. Estrada, Juez del Pueblo de San José, October 20, 1841, Pueblo Archives, San Jose Historical Museum.

[28]Complaint by Ignacio Peralta, May 24, 1845, Pueblo Archives, Vol. 4, 670-672, San José Historical Museum.

[29]Complaint by José María Amador, June 9, 1845, Pueblo Archives, Vol. 3, 54-55, San José Historical Museum.

[30]Suit by Eduardo Bale against José María Amador, Jul. 30, 1847, Pueblo Archives, Vol. VI, 448–49, San José Historical Museum.

ly, Amador explained the regional struggles that took place between the *Aba-jeños* and the *Arribeños* for control of the state government.

Part of the Amador dictations that caused him much anger and displeasure is the account in which he says that the native Californios had little ability to govern and admister their homeland. Amador fervently believed that the native-born governors that took office in the 1830s and 1840s ruined the economy while enriching themselves and their cronies. Amador also blamed them and the military commanders for displaying poor leadership in defending California from the American invaders during the Mexican War of 1846. While many scholars of California history assume that the Californios readily accepted the United States' occupation of their homeland, Amador argues that many of his countrymen were willing to fight for their homeland; they were even willing to sacrifice their lives to defend it. What led to the relative ease by which the United States took over California was that Governor Pío Pico and Commander General José Castro fled to México, leaving the Californios leaderless. With their departure, all military resistance broke down. Amador reserves most of his bitter contempt for Pico for running away and absconding with 22,000 pesos obtained from the sale of mission property.

Surprisingly, José María Amador did not have major complaints against the Anglo-American newcomers who took possession of California. He was well aware that Anglo irregular soldiers were appropriating the livestock and property of Mexicans but he only had one serious confrontation with them. One day, an Anglo-American force headed by John C. Frémont came to his ranch and took about sixty fine horses. He was never compensated for them.[31] With the exception of this incident, Amador claims that white Americans always treated him with respect. Because he did not have property confiscated by Anglo-Americans, some of his fellow Mexicans accused him of having pro-American sympathies.

During the Gold Rush, José María Amador, like many other native Californios, went to the gold fields. He made several trips to the area now called

---

[31]Francisco Eloy Amador writes in his memoirs that one leader of the Indians who were working on his father's Rancho de San Ramón offered his services to avenge Frémont's action but that his father dissuaded him from doing so. Francisco Amador writes: "At that time my father had a large collection of friendly Indians working at his Rancho San Ramon and their chief wanted my father's consent to having Indians follow General Frémont and ambush him. My father wanted no trouble as he easily saw that this could retaliate against Spanish settlers in this territory, and so consent could not be given."

Amador County to try his luck; at different times he was accompanied by friends like Antonio Suñol, Pierre Sansevain, and Suñol's son, José Antonio. Amador claims that he was easily able to amass a good fortune but a huge part of it was lost when one of his partners took it to Peru without his permission. After awhile, Amador returned to his ranch, claiming that his wife had fallen ill. He never went back to the gold fields.

Although he lived until the early 1880s, Amador does not discuss the period of his life after 1850. In the latter part of his memoirs, he returns to recollecting events that took place during his years as a soldier and administrator for the missions. The questions must be asked: Why did Amador choose not to discuss his later life? Was it because nothing of interest to him took place? Or, was it because this period was too tragic for him since he would have had to explain the loss of his Rancho San Ramón and his impoverishment? His *Memorias* did not answer these questions. It could be inferred that Amador did not feel comfortable recounting to an Anglo-American his true feelings about how Anglo-Americans abused and mistreated Mexicans, like himself.[32] It is possible that Amador's distrust of Savage as an Anglo-American kept him from revealing what happened to him and other Mexicans once the U.S. occupied California. It is also possible that Savage himself was quite aware that the loss of land was a touchy issue for the Californios and chose not to ask Amador about this matter.[33] Amador was not the only Californio who refused to talk to Savage about the loss of his property. Genaro Padilla writes that Apolinaria Lorenzana was "loath to speak to Savage on this subject" and she assured him that she did not want to think about it.[34]

No doubt Amador was quite aware of the Mexicans' land dispossession because he had seen many close relatives and old friends become immersed

---

[32]In the Amador Family Papers stored at the Amador County Archives, there is a letter by one of his descendants, Steven Graham, who claims that José María Amador was "a victim of the changing times." Graham, no doubt, was suggesting that the Mexican property holders were powerless to protect their lands against Anglo-American encroachers.

[33]Apparently, some scholars believe that Amador did not address his life after 1850 because Thomas Savage did not ask him questions on that period. These historians argue that Hubert H. Bancroft's research assistants received specific questions from Bancroft that only dealt with the Spanish and Mexican periods of California history.

[34]Padilla, 145. Padilla states that Lorenzana told Savage: "It is a long story and I don't even want to discuss it. The other two ranches they somehow took from me. So, that's the way it turns out, that after working so many years, after having acquired an estate, which I certainly didn't dispose of by selling or by any other means, here I find myself in the greatest poverty, living only by the grace of God and through the charity of those who give me a mouthful to eat."

in legal battles or lose their lives warding off Anglo-American encroachers. His brothers-in-law Juan P. Bernal and Antonio Suñol spent years in courts seeking to validate their property titles or attempting to evict Anglo squatters from their ranch properties.

Amador's family members were not the only Mexicans who were facing attacks on their properties, but instead these assaults were directed against individuals who held Mexican or Spanish property titles. In a petition submitted to the U.S. Senate and the House of Representatives on February 21, 1859, forty-eight signers, mostly Mexican but including several Anglo-Americans, asked these bodies to "honor, respect, protect, and uphold" the guarantees of the Treaty of Guadalupe Hidalgo. These signers, including Antonio Suñol, who was a close personal friend of Amador, claimed that having Mexican property titles confirmed by the California Land Commission, which was created by the U.S. Congress, was causing them incredible hardship and had brought them disastrous effects.

> Though this honorable body has doubtless had the best interest of the state at heart, still it had brought about the most disastrous effects upon those who have the honor to subscribe their names to the petition, for, even though all landholders possessing land titles under the Spanish and Mexican governments were not forced by the letter of the law to present them before the Commission for confirmation; nevertheless all those titles were at once considered doubtful, their origin questionable, and, as a result worthless by the Commission; all landholders were thus compelled de facto to submit their titles to the Commission for confirmation, under the alternative that, if they were not submitted, the lands, would be considered public property.[35]

To prevent the government from rendering their lands public properties, the Mexican titleholders had to submit them to the California Land Commission. Yet, this Commission often tended to question the legality of the Mexican titles and rejected them. In their petition, the signers noted that to validate their titles by American courts, they had to hire Anglo-American lawyers who would charge them substantial fees. Often, the titleholders would be forced to transfer sizeable amounts of their lands in payment for their services to their lawyers. Because their legal cases could last many years before they were settled, they also lost their land by failing to pay excessive property taxes or by incurring large loans at high interest rates.

---

[35]James P. Delgado, *Witness to Empire: The Life of Antonio María Suñol* (San José: Sourisseau Academy for California State and Local History, 1977), 97.

In addition to spending large sums of money in legal costs, the petition signers stated that they also had to contend with Anglo-American squatters who believed that the "old inhabitants'" titles were "doubtful" and their validity "questionable." They wrote:

> They [squatters] spread themselves over the land as though it were public property, taking possession of the improvements made by the inhabitants, many times seizing even the houses (where they had lived for many years with their families), taking and killing their cattle and destroying their crops; so that those before had owned great numbers of cattle that could have been counted in the thousands, now found themselves without any, and the men who were the owners of many leagues of land now were deprived of the peaceful possession of even one vara.[36]

Conflict with the squatters frequently led to violence and the loss of life among Mexican property holders. Several Santa Clara Valley ranch families, for example the Berreyessa family, lost members in conflicts with Anglo-American squatters. Moreover, José Antonio Suñol, who had traveled with José María Amador to the gold fields during the Gold Rush, was killed by a squatter near Mission San José while trying to protect his father's property, Rancho El Valle de San José. James P. Delgado claims that the stress of the legal conflicts killed Antonio Suñol in 1865.[37]

Martha Menchaca argues that the passage of the Homestead Act of 1862 made it even more difficult for Mexican property holders to retain their land.[38] The act allowed any citizen of the United States to claim 162 acres of public land. Under the act, citizens in possession of a tract of land could file a homestead claim with the California Land Commission even if it was held by a Mexican landholder. The homesteader could not be evicted unless the state or federal courts instructed him to leave. If the homestead petition was challenged by the property holder, the dispute had to be settled by a court. In the meantime, the landholder was still liable for all the taxes of the disputed property.

Mexican landholders were fully cognizant that Anglo-Americans were determined to dispossess them of their land by whatever means necessary. Of the 813 cases presented to the California Land Commission, 521 were confirmed by the time it adjourned in 1856.[39] This number increased to 604 by successful appeals to the courts. Nonetheless, of these 604 cases, only 330

---

[36]Delgado, *Witness to Empire*, 98.
[37]Ibid, 78
[38]Menchaca, *Recovering History, Constructing History*, 265.
[39]Mario Barrera, *Race and Class in the Southwest: A Theory of Racial Inequality* (South Bend: University of Notre Dame Press, 1979), 19.

were confirmed to Mexicans. Realizing the tremendous legal difficulties that their countrymen were encountering, it is likely that many Mexicans decided not to contest their properties and surrendered them to squatters. Other Mexicans, as was probably the case with José María Amador, pragmatically chose to sell off their property at whatever price they could obtain.

An interesting source revealed what happened to Amador's 16,517-acre Rancho San Ramón. The grave marker for Leo Morris, who is buried in the oldest Catholic cemetery of Dublin, California, states that he purchased 10,000 acres of Amador's ranch for $20,000 and "a white horse." [40] One has to wonder if it was Amador who insisted that Morris' "white horse" be a part of the sale transaction. There is little doubt that for the next few years, an aging Amador divested himself of the rest of his ranch. In his youngest son's memoirs, it can be established that by 1864 José María Amador had relocated his family to the town of Whiskey Hill, on the California coast. It is possible that Amador, by then in his early seventies, had moved into the area a few years earlier. A story that appeared in the *Santa Cruz Sentinel* on June 13, 1862, reported that Amador was working at a place called Chuchitas. He was in charge of extracting coal samples to see if the quality was good enough to be mined profitably. It appears that either this venture failed or Amador got too old to continue working it. By the mid-1870s, Amador—now partly paralyzed by stroke and living at the home of his daughter María Antonia Rodríguez—was dependent on his younger boys for the care and survival of the family. According to Francisco Eloy, Amador's teenage sons were working to feed the family. After his older brothers left the area in search of work, Francisco Eloy himself stopped his education at age fourteen to go to work. To supplement the family's meager income, he would use his father's muzzleloader to hunt for rabbits and quail.

Family records do not show how long Amador stayed in Whiskey Hill. Francisco Eloy's memoirs, however, reveal that by the early 1880s, Amador and his family had moved to Gilroy. Francisco Eloy notes that by then he was the family's primary breadwinner and worked as a woodcutter for the cattle kings, Miller and Lux. On June 12, 1883, José María Amador died. He was buried at St. Mary's Cemetery with a simple wooden cross, a symbol of his impoverishment, marking his grave. With the passage of time, the cross rotted away, leaving no trace of the location of his grave. Although Don José María Amador's gravesite was nearly forgotten, his indomitable spirit and his memory live on. [41]

---

[40] It appears that in the early 1850s, Amador sold 246 acres of land to Jeremiah Fallon for $1,500 and another 1,000 acres to Michael Murray.

[41] On August 12, 1976, the Amador County Historical Society and José María Amador's descendants honored him by locating his gravesite and collaborated to place a headstone on it.

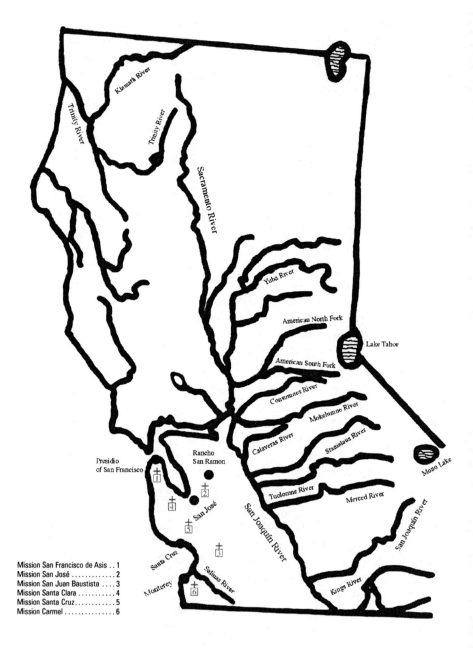

Mission San Francisco de Asis . . 1
Mission San José 2
Mission San Juan Baustista 3
Mission Santa Clara 4
Mission Santa Cruz 5
Mission Carmel 6

Map of Northern Alta California

SPANISH LANGUAGE MANUSCRIPT

EDITOR'S NOTE

The punctuation in the Spanish version of the José María Amador Memoria has been modified to make it more readable. The accents have also been changed to conform to modern standards.

ÍNDICE

Memorias Sobre la Historia de California

José María Amador:
Natural del País que nació en el año de
1781 y vive hoy cerca del pueblito de Whiskey Hill

Lo escribió, dictado por el autor,
Thomas Savage

Para la
Bancroft Library
1877

[Because Savage's Introduction to the Amador *Memorias* is in English, it will not be edited and will contain his original abbreviations. Some Spanish words were kept in the English translation of the *Memorias* for stylistic purposes. These words will be put in boldface and defined in the Glossary.]

THOMAS SAVAGE'S INTRODUCTION

One of the main objects I had in view in visiting Santa Cruz, in June 1877, was to see this ancient Californian said to have been born in 1781, that is, 12 years after the foundn. of the first mission in this Cal., and only abt. 5 years after that of San Francisco.

I had been assured that Amador had a clear head, an amiable disposition, and a large stock of informn. which he would notwithholdg.

My disappointmt was great on discovering that he had moved away from Sta. Cruz years before, but was living in Watsonville. I went to seek him, and found him on a small farm about 4½ miles from town, in great poverty under the care of his youngest daughter, who is married and burdening with many children. Amador is also quite crippled from the effects of paralysis which attacked him two or three years ago. The house was such as is found inhabited by the poorest class of Californian rancheros.

Such was the condition of named, of the son of one of the original founders, Pedro Amador.

He had heard of Mr. H. H. Bancroft's library in collecting material for a Hist. of California and did not hesitate one instant in furnishing what he rememberd abt. the past of his country during the Sp. and Mexn. domination.

I rode to his dwelling place every morning and returnd. to town in the evening. The intervening hours, during 7 or 8 days were industriously employed by me in recording what he dictated. All of which appears in the following pages under the title of Memorias sobre Hist. de California.

Amador's memory was quite fresh and had it been possible for me to make a longer stay in that vicinity, I dared not that from time to time he would have supplied me incidents, anecdotes as they came to his mind, to fill up many more pages. As it is, his contribution may be called a substantial one.

Thomas Savage (signature)

CAPÍTULO 1

LA VIDA DE LOS SOLDADOS DE CUERA EN El PRESIDIO DE SAN FRANCISCO

Yo, José Ma. Amador, nací en el presidio de San Francisco, el año de 1781. Tengo en la actualidad 96 años, y gracias a la Divina Providencia, conservo aún una memoria bastante fresca, y un recuerdo de los sucesos antiguos de mi país.[1] Fueron mis padres el Alférez Don Pedro Amador y María Ramona Noriega.[2] El primero fue natural de la vieja España y la segunda hija de Loreto en la Baja Cal. Mi señor padre sirvió algunos años como Sargento en el presidio de Loreto, y vino a la fundación de San Diego en 1769 con el Gobr. Portolá y el Capn. Rivera y Moncada, y con ellos se halló presente en la fundación del presidio y misión de Monterey en Junio de 1770. Después de esto se volvió a la B. Cal. con el Capn. Rivera y Moncada, y siguió hasta México no sé con certeza si fue hasta la capital, o hasta Guadalajara solamente.

En este viage enviudó él de su primera muger Ma. de la Luz con la que tuvo dos hijos. María de la Luz, a quien nunca conocí, y Jacinto Amador que sirvió con el grado de Sargto. en la Compa. de Caballería de Loreto. Una vez lo mandaron en comisión a Monterey, y estuvo allí unos 20 y tantos días.

Cuando tuve el gusto de conocer a este hermano, era yo entonces de unos 12 años de edad; no volví a verle más nunca.

---

[1]Esta anotación es de Thomas Savage. Savage cree que Amador estaba exagerando. Savage escribe: "Un error serio. Él [Amador] nació el 18 de diciembre de 1793 en San Francisco y fue bautizado el 20."

[2]Esta anotación es de Savage. Él escribió: "Otro error. Él [Pedro] era nativo de Cocula, en Nueva Galicia, ahora México."

CHAPTER 1

THE LIFE OF SOLDADOS DE CUERA AT THE PRESIDIO OF SAN FRANCISCO

I, José María Amador, was born in the Presidio of San Francisco in 1781. I am presently 96 years old, and thanks to Divine Providence, I possess a very fresh memory with recollections of ancient events that took place in my country.[1]

My parents were the Second Lieutenant Don Pedro Amador and María Ramona Noriega. My father was from Old Spain and my mother was a native of Loreto in Baja California.[2]

My father served several years as a sergeant in the Presidio of Loreto and came to the founding of San Diego in 1769 with Governor [Gaspar de] Portolá and Captain [Fernando de] Rivera y Moncada; he accompanied them to the establishment of the Presidio and Mission of Monterey in June of 1770. Afterwards, he went back to Baja California with Captain Rivera y Moncada and then proceeded to México, but I am not certain he went all the way to the capital or just to Guadalajara.

During this trip, he became a widower since his first wife María de la Luz died; he had two children with her, María de la Luz, whom I never met, and Jacinto Amador who obtained the rank of Sergeant in the Cavalry Company of Loreto. One time, he was sent on a commission to Monterey, staying there for about twenty or more days.

[While he was there] I had the pleasure of meeting this brother. I was about twelve years old. I never saw him again.

---

[1]This is a note from Thomas Savage. He believes that Amador is stretching the truth. Savage writes: "A serious error. He [Amador] was born Dec. 18, 1794 at S. Fco. & baptzd. on the 20th."

[2]This is another note by Savage. He writes: "Another mistake. He [Pedro] was a native of Cocula, in Nueva Galicia, now México."

A los pocos años de la ida de mi padre a México, volvió a esta California casado en segundas nupcias con mi madre, y destinado con el rango de Alférez vivo y efectivo a la compa. Presidial de San Franco.,[3] pero como estuvo sirviendo en Loreto bastante tiempo, ya trajo a San Francisco 3 hijos de su segunda esposa, que los condujo en alforjas, dos en una, y el otro en la otra alforja, y para emparejar el peso, puso una piedra en la última. Mi madre [María Ramona Noriega] arreaba la mula en que venían los niños, y mi padre la tiraba. Así marcharon por tierra todo el camino desde Loreto hasta San Francisco, tardando en el viaje 2½ ó 3 meses. Los hijos que trajeron mis padres se llamaban Juan Pablo, María Antonia, y Fructuoso (este últo. fue el que trajo a la piedra por compañera). Tuvo mi padre varios hijos que nacieron todos en San Francisco: María del Cármen (que a su tiempo se casó con un soldado volunto. de México llamado Mendoza, y con él se fue a México, nunca la vi más porqe. murió allá cuando estaba de vuelta pa. Cal.), Sinforosa (ésta casó también con un voluntario Mexicano (artillero) llamado Claudio Galindo con quien pasó a México y no volvió más a su país), Marcos (éste fue soldado de la compa. de cuera de San Francisco), yo, José María, Honesíforo (éste tuvo la desgracia de morir quemado con pólvora a los 10 u 11 años de edad), María Rosa (ésta casó con Francisco Albiso, soldado de la Compa. presidial de San Francisco).

Se me olvidaba María Ignacia, que nació antes de Sinforosa, y casó con Nicolás Berreyessa, que era soldado inválido de San Francisco residente en San José. (Ella tenía 12 años, y él 60 cuando se casaron, duraron un año casados, muriendo él; del matrimonio tuvieron una hija, que fue después muger de Agustín Bernal). Después de María Rosa, nació el último de mis hermanos, Lázaro, y a los ocho días murió nuestra venerada madre [María Ramona], el año de 1801, el día 6 de Septiembre. Su enfermedad no pasó de 24 horas, murió de pasmo por haberse mojado los pies a tan pocos días de parida. Lázaro murió chico, como a los dos años.

---

[3]Savage cree que Amador cometió otro error. Savage escribe: "Otro error. A [Pedro] Amador, se dice, se le ofreció un nombramiento a alférez en Loreto pero lo rechazó. A él se le consideró varias veces para ese cargo pero nunca se le concedió. Al final se retiró como . . .[lo que sigue no es leíble]" Como prueba de su creciente respeto por capacidad de recordar de José María Amador y su buen conocimiento de la historia, Thomas Savage ya no hizo más anotaciones tratando de corregirlo en el resto de la memoria.

A few years after my father left to go back to México, he returned, married to his second wife, my mother, to this [Alta] California. He had the rank of active second lieutenant in the presidial company of San Francisco with all its rights and responsibilities.[3] Since he had served in Loreto for a long time, he brought to San Francisco three children by his second wife. He carried them in **alforjas**: two in one alforja and the other in the other alforja; a rock was placed to even the load. My mother guided the mule that carried the children and my father pulled it. In this manner, they trekked the entire road from Loreto to San Francisco; the trip lasted about two-and-a-half to three months. The children that my parents brought with them were Juan Pablo, María Antonia, and Fructuoso (this last one was the one who had the rock for a companion). My father had several other children, all of whom were born in San Francisco: María del Carmen (who in time would marry a volunteer soldier from México by the name of Mendoza and with whom she went to México. I never saw her again because she died over there as she was returning to California); Sinforosa (who married a Mexican volunteer [artillery-man] by the name of Claudio Galindo, whom she accompanied to México and never came back to her homeland); Marcos (he was a soldier in the Leatherjacket Company of San Francisco); I, José María; Honesífero (he had the misfortune of having been burned to death from gunpowder at the age of ten to eleven years); and, María Rosa (she married Francisco Albiso, a soldier in the company of the Presidio of San Francisco).

I forgot to mention María Ignacia, who was born before Sinforosa, and who married Nicolás Berreyessa, a retired soldier now residing in San José. (She was twelve years old and he was sixty years old when they got married. They had been married one year when he died; they had one daughter who later became the wife of Agustín Bernal.) After María Rosa, Lázaro, the last of my siblings was born. Eight days after his birth, on September 6, 1801, our venerable mother died. Her illness did not last more than twenty-four hours; she died from a spasm after wetting her feet only a few days after having given birth. Lázaro died young, when he was two years old.

---

[3]Savage believes that Amador made another mistake. He notes: "Another error. [Pedro] Amador was, it is said, offered a promotion as **Alférez** at Loreto, which he declined. [He] was several times proposed for such promotion but did not get it. At last he was retired as a . . . [illegible]" As an indication of the increasing respect that Thomas Savage has for Amador's excellent memory and his historical knowledge, he would no longer make further notations seeking to correct him in the rest of the **Memorias.**

Toda esta familia nuestra ha desaparecido de la tierra, hombres y mugeres. Solamente yo existo, siguiendo a mi Señor padre en la longevidad, porqe. es de advertir que él vivió 99 años y un mes, en cuyo tiempo sirvió al Rey de España 47 años en compañías de caballería presidiales. Creo que fue en 1800 cuando él se retiró del servicio, estableciéndose en el pueblo de San José, con 200$ anuales que le abonaba la hacienda. Allí vivió hasta su muerte el 8 de Mayo de 1825.

Sé que mi padre se halló presente en innumerables campañas de indios y mariscados, antes de su retiro, pero no puedo dar cuenta más que de una que fue en el sitio del Hambre en la ranchería de Apalames. Aquí, un soldado de la compa. perdió un ojo de un flechazo que le dispararon los indios, y se perdió uno de mis hermanos (Fructuoso) acompañado con otro soldado (Hilario Miranda). Estuvieron perdidos 6 días; por esta causa se le dio al parage donde estuvo la tropa acampada el nombre de El Hambre. Estuvo la tropa allí hasta que se encontraron los perdidos. Los indios fueron severamente escarmentados, varios de ellos perecieron en la campaña a manos de nuestra gente y 50 más o menos, hechos prisioneros, presos llevados a San Francisco y puestos a trabajar en las obras públicas. Las rancherías de aquella región no eran muy populosas. El sitio del Hambre es una cañada situada a este lado de Martínez.

Si mal no recuerdo gobernaba las Californias Dn. Felipe de Neve cuando yo nací. Yo senté plaza en la compañía de artillería, destacamento de San Francisco; me filió el Alférez José Roca. En esa compañía serví ocho años; obtuve mi licencia del Gobr. Don José Joaquín de Arrillaga en 1809 o 10,[4] y despúes tomé plaza el año de 1817 en la compa. de caballería de cuera de San Francisco que mandaba el Capitán Dn. Luis Antonio Argüello.[5]

---

[4]Rose Marie Beebe y Robert M. Senkewicz, *The History of Alta California: A Memoir of Mexican California, Antonio María Osio* (Madison: The University of Wisconsin Press, 1996), 317. Los autores hacen la anotación que Arrillaga fungió como gobernador del Alta California desde1804 hasta su muerte en 1814.

[5]Apararentemente, José María Amador le tenía un gran respeto y admiración al Capitán Luis Antonio Argüello. Según Beebe y Senkewecz, Argüello nació en San Francisco en 1784 (316). Su padre, José Darío Argüello, sirvió como comandante militar en San Francisco y en Monterey durante la década de 1790 y los primeros años de 1800. Luis Argüello, como su padre, se dedicó a la carrera militar y fue nombrado capitán de la compañía de San Francisco en 1818. Luis después fue nombrado gobernador interino de Alta California en 1822. Después de haber dejado la gubernatura, él ocupó varios cargos militares y murió en San Francisco en 1830.

All [members] of my family have parted this earth—women and men—only I survive. I follow my Señor Father in longevity for it is necessary to note that he lived for ninety-nine years and one month. In his lifetime, he served the King of Spain forty-seven years in the presidial cavalry companies. I believe that it was in 1800 when he retired from military service, settling in the pueblo of San José, with a 200 peso annual retirement pension from the [Royal] Treasury. He lived there until his death on May 8, 1825.

My father was present in numerous campaigns against Indians and other military raids before his retirement, but I can only recount one that took place at El Hambre site in the Apalmes **Ranchería**. There, a soldier of the company lost an eye due to an arrow that Indians shot at him, and one of my brothers (Fructuoso) got lost in the company of another soldier (Hilario Miranda). They were lost for six days; the place where the troops camped became known as El Hambre [the Place of Hunger]. The troop stayed there until they found the lost ones. The Indians were severely punished; several of them were killed during the campaign at the hands of our soldiers, and about fifty, more or less, were taken prisoners—prisoners who were sent to San Francisco and put to work on public projects. The rancherías of that region did not have large populations. The El Hambre site is a ravine located on this side of Martínez.

When I was born, if I remember correctly, Don Felipe de Neve governed the Californias. I obtained a place in the artillery company of San Francisco; Second Lieutenant José Roca recruited me. I served eight years in that company and I got my discharge [from it] from Governor Don José Joaquín de Arrillaga in 1809 or 1810.[4] Afterwards, in 1817, I took an assignment in the **soldado de cuera** company of San Francisco that was commanded by Captain Don Luis Antonio Argüello.[5]

---

[4]Rose Marie Beebe and Robert M. Senkewicz, *The History of Alta California: A Memoir of Mexican California by Antonio María Osio* (Madison: The University of Wisconsin Press, 1996), 317. Arrillaga served as governor of Alta California from 1804 until his death in 1814.
[5]Beebe and Senkewicz, 316. José María Amador had a deep respect and admiration for Captain Luis Antonio Argüello. The authors note that Argüello was born in San Francisco in 1784. His father, José Darío Argüello, served as military commander in San Francisco and in Monterey in the 1790s and early 1800s. Luis Argüello followed his father into the military; he became the captain of the company of San Francisco in 1818. Luis was chosen to be acting governor of Alta California in 1822. After leaving office, he held several military posts. He died in San Francisco in 1830.

Lo hice huyendo de un sorteo que se hacía para aumentar las compañías presidiales. La de Monterey estaba a la sazón al mando del Capn. José de la Guerra y Noriega. Una de las causas que me hicieron huir de ese sorteo era que trasquilaban a los que sorteaban, y les había cabido en suerte servir. Este sorteo se hizo porque ningún joven quería entrar voluntariamente a servir, ni recibir enganche.

Después de filiado el recluta le hacían tupé y valcarra. El tupé era que le afeitaban toda la mitad del frente de la cabeza, dejándole sólo a los lados la valcarra que caía sobre la cara y servía de patilla. La parte de atrás formaba la coleta que era entrenzado. Esto era tan ridículo que nadie se prestó a ello por su voluntad. Todos los que sufrieron esa trasquila, fueron forzados. Esta ridícula invención fue obra del Gobr. Solá y del Capn. de la Guerra.[6] Para escaparme de eso (puesto que se me hacía la injusticia de obligarme a servir después de haber servido 8 años en la artillería) di una arrancada de San José, y me enganché voluntario en San Franco. La moda del pelado de Monterey no se estableció en San Francisco, porque el Capn. Argüello se opuso. Después se permitieron a nuestra compa. algunos de los de la Monterey con el sillar hecho como los caballos. Aquello fue cosa que produjo mucha indignación, porqe. era cosa que nunca se había visto antes en California. Mi enganche fue por 10 años. Después de servirlos me retiré el año de 1827 en Sept. después de la fundación de San Francisco Solano.

Yo era cabo habilitado de la escolta y mayordomo de la misión, y estuve encargado de los trabajos dos años y meses hasta que me retiré a la misión de San José, en donde serví 15 años de mayordomo de los temporalidades. Durante mi mayordomía fueron ministros de la misión los Padres Buenaventura Fortuni [sic] y Narciso Durán,[7] y últimamente cuando se retiraron

---

[6]Beebe y Senkewecz, 337. Los autores mencionan que Pablo Vicente de Solá nació en España y llegó a la Nueva España como oficial militar. En 1894, de Solá fue nombradao gobernador de Alta California, puesto que mantuvo hasta 1822. Supuestamente, él era de "peso normal, cuerpo grueso, cuello pequeño, de cabeza grande y un poco angosta y de cara ancha, con pocos dientes, de cabello casi blanco, y con una voz profunda y calmante."

[7]Maynard Geiger, *Franciscan Missionaries in Hispanic California, 1769–1848: A Bibliographical Dictionary* (San Marino, CA: Huntington Library, 1969). Según Geiger el padre Narciso Durán nació en España y llegó a la misión de San José en 1806 y allí permaneció hasta 1833. Durante ése tiempo Durán, en colaboración con Fray Buenaventura Fortuny, convertion a la misión a una de las más prósperas. Después de que se trasladó a la misión de Santa Bárbara, Durán se opuso al plan del gobernador Echeandía para emancipar a los indígenas.

I did it to escape the lottery that was established to increase the presidial companies. The Monterey Company was at that time under the command of Captain José de la Guerra y Noriega. One reason that I fled the lottery was that they sheared [the hair] of the lottery draftees who were unlucky enough to have been chosen to serve. This lottery was done because no youth wanted to voluntarily serve, nor be recruited.

After being enlisted, the recruits were given a toupee and a **valcarra**. The toupee was when the entire front half of the head was shaved, leaving only the valcarra on the sides. The valcarra would drop on the sides of the face and would serve as sideburns. The hair behind the head was braided into a pigtail. This haircut was so ridiculous that no one would voluntarily accept it. Those who suffered this shearing were forced to have it. This ridiculous invention was the work of Governor [Pablo Vicente de] Solá and Captain de la Guerra.[6] To escape this (I thought it was an injustice to force me to serve after having served eight years in the artillery), I fled from San José and offered myself as a volunteer in San Francisco. The Monterey haircut was not introduced in San Francisco because Captain Argüello was opposed to it. Later, some of the [soldiers of Monterey] joined our company with the saddle [haircut] made like those of horses. This was something that produced much indignation because it was something that had not been seen before in California. My enlistment was for ten years. After serving them, I retired in September 1827, after the founding of Mission San Francisco de Solano.

I was the active corporal of the guard and foreman of the mission; I was in charge of the work detail for two years and several months until I retired to Mission San José where I served fifteen years as a foreman of daily operations. During the time I served as the foreman, Fathers Buenaventura Fortuni and Narciso Durán were the priests.[7] Later, when the previously mentioned retired

---

[6]Pablo Vicente de Solá was born in Spain (Beebe and Senkewicz, 337). He came to New Spain as a military officer. In 1814, he was appointed governor of Alta California and remained in office until 1822. He was supposed to be of "normal weight, heavy build, short neck, large and somewhat long head, wide face, very few teeth, hair almost white, with a deep and calm voice."

[7]Maynard Geiger, *Franciscan Missionaries in Hispanic California, 1769–1848: A Bibliographical Dictionary* (San Marino, CA: Huntington Library, 1969). Geiger points out that Father Narciso Durán was born in Spain. He arrived at Mission San José in 1806 and stayed there until 1833. During this time, in collaboration with Fray Buenaventura Fortuny, he developed the mission into one of the most successful ones. After moving to Mission Santa Barbara, he opposed Governor Echeandía's plan for the emancipation of Indians.

los citados de la misión, entró el Padre José Ma. de Jesús González, quien quedó allí hasta mucho después de secularizada la misión.[8] Cuando se secularizó ésta y la recibieron José de Jesús Vallejo y Amesti, yo me retiré a mi rancho llamado de San Ramón.[9] Volví a la misión por llamado del Padre González a recibir las temporalidades de nuevo, por empeños del mismo Padre y de Dn. José de Jesús Vallejo. Estuve dos años más con ellos, y entonces el Visitador General Dn. Guillo. E.P. Hartnell me entregó la misión nombrándome Admor., después de echar de ella a los Sres. Vallejo y Amesti. Esto fue por 1840.

A los dos años de desempeñar ese cargo me sacaron de la misión honradamente por orden del Gobr. Alvarado, porque no quise entregar indebidamte. 1300$ pertenecientes a la comunidad, para sufragar los gastos de un gran baile que el Sr. Gobernador había dado en Monterey.[10]

Vino a exigírmelos un yerno de Dn. Luis Argüello (Don José Eulogio Celis) en nombre de Alvarado, y yo le contesté que le entregaría las existencias de tejas y adobes (que era lo que había en la misión en ese tiempo) a la hora que quisiera. Se enfureció el hombre y arrancó pa. Monterey a dar cuenta de mi respuesta al Sr. Gobr. Le había yo advertido a Dn. José que yo había recibido la misión con una deuda de $15.000 y la había pagado a

---

[8]Geiger, 115. De acuerdo a Geiger el padre José María de Jesús González nació en Guadalajara, México. En 1833, él y otros franciscanos provenientes del Colegio de Zacatecas llegaron al puerto de Monterey. González fue el que reemplazó al padre Narciso Durán en la misión de San José. González permaneció en ella hasta 1842. El historiador Geiger indica que González escribió una carta en 1864 al Reverendo Joaquín Adam en la cual dá una descripción de la misión de San José durante el tiempo de su llegada a ella. González escribió: "En el inventario hecho en enero de 1837, los resultados indicaron que la misión enumerban 1,300 neófitos; un gran tramo de tierra, bien labrada; el granero lleno con semillas; dos huertos, uno con 1,600 arboles frutales; dos viñedos—uno con 6,039 parras y el otro con 5,000; herramientas para agricultura en abundancia; talleres para carpinteros, herreros, zapateros y también para curtidores, y todas las herramientas para esos trabajos." González añadió que la misión era dueña de miles de cabezas de ganado.

[9]Beebe y Senkewicz, 341. Los escritores apuntan de que José de Jesús Vallejo, hijo de Ignacio Vallejo y María Antonia Lugo, nació en San José en 1798 y ocupó varios cargos militares y civiles. José de Jesús llegó a ser administrador de la misión de San José en 1836. Murió en 1882.

[10]Beebe y Senkewicz, 316. Los autores anotan de que Juan Bautista Alvarado, hijo de José Francisco Alvarado y María Josefa Vallejo, era originario de Monterey y nació en 1809. Él tuvo el cargo de secretario de la Deputación de California desde 1828 hasta 1834 y fungió como uno de sus miembros en 1835. En 1836, Juan Bautista encabezó una revolución en contra del gobernador interino, Nicolás Gutiérrrez. Más tarde, él sirvió como gobernador hasta 1842. En 1844, él participó en la revuelta en contra del gobernador Manuel Micheltorena.

from the mission, Father José María de Jesús González took over and remained there until long after its secularization.[8] When it was secularized and it was handed over to Misters José de Jesús Vallejo and Amesti, I retired to my ranch called San Ramon.[9] I returned to the Mission when Father González called me to resume supervision of the daily operations at the request of the same priest and Don José de Jesús Vallejo. I stayed an additional two years more with them and then Visitor General Don Guillo. E. P. Hartnell turned over the mission to me, naming me administrator after he ousted from it Misters Vallejo and Amesti. This was done around 1840.

After two years of working in this position, I was honorably dismissed by order of Governor [Juan Bautista] Alvarado because I refused to improperly give him 1,300 pesos that belonged to the community to cover the expenses of a grand dance that the governor had given in Monterey.[10]

A son-in-law of Don Luis Argüello (Don José Eulogio Celis), on behalf of Alvarado, came to demand the sum. I told him that I would give him the supplies of roof tile and adobe bricks (this is what was available at the mission at that time) whenever he wished. The man became furious and left for Monterey to inform the governor of my response. I had made it clear to Don José that I had received the mission with a debt of 15,000 pesos, which I had already paid to

---

[8]Geiger, 115. According to Geiger, Father José María de Jesús González was born in Guadalajara, México. In 1833, he arrived with other Franciscans from the College of Zacatecas in Monterey. He replaced Father Narciso Durán at Mission San José and remained there until 1842. Geiger notes that González wrote a letter in 1864 to Reverend Joaquín Adam giving him a description of the mission at the time of his arrival. González wrote: "In inventory made January 1837, the results showed that the said mission numbered 1,300 neophytes; a great piece of land, well tilled; the store house filled with seed; two orchards, one with 1,600 fruit trees; two vineyards—one with 6,039 vines, the other with 5,000; tools for husbandry in abundance; shops for carpenters, blacksmiths, shoemakers, and even a tanner, and all the implements of the work." In addition, González states that this mission owned thousands of livestock.

[9]Beebe and Senkewicz, 341. The authors note that José de Jesús Vallejo, a son of Ignacio Vallejo and María Antonia Lugo, was born in San José in 1798. He held several military and civilian positions in Alta California. José became the administrator of Mission San José in 1836. He died in 1882.

[10]Beebe and Senkewicz, 316. The writers state that Juan Bautista Alvarado, son of José Francisco Alvarado and María Josefa Vallejo, was born in Monterey in 1809. He served as secretary for the California Deputation from 1828 to 1834 and became one of its members in 1835. Juan B. Alvarado led a revolution against acting governor, Nicolás Gutiérrez, in 1836. Afterwards, Alvarado served as governor until 1842. In 1844, he participated in a revolt against Governor Manuel Micheltorena.

Dn. Pedro Arenas, residente en San Diego. Volvió algunos días después Don José con la misma exigencia y le di la misma respuesta que antes. Entonces a su regreso a Mont. el Sr. Alvarado mandó un oficial (Alfr. Julian Estrada) con 10 soldados armados a quitarme el encargo y obligarme a entregar las llaves sin formar inventario. Me sorprendieron a las 7 ó 8 de la noche abocándome las armas sobre mi cuerpo; yo tomé las llaves a las manos de todas las oficinas, y no las entregué. Dije a Estrada y sus soldados que me matasen, y después podrían apoderarse de las llaves pero que vivo no las daba.

En este acto entraron al cuarto donde me hallaba yo, el Señor Padre González y Dn. José de Jesús Vallejo, quienes le dijeron al oficial que yo tenía la razón, pues no podía ni debía entregar la misión sin inventariarla, porque yo la había recibido inventariada. Retiró el oficial su tropa al cuartel, y yo quedé libre habiéndoles dado un vaso de licor a cada uno. Ocupamos nueve días en la formación del inventario: era inmensa la cantidad de semillas y de herramientas, que como de efectos en el almacén, que tenía la misión, sin contar el ganado. Había 40,000 fanegas de todas semillas en los trojes, 16,000 cabezas de ganado mayor, 30,000 de borregada, 300 caballos de servisio, 500 o 600 yeguas; 100 yuntas de bueyes, 100 vacas mansas, fuera de las demás existencias, huertas ta. Después de hecho el inventario le entregué la misión con todas sus pertenencias a Joaqn. Castro y José Anto. Estrada, advirtiéndoles que me retiraba para mi rancho, y que la misión no duraría pasado dos años, como se verificó. Pues antes de los dos años se habían llevado pa. San Pablo hasta los estantes del almacén con todo y efectos. Del ganado no quedó nada, hasta los alembiques de la misión y las ollas en que se freían los untos podrían hallarse hoy mismo en San Pablo.

Volveré ahora a dar cuenta de los sucesos de Cal. en mi vida militar.

El año 1805 salieron el difunto Ignacio Higuera, Joaqn. Higuera, J. Anto. Sánchez a acompañar al Padre Ministro de la misión de San José, Pedro Cuevas, a catequizar los indígenas gentiles de la ranchería de Los Loechas, como 14 leguas al oriente de la misión, arriba del actual pueblo de Livermore, a 4 ó 5 leguas de dista.[11] Los indios, a la llegada del

---

[11]Geiger, 58. Aunque Amador recuerda a este misionero como Pedro Cuevas, Geiger lo identifica como Pedro de la Cueva. De la Cueva era nativo de Estremadura, España; él llegó a la misión de San José alrededor de 1804, y sirvió en ella hasta 1806. De acuerdo a Geiger, de la Cueva fue atraído a Las Loechas por un engaño de un indígena cristiano—un "traidor"— quien lo llevó allá reclamando que alguien estaba moribundo y que deseaba hablar con el padre. Geiger menciona que de la Cueva era un alcohólico habitual. Después de que fue aprobada su petición debido a enfermedad y fue relevado de su cargo en la misión, de la Cueva regresó al centro de la Nueva España en 1806.

Don Pedro Arena, a resident of San Diego. Don José came back a few days later and made the same demand and I gave him the same response that I had made earlier. After his [Celis'] return to Monterey, Sr. Alvarado sent an officer (Second Lieutenant Julian Estrada) with ten armed soldiers to remove me from my position and compel me to surrender the [mission] keys without performing an inventory. They took me by surprise around seven or eight at night, pushing their weapons against my body; I took in my hands the keys from every room and refused to surrender them. I told Estrada and his soldiers that only by killing me would they take possession of the keys but that as long as I was alive, I would not give [the keys] to them.

At that moment, Father González and Don José de Jesús Vallejo came to the room I was in and told the officer that I was correct and that I could not surrender the mission without an inventory being made because I had received it with an inventory. The officer removed his troops to his quarters and I was set free; I then gave each one of them a glass of liquor. It took us nine days to come up with an inventory: there was an immense quantity of grains and tools as well as other effects that the mission had in its warehouses, not counting the cattle. There were 40,000 **fanegas** of all types of grains in the granaries, 16,000 head of cattle, 30,000 head of sheep, 300 service horses, 500 to 600 mares, 100 pairs of oxen, and 100 domesticated cows. There were also orchards. After the inventory was completed, I turned over the mission, with all its belongings, to Joaquín Castro and José Antonio Estrada, forewarning them that once I retired myself to my ranch, the mission would not survive more than two years. This proved to be true. Before the two years had transpired, they had even taken the permanent fixtures and the effects of the warehouse to San Pablo. Nothing remained of the cattle, even the scanty remnants of the mission and the pots, where the **untos** were boiled, were found in San Pablo.

I now return to give an account of the events in California during my years in the military.

In the year 1805, the now departed Ignacio Higuera, Joaquín Higuera, and J. Antonio Sánchez left to accompany the Father Minister of Mission San José, Pedro Cuevas, to convert the Indian gentiles of **Ranchería** Los Loechas, located about fourteen leagues east of the mission, above the present-day town of Livermore, at the distance of some four or five leagues.[11] At the arrival of the

---

[11]Geiger, 58. Although Amador remembered this missionary as Pedro Cuevas, Geiger identifies him as Pedro de la Cueva. He was born in Estremadura, Spain. De la Cueva arrived at Mission San José around 1804 and continued serving there until 1806. According to Geiger, de la Cueva was lured to Las Loechas by a ruse from a Christianized Indian—a "traitor"— who took him there claiming that someone was dying and wanted to talk to a priest. Geiger notes that de la Cueva was a confirmed alcoholic. After authorities accepted his petition that he be relieved of his duties at the mission because of illness, de la Cueva returned to the center of New Spain in 1806.

Padre y los soldados, hicieron armas contra éstos. Jarearon al Padre y a uno de los soldados, y al mayordomo Ignacio Higuera. Este Señor Higuera se defendió hasta que se le acabó la munición, entonces los indios lo cogieron vivo, y lo mataron a flechazos.después de muerto, le cortaron las dos manos, y le arrancaron la cabellera; el Padre con el soldado Joaquín Higuera y la poca munición que le quedaba a éste, se escaparon ocultándose en una cueva de piedra, disparando algún tiro que otro a los indios estando en la cueva, para no agotar su munición. Allí estuvieron hasta la noche, heridos ambos. Los otros soldados Sánchez y Alviso huyeron y vinieron a la misión a dar cuenta de lo que había pasado. En el silencio de la noche se salieron de la cueva el Padre y Joaqn. Higuera y a pie lograron, caminando por las lomas y ocultándose de los indios, llegar a la misión. Entonces vinieron el Teniente Gabriel Moraga y su tropa a castigar a los malhechores. Éstos, se habían ya cambiado al río de San Joaquín a una ranchería que se llamaba de Los Pitemes. Hubo un lijero combate, y prontamente agarraron a los indios, hombres, mugeres y niños.

Las mugeres y los niños fueron reducidos a la misión de San José para ser cristianizados, y los hombres fueron puestos a hacer adobes pa. el cuadro del presidio de San Francisco. Cuando cumplieron sus condenas se hicieron todos ellos cristianos. En aquella espedición fuimos yo y varios otros vecinos del pueblo de San José pa. prestar ausilio, porque la tropa era poca.

El año 1818 salí yo con el Alférez José Antonio Sánchez a una campaña en el parage de Las Calaveras, un poco más adelante de donde está hoy la ciudad de Stockton.[12] La espedn. se componía de 25 soldados, y el alférez, y algunos indios cristianos ausiliares; allí tuvimos una acción reñida con los indígenas. De nuestra parte hubo un muerto (un indio ausiliar) y 5 heridos—José Higuera, Pablo Pacheco, Agustín Bernal, José Ma. Gómez y yo. Matamos 50 y tantos indios; cogimos presos otros 50 y nos retiramos con los prisioneros a San Francisco. La acción empezó en un arroyo y acabó en un roblar. Los que no cayeron en nuestras manos, se escaparon en un bosque, entre ellos deben haber muchos heridos. En el roblar después de dispararles una descarga

---

[12]Beebe y Senkewicz, 336. De acuerdo a los escritores, José Antonio Sánchez, nacido en Sinaloa, fue miembro de la compañía militar de San Francisco. Aparentemente, José Antonio ganó gran fama como un combatiente experimentado de indígenas; fue veterano de muchas campañas en contra de ellos. Él también sirvió como comandante militar en el presidio de San Francisco desde 1829 a 1833. Se jubiló del servicio militar en 1836 y murió algunos años más tarde.

priest and the soldiers, the Indians rose up in arms against them. They wounded with [arrows] the Father, some of the soldiers, and the foreman Ignacio Higuera. This Mr. Higuera defended himself until he finished all his ammunition; then, the Indians captured him alive and killed him with arrows. After he died, they cut off his two hands and they scalped his hair. The priest and the soldier Joaquín Higuera, with the remaining little ammunition that he had, escaped and hid in a rock cave. To keep from running out of ammunition, he shot only occasionally at the Indians who were already in the cave. The soldiers Sánchez and Alviso fled and reached the mission and reported what had happened. In the silence of the night the priest and Joaquín Higuera left the cave on foot, and by walking over hills and hiding from the Indians, they managed to arrive at the mission. Afterwards, Lieutenant Gabriel Moraga and his troops went to punish the attackers. These [Indians] had moved to the San Joaquín River to a ranchería called Los Pitemes. After a small skirmish, they quickly captured the Indians, including men, women, and children.

The women and children were sent to Mission San José so that they could be Christianized and the men were put to work, making adobe bricks for the walls of the Presidio of San Francisco. When they completed their sentences they all became Christians. In this expedition, I and various other **vecinos** from the town of San José, went to provide assistance because the troop was small.

In 1818, Second Lieutenant José Antonio Sánchez and I went on a campaign at the Calaveras place, just a little ahead where the city of Stockton today is located.[12] The expedition was made up of twenty-five soldiers, the second lieutenant, and some Christianized Indian auxiliaries. There, we had a real fierce fight with the Indians. On our part we had one death (an auxiliary Indian) and five wounded: José Higuera, Pablo Pacheco, Agustín Bernal, José María Gómez, and myself. We killed some fifty Indians and took another fifty of them prisoners, returning to San Francisco with them. The battle started near a brook and ended in an oak grove. Those who were not captured by us escaped into a forest; among these [Indians] there had to have been many who were wounded. At the oak grove, after simultaneously discharging

[12]Beebe and Senkewicz, 336. According to the authors, José Antonio Sánchez, who was born in Sinaloa, was a member of the military company of San Francisco. Apparently, he had earned the reputation as a skilled Indian fighter; he was a veteran of many campaigns against them. José Antonio served as military commander at the Presidio of San Francisco from 1829 to 1833. He retired from the military in 1836 and died several years later.

de fusilería cargamos sobre ellos con nuestras lanzas y les hicimos una gran carnicería. La causa de haber ido a atacarlos, fue el que ellos habían asesinado a unos cristianos de la misión de San José. Los prisioneros fueron puestos en los trabajos. En aquel tiempo se estaba haciendo el cuadro del presidio con adobes, pues el que existió antes era de palo parado.

Dos años despúes (en 1820) salimos a otra campaña, a una ranchería llamada de Los Cosumnes, por un robo que habían hecho aquellos indígenas en el pueblo de San José. Mandaba la espedn. que se componía de 25 solds., 15 vecinos del pueblo, y 50 indios cristianos, el Alfz. José Anto. Sánchez. Los vecinos estaban al cargo del alcalde Juan Alvires. Caímos sobre la ranchería a la madrugada. Aquí advertiré que los indios no dormían de noche, y sí en la madrugada, así es que esta era la hora propicia para cogerlos desprevenidos. Matamos 8 ó 10 de los indígenas, los demás cogieron un tular grande y se escaparon. Recogimos 70 caballos, y nos volvimos al presidio sin prisioneros. Si habíamos cogido al principio dos Capitanejos, a quienes mandó el Alférez aplicarles 200 azotes a cada uno en el mismo campo, dándoles libres con la advertencia de que si volvieran a robar ó a hacer armas lo habrían de pagar con la vida.

El año de 1824 estuve en otra espedn. con el Tente. Moraga por la parte opuesta del río, hasta un parage llamado de los Cerritos Cuates. De allí nos volvimos para el Sur, sin haber tenido encuentro con los indios. En el diario que llevaba el Tente. y a nuestro regreso se dio nombres a los ríos. Al río de los Cerritos Cuates se le nombro Jesús María, más acá al río que está en Marysville se dio el nombre del Sacramento. A un brazo del Sacramento se le nombró el río Americano. En la ranchería de Cosumnes se llamó al río La Pasión. En Moquelemnes llamamos al río Guadalupe. Al pasar por Estanislao se llamó San Francisco al río que allí existe. Despúes pasamos a Jabalumes, al que se llamó río de Dolores. Despúes fuimos al río Reyes.

En seguida a un zanjón inmediato lo titulamos Arroyo del Zanjón de San José. Más adelante dimos a un río el nombre de Mariposas. Después en el tular que hay se puso a la laguna el nombre de Buena Vista. Su nombre géntil era de Los Taches. Más luego pasamos la laguna para acá pa. Sta. Bárbara, y nos hallamos con la novedad del alzamiento de los cristianos de La Purísima y Santa Inés. Entonces el Tente. Moraga tomó 14 prisioneros de los cabecillas y los hizo fusilar contra una pared. De allí pasamos a Santa Bárbara. De allí regresé

a fusillade of our firearms, we charged at them with our spears and commenced a great butchery. The reason for having gone to attack the Indians was that they had killed some Christians from Mission San José. The prisoners [from this attack] were put to work. At that time, the walls of the Presidio were being built with adobes since the old [walls] that had existed before were made from wooden stakes.

Two years later (in 1820), we went on another campaign to a **ranchería** called Los Cosumnes due to a robbery that those Indians had committed in the Pueblo of San José. Second Lieutenant José Antonio Sánchez was in command of the expedition that was composed of twenty-five soldiers, fifteen **vecinos** of San José, and fifty Christianized Indians. The vecinos were led by the **alcalde,** Juan Alvires. We reached the rancheria at dawn. Here I would like to note that the Indians did not sleep at night but at dawn. Hence, it was the proper time to catch them unprepared. We killed eight or ten Indians; the others escaped on a large tule raft. We picked up seventy horses and returned to the presidio without prisoners. At the beginning [of the raid], we captured two Indian captains, for each of whom the Second Lieutenant ordered 200 lashes be given out in the field, before letting them go with a warning that if they continued to rob or take up arms, they would pay with their lives.

In 1824, I was involved in another expedition with Lieutenant [Gabriel] Moraga on the opposite side of the river until reaching a place called Los Cerritos Cuates. From there we turned south, without having any clashes with the Indians. In the diary that the lieutenant kept and after our return we gave names to the rivers. The river of the Cerritos Cuates was named Jesús María. A closer river, the one that is in Marysville, became the Sacramento; a tributary of the Sacramento was named Americano. At the ranchería Cosumnes, the river was called Pasión. In Moquelemnes, we called the river Guadalupe. When we passed through Estanislao, the river that still exists here was named San Francisco. Afterwards we passed to Jabalumes, at which point we called the river Dolores. From there we went to the Reyes River.

A gully immediately next to it we called **Zanjón** de San José Creek. Further on, we came to a river by the name of Mariposas. Beyond [this point], in the water-reeds that are there we gave the lagoon [there] the name of Buena Vista; its Indian name was Los Taches. We proceeded to cross the lagoon on this side of Santa Bárbara. We got the news of the uprising of Christian Indians at La Purísima and Santa Inés Missions. Lieutenant Moraga took fourteen prisoners among their captains and had them executed against a wall. From there we went to Santa Bárbara. After reaching it,

yo con un correo extraordinario pa. San Francisco, dejando la espedn. en Sta. Bárbara preparándose para ir en persecución de los indios que se habían refugiado en la laguna de Buenavista. Mis compañeros me informaron después que habían logrado capturar a todos los cabecillas y los habían sentenciado a obras públicas en los presidios.

En el año de 1819 salió de San Francisco una espedn. al mando del Capitán Dn. Luis Anto. Argüello con 73 soldados, un oficial el Alférez Sánchez, y el Sargento Francisco Soto. Entre los soldados iban como 25 de infantería de la campa. de San Blas, aunque todos iban montados. Yo era a la sazón cabo habilitado comandante de la escolta de Sta. Cruz, y me relevaron para ir en la espedición. Como en efecto, fui de asistente del Capitán Argüello. Llevamos 400 bestias por delante, pasadas por el estrecho de Carquinez. Anduvimos por el valle del río de Jesús María 21 días hasta llegar al río de la Trinidad. Tuvimos en el camino una ligera escaramuza con unos indígenas sobre un temascal (los temascales de allí eran bajo de y parejos con la tierra).

El comandante nos había prohibido disparar ni un solo tiro, pero los indios comenzaron a jarearnos con fuerza, y entonces el Capn. Argüello dispuso bajar un cañón de a 6 que iba en una mula, y su cureña.[13] Lo hizo abocar al temascal con orden de no ofender a los indígenas, sino de dispararlo al aire. Yo le metí la punta de la cuña a la colilla del cañón, y me llevé 7 Indios, por lo cual después quiso castigarme el capitán; pero no me lo pudo probar, y así me escapé del castigo. Enseguida, se me fue una mula cargada con 500 cartuchos al río y no fue posible detenerla. Se perdió en el río con toda y carga, no se vio más la mula. Después, había un soldado medio loco, llamado José Navarrete. Se le disparó la carabina dentro de la misma funda, y le dio el tiro a uno de los de a pie; le pasó la cartuchera de la cintura, siete cañones de hoja de lata, y arrancándole del caballo, la bala le tiró cosa de seis varas. Nosotros nos echamos a pie porque el tiro le prendió la ropa al infante, llamado Juan Miranda; éste creía que la bala le había pasado el cuerpo, y daba gritos, clamando, "¡por Dios, tráiganme al padre, que me muero!" y con todo, no fue más que un puro susto, pues no tenía el hombre ni siquiera un rasguño. A esto el Capitán mandó castigar

---

[13]Amador usa la palabra "jarar" para describir el lanzamiento de flechas. El historiador H. H. Bancroft pensó que "jarar," en la forma que la usaba Amador, era un "californismo," una corrupción de la palabra en español que indicaba un dardo o un tipo de flecha.

I returned with a special courier to San Francisco, leaving the expedition in Santa Bárbara as it was readying itself to go in pursuit of Indians who had taken refuge at the Buenavista Lagoon. My fellow soldiers later informed me that they had managed to capture all the leaders and that they had been sentenced to perform public works in the presidios.

In 1819, an expedition left San Francisco led by Captain Don Luis Antonio Argüello and composed of seventy-three soldiers, one officer, Second Lieutenant Sánchez, and Sergeant Francisco Soto. Among the soldiers were twenty-five infantrymen from the San Blas Company, yet every one of them was mounted. At that time, I was the active corporal of the guard of Santa Cruz; I was relieved of my post to be a part of the expedition, and in effect, I became the assistant to Captain Argüello. We took 400 horses with us, which we crossed at the Carquinez Strait. We traveled through the valley of the Jesús María River for twenty-one days before reaching the Trinidad River. On the way we had a minor skirmish with some Indians near a **temascal**. (The temascales there were low and level to the ground.)

The commander had prohibited us from discharging even a single shot, but when the Indians started showering us with arrows Captain Argüello issued orders to unload a size six cannon and its mounting, which was being carried by a mule.[13] He commanded that it be aimed at the temascal, making it clear not to bother the Indians; he just wanted it discharged in the air. I used the match-cord to light the fuse of the cannon and I hit seven Indians; later on, the Captain wanted to punish me. He could not prove anything and so I managed to escape punishment. Afterwards, I lost a mule carrying 500 cartridges when she ran away into the river and I was unable to stop her; she was lost in the river with the entire load. We never saw the mule again. There was a soldier, who was a fool, by the name of José Navarrete. His carbine was discharged in its holster and the shot hit one of the foot soldiers; it went through [Navarrete's] cartridge belt and seven cartridges made of tin, knocking him off his horse. The bullet threw him a distance of six **varas.** We got on our feet because the bullet set fire to the clothes of the infantryman named Juan Miranda; he thought that the bullet had gone through his body and was shouting, begging "By God, bring the priest, I am dying." After all this, it was nothing but a scare, since the man suffered nothing, not even a scratch. The captain sent Navarrete to be punished,

---

[13]Amador uses the word "jarar" to describe the discharging of arrows. Historian H. H. Bancroft believed that "jarar" in the way that Amador used it was a "Californism" since in formal Spanish it means an arrow or a dart.

a Navarrete poniéndole cuatro cueras, y que fuera a batir el camino porqe. no cuidaba de sus armas.

Siguió la tropa su marcha por toda la vega del rió pa. el norte, y los indígenas, asustados del cañonazo (diciendo un toro ha bramado y nos ha asustado) salían a encontrarnos a cada momento con banderas de tapojos o plumas de pájaros y pita de inmortal (muy blanca a manera de la del maguey) pa. regalarnos, y nos acompañaban hasta la siguiente ranchería. En este intermedio, a los 8 días de camino, nos encontramos con un temascal que tenía como 200 varas en circumferencia al raso de la tierra. El Capitán, por curiosidad, mandó salir toda la gente, entrando los soldados y sacándolos del temascal; hizo poner en fila todos los indios, los hombres en una línea, las mugeres en otra, y los niños en otra; se contaron al pie de 3000 almas. Esto parecerá fábula, pero es la pura verdad sin exageración ninguna. Seguimos adelante, sin haberles regalado nada a esos indios, porque no llevábamos más que la provisión necesaria. La verdad es que esta espedn. desde que salió no llevaba otra cosa que los bastimentos necesarios para alcanzarnos hasta llegar al Columbia. Nuestro guía era un inglés llamado John Gilroy, el mismo que ha dado su nombre al pueblo de Gilroy. Él había dicho que conocía bien la ruta al Columbia, y era verdad, pero por un camino diferente del que nosotros llevábamos. El camino de él era por la sierra, y nosotros íbamos por el valle.

Descubierto esto, tomamos por guía a un indio desde el río de la Trinidad; quien en dos días nos llevó al Columbia atravesando la Sierra. De allí volvimos atrás, y tomamos la sierra que viene a caer a la línea del presidio de Ross. Gastamos 12 días en atravesar la sierra, matando a lanzadas el caballo o mula que se cansaban, y quemando el aparejo, pa. que ni unos ni otros fuesen a manos de los indios.

Llegamos, por fin, a San Rafael, y nos retiramos pa. San Francisco. En seguida, a poco tiempo volvimos al descubrimto. de Bodega con el Tente. Moraga (sería esto por abril o mayo de 1820), y pasamos a Ross, en donde nos dieron un cordial recibimto. Estábamos en el año de la pobreza (porque hacía mucho tiempo que no venían los situados de México). Al regreso de Ross volvimos a Bodega en donde había dos buques, fragatas, anclados, los que nos dieron un escelente recibimto. Después de las salvas que nos hicieron las fragatas, Moraga nos mandó corresponder a ellas con otra de

ordering that he be given four lashes and to go scout ahead of the group because he did not take care of his weapons.

The troops continued their march all along the side of the river to the north, and the Indians, [who got] scared by the boom of the cannon (they were saying that a bull was bellowing and that he had scared them) would come out to meet us. They would at every moment give [us] **tapojo,** bird feather and **pita de inmortal** (very white in the manner of the maguey plant) flags. Then, they would accompany us to the next ranchería. During this part of the expedition, on the eighth day of our journey, we came upon a **temascal** that was 200 **varas** in circumference at ground level. The captain, out of curiosity, ordered all of the people out of it; the soldiers entered it and took them out. He forced all the Indians to form lines; the men on one line, the women on another one, and the children in still another one. We counted around 3,000 souls. This appears to be a fable, but it is the whole truth, without exaggeration. We continued the expedition, without having given anything to those Indians because we carried only the necessary provisions. The truth is that this expedition from the start did not carry anything but only the necessary supplies to allow us to reach the Columbia [River]. Our guide was an Englishman by the name of John Gilroy, the same one that has given his name to the town of Gilroy. He had said that he knew the route to the Columbia well, which was true but through a road that was different from the one we were on. His route was through the mountains but we took the one through the valley.

After becoming aware of this, we took an Indian guide at the Trinidad River who in two days time took us to the Columbia by crossing the mountains. From there we turned back and we took the mountains that level off at the Ross Presidio. It took us twelve days to cross the mountains, spearing to death the horses or the mules that got tired and burning the harnesses so that neither could fall in the hands of the Indians.

Finally, we reached San Rafael and retired to San Francisco. Almost immediately thereafter, we returned to the discovery of Bodega Bay with Lieutenant [Gabriel] Moraga (this was around April or May of 1820) and then we went on to [Fort] Ross where we received a warm welcome. We were living in impoverished times because we had not received our salaries coming from México for a long time. Coming back from [Fort] Ross, we returned to Bodega where there were two ships (frigates) anchored there; they gave us an excellent welcome. After the frigates gave us a cannon salute, Moraga ordered us to reciprocate with our own

fusilería, la que hicimos los 30 hombres que estábamos con él. Saltaron a tierra los oficiales rusos, y se llevaron a bordo a Moraga y a nuestros dos sargentos José Anto. Sánchez y Francisco Soto. Allá les regalaron, haciéndoles, además, presentes de considerable valor. A nosotros los de la tropa nos mandaron los de los buques dos lanchas que nos llevaron abordo quedando dos soldados en el pabellón de las armas, que a su tiempo fueron relevados y pasaron también abordo. Nos dieron un avío considerable. Salimos provistos de todo, mantas, cortes de indiana o calico, zapatos to to. Al casado como casado, y al soltero como soltero. Vinimos a tierra con camisas de saya saya, (género de seda color de rosa oscuro-claro), con lo que se vio el espectáculo algo raro de pobres con camisas de seda. Llegamos al fin a San Francisco al segundo día hechos unos galantes causándole envidia a nuestros pobres compañeros que se habían quedado en el presidio.

En 1828 hicieron un robo los indios en mi rancho y en el de los Castros. Salimos en pos de ellos 14 hombres a darles alcance, y cuando llegamos a la ranchería ya se habían comido la mayor parte de las bestias.

Rodeamos la ranchería y un temascal (la ranchería de Los Telamas, río arriba del Moquelemne) y negándose los indígenas a rendirse, le prendimos fuego al temascal con ceras de ellos mismos. Algunos salieron, huyendo del fuego, pero batiéndose, y jarearon a 3 compañeros, vecinos del pueblo de San José (el español José Noriega, Anastacio Mendoza y Anastacio Chabolla). Al día siguiente marchamos pa. la sierra a la orilla de un bosque. Allí tuvimos un combate con los indios, y salió herido un vecino llamado José Galindo (éramos vecinos todos los de esa espedn. y la mandaba el Sor. Noriega). Galindo recibió un jarazo en el lagarto del brazo izquierdo, porque no supo o no pudo impedirlo con su adarga.

Debo hacer aquí la advertencia que todos los vecinos llevábamos cueras y adargas, además de las armas. Casi todos los de la espedn. habíamos sido soldados de cuera, y poseíamos esos utensilios o armas de defensa, a más de las ofensivas porque, si bien es cierto que el soldado al retirarse del servicio tenía el derecho de venderle todo al habilitado, y éste tenía obligación de tomar caballos y armas por su costo, muchos soldados, o por lo menos algunos retenían las armas en su poder. Es verdad que esto no lo hacían sino los que les tenían amor a las armas. Continuó el combate en otra ranchería, fue cosa de cuerpo a cuerpo en un roblar y en un chamizal. Agustín Albiso

fusillade of firearms, which we, the thirty-six men that were with him, did. The Russian officers came to shore and they took Moraga and our two sergeants, José Antonio Sánchez and Francisco Soto, on board. While there, they gave them gifts of considerable value. For us, troops, two boats from the vessels were sent to take us aboard, leaving two soldiers at our Bell tent. Later, they were relieved from duty and they, too, went aboard. They gave us a considerable [amount] of provisions. We left with supplies of all types: **mantas**, pieces of Indiana or Calico [fabric], and also shoes. Those who were married got supplies for the married; those who were single, received supplies for the single. We came ashore with shirts of **saya saya** (a type of silk in a light/dark pink color), which made us into a spectacle—poor people in silk shirts. We came back to San Francisco on the second day, transformed into gallant men and causing much envy amongst our poor fellow soldiers who had stayed behind at the presidio.

In 1828, the Indians committed a robbery at my ranch and at Castro's ranch. We, fourteen men, went in their pursuit, but when we got to the ranchería they had already eaten most of the beasts.

We surrounded the ranchería and a **temascal** (Los Telamas Ranchería was upstream on the Moquelemne) and after they refused to surrender, we set fire to the **temascal** with their own candles. Some of them came out, fleeing the fire but fighting and wounding with arrows three of our companions, **vecinos** from the pueblo of San José (the Spaniard José Noriega, Anastacio Mendoza, and Anastacio Chabolla). On the following day we marched to the mountains, at the edge of the forest. There, we combated the Indians, and a civilian José Galindo was wounded. (We were all **vecinos** in this expedition and we were commanded by Mr. Noriega.) Galindo received an arrow in a large muscle of his left arm because he did not know how or could not deflect it with his shield.

At this point I would like to note that all the **vecinos** were carrying leather jackets and shields in addition to weapons. Almost everyone in the expedition had been a **soldado de cuera**, and we owned our equipment and defensive weapons as well as offensive weapons because although it is true that a soldier upon retiring from military service had the right to sell everything to the company paymaster (this individual had the obligation of taking horses and weapons at cost), many soldiers, or at least some, chose to keep weapons in their possession. It is true that they would only do this if they had a love of weapons. The fight continued in another ranchería—it was man-to-man combat at an oak grove and at a **chamisal** thicket. Agustín Albiso was

bregaba con un indio a quien no podía matar, y yo con otro. Agustín quedó en un arroyo con su indio pa. matarlo si podía; yo con el mío a quien disparé un tiro al pulmón, pero me falló el tiro de mi carabina. Era indio pelón, a quien no podía yo agarrar de las greñas, y así lo atropellé con mi caballo echándolo a tierra.

Yo me monté a caballo encima de él, y lo trabé con las espuelas dándole con la culata de la carabina en la cabeza sin poderle rendir. El valiente indio se incorporó llevándome montado sobre su espalda trabado con las espuelas y sin poder yo hacerle rendirse a pesar de los golpes que seguía yo dándole. Él casi me iba metiendo en el bosque, y me llovían flechas como buñuelos en noche buena, hasta que me acordé de mi puñal que llevaba en la cintura. Se lo metí en el estómago, echándole fuera todas las tripas; entonces cayó él rendido, y yo encima de él. Así me retiré andando pa. atrás hacia donde estaba mi caballo asegurado con la rienda, defendiéndome siempre de las flechas que me disparaban de todos lados. Logré escapar sin herida ninguna. Fui en busca del compañero Agustín Alviso, a quien encontré en el mismo sitio en que lo había dejado. Ya había él matado a su indio rompiéndole la cabeza y echándole fuera los sesos con una piedra. Durante el combate no había él podido disparar al indio ni un solo tiro con la carabina. Después de este combate singular, se huyeron los indios (sin que los hiciésemos ningún prisionero), y nosotros nos reunimos y marchamos a pernoctar en el río de San Joaquín. En la noche murió José Galindo, lo atravesamos sobre una silla y lo tragimos a enterrar a San José.

Creo que en el año de 1837 (estaba Alvarado de Gobernador) vinieron los indios y me robaron 100 bestias de mi rancho de San Ramón. Salí con 15 hombres en persecución de ellos. En el río de Taualomes, como a las 3 de la tarde caímos en la ranchería, y les quitamos 60 bestias, las que tuvimos que velarlas toda aquella noche, hasta que amaneció. Entonces seguimos el rastro de los indios arriba pa. la sierra, y no les pudimos dar alcance.

Nos volvimos a un parage nombrado El Barro en la misma sierra. Allí había un corral de piedra y un ojo de agua. Llegamos allí como a las 4 p.m. y emprendimos marcha para vigiar a los indios. No pudimos encontrar ninguno de ellos, pernoctamos en ese lugar, éramos 16, esto es, el Alférez Prado Mesa con 10 soldados, y nosotros 5 vecinos. Pusimos de guardia ocho hombres, 4 en el campo y 4 en la caballada. Nos cayeron como 200 Indios

occupied with an Indian whom he could not kill and I was doing the same with another. Agustín ended up in a stream with his Indian to kill, if only he could. I was fighting my own, whom I shot in the lungs, but my shot from the carbine failed. He was a bald Indian, so I could not grab him from the hair; hence, I had to run him down with my horse, knocking him down to the ground.

I mounted myself on top of him, jammed him with my spurs, and hit him in the head with the stock of my carbine, but I could not make him surrender. The brave Indian got up, carrying me on his back although my spurs were locked unto him. I was unable to make him surrender despite the blows that I kept giving him. He kept taking me into the forest and arrows kept raining on me like **buñuelos** on Christmas Eve. I finally remembered that I was carrying a dagger on my waistband and I stuck it in his stomach, letting out all his intestines; it was then that he fell fatigued and I landed on top of him. I then retreated, walking back to where I had left my horse secured with the reins, always defending myself against the arrows that were being shot at me from all directions. I managed to escape without a single wound. I went searching for my partner Agustín Alviso, whom I found in the same place where I had left him. He had already killed his Indian with a stone that broke open his head, letting the brains ooze out. During the battle, he had not been able to discharge a single shot with his carbine at the Indian. After this singular battle, the Indians fled (we did not take one prisoner) and we got back together and marched to explore the San Joaquín River. José Galindo died that night. We laid him over the saddle [of a horse] and brought him to be buried in San José.

I believe that it was in 1837 (Alvarado was governor) when the Indians came and stole 100 beasts at my Rancho San Ramón. Together with fifteen men, I went in pursuit of them. At the Taualomes River, around three in the afternoon, we reached the ranchería, and took back sixty beasts that we had to guard all night long until dawn. Afterwards, we followed the tracks of the Indians up into the mountains, but we could not catch up to them.

We turned back towards a place called El Barro on the same mountain. We reached a corral made of stones and a water spring around four in the afternoon and started a march to search for the Indians. We could not find a single one of them. We explored the area. We numbered sixteen, that is, the Second Lieutenant Prado Meza with ten soldiers and we five civilians. We put eight men as guards, four out in the field and four with the horse herd. Two hundred Indians

esa noche entre 12 y 2, noche muy oscura. Me dieron 4 jarazos todos a la vez; jarearon a Prado Mesa, al inglés Roberto Livermore que iba con nosotros; a otro inglés, a quien nosotros conocimos con el nombre Pérez Nicu, a Inocencio Romero; a Domingo Altamirano, a Desiderio Briones. Los guardas de la caballada echaron a huir, y los indios se la llevaron toda dejándonos sólo con las 12 bestias de guardia. Yo estuve sin sentido más de un cuarto de hora, y cuando volví en mí me preguntó el Alfz. cómo me sentía. Yo le dije que bueno aunque herido. Me preguntó qué debíamos hacer, si quedarnos o irnos con las bestias de guardia; yo me opuse, porque estaba seguro de que cada individuo tan pronto como se viera a caballo, tomaría camino, cada uno por su lado. El alférez no conocía a esa gente tan bien como yo. Entonces el alférez me lo dejó a que yo dispusiera y yo le respondí que pasara revista a sus soldados, a ver si tenían suficiente munición, que si les faltaba, yo tenía un chifle de pólvora con 90 tiros, y 22 cartuchos en mi cartuchera. Admitió él lo propuesto por mí. Cargaron dos hombres en los cañones de sus escopetas a Desiderio Briones que estaba herido en las dos rodillas, llevándolo por un arroyo abajo como dos millas: lo metimos debajo de un raicero de un roble, en donde había en el arroyito al pie del roble un ojito de agua.

Le arrimamos bellotas pa. que comiera. (No teníamos otra cosa. Los indios nos habían quitado todos los comestibles.) Más aún, la tropita moderna de Alvarado, Vallejo y Castro, en la estampida que dieron del susto que llevaron, dejaron abandonados capotes, zapatos, ta. Era gente bizoña, y absolutamente sin disciplina, porque los jefes no habían sabido dársela.

Anduvimos el resto de la noche rumbo al río de San Joaquín, todos a pie. Al amanecer nos gritó José Romero que venían los compañeros a alcanzarnos con la caballada. Yo le dije al alférez que pasara revista a su tropa, y diera orden que nadie disparase un tiro hasta tener la carabina al pecho de los enemigos, porque aquellos eran los indios que se nos venían encima. En efecto, venían 70 a caballo. Nos salimos de la vereda como 500 varas en un monte de estafiate, y nos escondimos. Los indios llegaron al lugar en donde habíamos estado y no pudieron hallar nuestras huellas por donde habíamos salido de la vereda. Ellos se fueron entonces para la estacada que tenían en Estanislao. Caminamos todo el día muertos de sed y de hambre hasta cerca del río de San Joaquín, en donde hicimos noches, completamente fatigados y sufriendo de nuestras heridas. Emprendimos camino al amanecer; alcanzamos

attacked us at night between twelve and two in the morning; it was a real dark night. Four arrows hit me at the same time; also wounded were Prado Meza, the Englishman, Roberto Livermore, who was accompanying us, another Englishman, whom we used to know as Pérez Nicu, Inocencio Romero, Domingo Altamirano, and Desiderio Briones. The horse herd guards fled and the Indians took the horses, leaving only the guards' twelve. I was unconscious for more than a quarter of an hour, and when I regained consciousness the second lieutenant asked me how I was feeling. I told him I was fine, but wounded. He asked me what we should do and if we should stay or leave with the guards' horses. I was opposed to leaving because I was certain that each individual, once on his horse, would take off on his own way. The second lieutenant did not know these people as well as I did. The second lieutenant left it up to me to decide, and I told him that he should review his troops, to check if they had sufficient ammunition, and if they were short, that I had one gunpowder bag with ninety shots and twenty-two cartridges in my cartridge belt. He accepted my proposal. Two men carried Desiderio Briones, who was wounded in both knees, with the barrels of their carbines, taking him downstream for about two miles. We put him under the cover of an oak tree, where next to the trunk there was a water spring that fed a small stream.

We collected acorns so that he could eat (we did not have anything else since the Indians had taken all our food). [It should be noted that] the little modern troops of Alvarado, Vallejo, and Castro had abandoned all their ponchos, shoes, etc. when fear overtook them and set off the stampede. They were inexperienced people, who had absolutely no discipline because their own leaders had not known how to teach it to them.

We walked the rest of the night in direction of the San Joaquín River. At dawn, José Romero shouted to us that our comrades were coming with the horse herd. I told the second lieutenant to review his troops and issue the command that no one should fire a single shot until their carbines were in front of the enemies' chests because those were Indians that were coming against us. In effect, there were seventy mounted on horses. We got off the path about 500 **varas** away and went into a thicket where we hid ourselves. The Indians came to the place where we had been and they could not find our tracks where we had left the path. They then went to their stockade in Estanislao. We walked all day, dying of thirst and hunger, until we got close to the San Joaquín River, where we camped for the night, completely tired and suffering from our wounds. We started marching at dawn and reached

el río a las 11 a.m. Hicimos unas balsas de palos atados con nuestras fajas, en las que pasamos el río, y nos acampamos dentro de un monte. Pasamos el día allí. Un tal Higuera logró matar un venado allí en el bosque, y eso comieron. Yo estaba postrado con mis heridas y el cansancio sin poder dar ni un paso. Así quedé hasta que se ocultó el sol, y entonces me despertaron para continuar la marcha. Caminamos esa noche atravesando el valle pa. un punto que se llama Buenos Aires.

En la mitad del llano nos paramos a descansar, unos por estar estropeados, y otros por sus heridas. Muy pocos estaban [con] calzados, y aún los había sin calzones. Al mismo tiempo de esta sesteada, oí yo un tiro, que fue disparado por gente del pueblo que venía a ausiliarnos, pues los que habían huido del ataque de los indios habían llegado allí diciendo que habíamos perecido todos. A poco rato correspondí a ese tiro con otro, al que me contestaron inmediatamte. El que había disparado el primer tiro era mi hijo Valentín Amador. El ausilio se reunió con nosotros, y juntos fuimos a Buenos Aires. Allí pasamos la noche. En la mañana siguiente vino el médico indio y me sacó los pedernales. Quedé medio muerto.

Para esa operación se valió el indio de unas raíces que trajo de las lomas. Una de ellas era muy larga de más de una cuarta, y muy encarnada. Se llamaba yerba de jarazo.

Otra raíz era amarilla del mismo tamaño de la otra. Se cree que es de la misma familia, aunque de distinto color.

La 3a. raíz era delgadita y larga, muy ondeble.

El indio mascó la colorada y me la untó en las heridas.

La delgadita me la dio a mascar a mí, con orden de tragarme el jugo. Este jugo me hacía correr la sangre a chorros por las heridas.

La yerba mascada que me puso el indio en las heridas, hizo enanchear las bocas de estas, y entonces él con unas tenazas de madera me estrajo los pedernales. Estas operaciones fueron tan estremadamte. dolorosas que me hicieron perder el sentido.

La raíz amarilla la usó el indio lo mismo que a la colorada.

Después que volví en mí se hizo una escalera de hombres para llevarme cargado. Me cargaron 4 indios que eran relevados por otros 4 a ciertas distancias; los que caminaron 12 leguas conmigo hasta dejarme en mi casa en mi rancho. Allí mandé dar un par de pesos y una buena cena a cada uno de los indios cargadores. A los 25 días de esa cura estaba yo bueno y sano.

Ya, el Sargento Nazario Galindo, Francisco Palomares, y otros dos más habían ido por Briones con un carrito. Lo encontraron vivo y lo trajeron. El mismo indio que me curó a mí lo sanó a él por el mismo procedimto.

the river at eleven in morning. We made a raft of logs that we tied together with our waistbands to cross the river, making camp in the woods. We spent the day there. Someone by the name of Higuera managed to kill a deer there in the forest, and that is what they ate. I was weakened by my wounds and fatigue, and was unable to take a single step. I remained in that condition until sunset when the others awoke me to continue the march. We walked through the night, crossing the valley to a place called Buenos Aires.

In the middle of the plain we stopped to rest, some from fatigue and others because of their wounds. Very few of them had shoes and some did not have pants. As we rested, I heard a rifle shot, which was discharged by the people from the pueblo that had come to rescue us, since those that had fled during the Indian attack had arrived at the town telling the people that all of us had perished. A little later, I answered the first shot with another one to which they returned a shot immediately. The one that had fired the first shot was my son, Valentín Amador. The rescuers joined us and together we went to Buenos Aires. We spent the night there. The following morning the Indian doctor came and took out the arrowheads. [As a result of the operation], I ended up half-dead.

For this operation, the Indian used some roots that he brought from the hills. One of them was very long, more than a **cuarta** in length and very reddish in color. It was called the **jarazo** plant.

Another root was yellow and the same size as the other. It is believed that they belonged to the same family although of a different color.

The third root was very thin and long, very flexible.

The Indian chewed the red one and rubbed it on my wounds.

He gave the thin one to me to chew, ordering me to swallow the juice. This juice made my blood gush out through my wounds.

The chewed plant that the Indian put on my wounds enlarged the mouths of the wounds; he then removed the arrowheads with some wooden pliers. The operation was so extremely painful that I lost consciousness.

The Indian used the yellow root in the same manner as the red one.

After I regained consciousness, a ladder of men was made to carry me. Four Indians carried me and, after traveling a certain distance, they were relieved by another four. They walked twelve leagues with me until leaving me at the house of my ranch. There, I ordered that each Indian carrier be given a couple of pesos and a good dinner. Twenty-five days after the treatment I had recovered and I was in good health.

By then, Sergeant Nazario Galindo, Francisco Palomares, and two others had gone to get Briones in a small cart. They found him, still alive, and they brought him back. The same Indian who had cured me healed him using the same procedure.

A los 25 días que pasó esto vino el Alfz. Prado Mesa a buscarme para volver a vengar el agravio que nos habían hecho los indios. Caímos al río de Estanislao 70 hombres entre soldados y vecinos, y 200 indios ausiliares. Tomamos a los indios hóstiles, que eran 200 y pico entre gentiles y cristianos prófugos, con la traición de que nuestros indios ausiliares comprasen todas las flechas de los otros aunque se quedasen sin camisa. Se verificó la compra. Invitamos a la gentilidad y a sus compañeros cristianos a que viniesen a comer pinole y carne seca. Todos vinieron a nuestro lado del río, entonces cuando estaban a nuestra banda, los hice rodear por la tropa, vecinos e indios ausiliares, y los puse a todos en collera. Yo era el 2º gefe de la espedn., el 1º era Prado Mesa.

Marchamos con nuestros prisioneros a la sierra, lloviendo a cántaros, pa. ir a caer sobre otra ranchería. Pernoctamos dentro de un chamizal, rodeando a los presos toda la gente en pie, porqe. aquellos habían tratado de fugarse. Estábamos todos atascados con el lodo hasta la rodilla.

Cuando amaneció conté la caballada y faltaban nueve bestias. Salí a buscarlas, a la derecha rumbo al oriente, y el alférez salió a la izquierda, rumbo al oeste, con el mismo objeto. Me salieron al encuentro 10 indios ausiliares moquelemnes, (de la misma partida nuestra) emplumados y armados en guerra para sorprenderme; pero yo, como les entendía el idioma, cuando me gritaron les conocí, y le hablé por su nombre al que hacía cabeza, que se llamaba Heleno. Llegaron a donde me hallaba; les pregunté qué querían, y ellos me respondieron que querían justicia; que les entregasen los cristianos prisioneros para matarlos a flechazos. Les respondí que diesen vuelta al chamizal, sorprendiesen al alfz. Prado Mesa, y le pidiesen la justicia a él. Así lo hicieron, y el alférez no tuvo tiempo ni de tocar sus pistolas con la mano, se creía perdido, que lo mataban sin remedio. Entonces el indio Heleno le habló en castellano y le dijo que demandaba justicia. Llegamos el alférez y yo al campo. Separamos de la collera 100 cristianos, y en cada media milla o milla se ponían seis de rodillas a rezar el credo, haciéndoles entender que iban a morir. A cada uno de ellos se le ponían cuatro flecheros, de frente dos, y dos a la espalda. Los que no quedaban muertos en el acto, los mataban a lanzadas. El Alférez no quería hacer la ejecución porque no tenía ánimo, pero yo le contesté que si a mi padre me lo ponía delante, a él mismo mataba. En la caminata fueron muertos en la forma esplicada los 100 cristianos. Llegamos al campo en donde íbamos a parar con la collera de 100 gentiles.

Twenty-five days later, Second Lieutenant Prado Meza came looking for me to avenge the offense that the Indians had committed against us. We came to the Estanislao River; seventy men, both soldiers and civilians, and 200 Indian auxiliaries. We took the hostile Indians, who were comprised of 200 gentiles and Christian runaways, through the betrayal by our Indians auxiliaries who, by offering everything, even their own shirts, bought all the arrows from them. The purchase was verified. We invited the gentiles and their Christian friends to come and eat **pinole** and dried meat. All of them came to our side of the river. When they reached our own side, I ordered the troops, civilians and Indian auxiliaries to surround them, and we put collars on all of them. I was the second leader of the expedition; the first one was Prado Mesa.

While it was raining buckets, we marched with our prisoners to the mountains to reach the other **ranchería**. We searched a **chamizal** thicket while encircling the prisoners with all the troops on foot because they [Indians] had tried to escape. We were all stuck in the mud, knee-deep.

At dawn, I counted the horses, and nine beasts were missing. I went searching for them to the right, in an easterly direction, and the second lieutenant headed left on a westerly direction, with the same objective. Ten Moquelemne Indian auxiliaries (our allies) came to meet me. Feathered and armed for battle, they tried to surprise me, but since I understood their language, when they yelled at me, I knew who they were, and I called their leader by his name. He was called Heleno. They came to where I was, and I asked them what was it that they wanted and they answered that they wanted justice. They wanted us to give them the Christian prisoners so that they could kill them with arrows. I told him to turn around and go into the chamiso thicket and surprise Second Lieutenant Prado Mesa and demand justice from him. They did so accordingly and the second lieutenant did not have time to reach out for his guns; he felt that he was lost, that they would certainly kill him. Then, the Indian Heleno spoke to him in Spanish and told him that he wanted justice. The second lieutenant and I came to the camp. We separated from the collars 100 Christians and every half-mile to a mile six of them were placed on their knees so that they could say the prayer, "Our Father," letting them know that they were going to die. Each one had four bowmen, two in front and two in back. Those who did not die right away were speared to death. The second lieutenant did not want to carry out the executions because he lacked the courage, but I told him that if my father were put before me I would kill him. In the march, 100 Christians were killed in the manner just described. We reached the place where we were going to make camp with 100 collared gentiles.

Allí, antes de oscurecer, como llovía tanto, le propuse al alférez que se hiciera cargo de la collera, porqe. en la noche debía haber desgracias entre los ausiliares y la gente nuestra, porque se había perdido una mula aparejada cargada con una olla que llevaba cucharas y otros utensilios. Esta mula debía caer al campo en donde estaba la caballada, esto produciría un desorden espantando la caballada, se alarmaría la gente y en la confusión se balearían unos a otros. El alférez me dijo que determinase yo lo que me pareciera más conveniente. Y yo le contesté que estaba porque se fusilara a la presa, haciéndolos cristianos primeramte., que se les hiciese saber que iban a morir, y se les preguntase si querían hacerse cristianos. Mandé a Nazario Galindo que tomase una botella de agua, yo tomé otra. El empezó por una punta de la collera y yo por la otra. Bautizamos a todos los indios, y después fueron fusilados por la espalda: en una descarga cayeron 70 muertos. Doble la parada pa. los 30 que quedaban, y se tumbaron todos. Desatando la collera, resultó uno vivo sin que le hubiera dado el balazo, quien de un salto se echó en el río. Se le tiraron más de 40 tiros en el agua que no le tocaron. Al fin cuando iba a salir lo hirieron, pero él se escapó a su ranchería.

En la tarde del día sigte. me obligaron los indios ausiliares a que pasase el río a tomar la ranchería de aquellos 200 indios, y apoderarnos de las mugeres e hijos. Me hicieron pasar el río nadando con ellos, advirtiendo que todo me volteaba con los peñascos qe. había en el agua, con mi carabina amarrada en la cabeza con un pañuelo; mi ropa la llevaba un indio amarrada en la cabeza del mismo modo.

Habiendo pasado el río, me hicieron atravesar el río otra vez de vuelta, parece que ellos creyeron que yo tendría recelo de acompañarlos en pasar el río. Ellos se comprometieron aquella noche (ya era oscuro cuando yo pasé el río) a ir a la ranchería, matar los hombres, y traer todo el mugerío y los niños. Aclarando el sigte. día, llegaron a mi campamto. con 160 almas entre mugeres y niños, con las que pasaron el río. Cada muger pasó el río nadando con sus chicos en coras, todos los niños y niñas de 7 años arriba pasaron nadando como peces. Entonces levanté yo el campo con el alfz. Prado Mesa, y nos vinimos pa. la misión de San José, en donde fueron bautizadas todas las mugeres y criaturas que tragimos. Los indios ausiliares me dijeron que habían matado en aquella rancha. como 24 hombres, incluso el que escapó herido del río, cuando fueron fusilados sus compañeros.

There, before sunset, since it was raining considerably, I proposed to the second lieutenant that he should take charge of the collars because that night there was going to be a misfortune between the auxiliaries and our own people, since a mule that was already harnessed and loaded with a pot that contained spoons and other utensils had been lost. When this mule reached the field where the horse herd was being kept, this would cause chaos, scaring the horse herd. The people, then, would become alarmed and in the confusion they would start shooting at each other. The second lieutenant told me to decide what I thought would be convenient. And I told him that I was in favor of executing the prisoners but that they would have to become Christians first. They were to be told that they were going to die and that they should be asked if they wanted to become Christians. I ordered Nazario Galindo to go get a bottle of water and I got another one. He started on one end of the collar chain and I from the other end. We baptized all of the Indians, and then they were executed from behind. In one discharge [of guns] seventy of them fell dead. I doubled the guard on the remaining thirty and all of them were brought down. After we cut the collars, one survivor, who had not been hit by a single shot, leaped into the river. More than forty shots were fired at him in the water but none hit him. In the end, right before he got out of the water, he was wounded, but he managed to escape to his ranchería.

In the evening of the following day, the auxiliary Indians forced me to cross the river and take the ranchería of 200 Indians and take possession of the women and children. I swam the river with them, and I should note that I was constantly losing my balance with the rocks that were in the water since I had my carbine tied to my head with a handkerchief; an Indian was carrying my clothes tied to his head in the same manner. After crossing the river, they made me cross the river back again; I felt that they thought that I would hesitate to accompany them in crossing the river. They made the decision to go that night (it was already dark when I swam the river) to the ranchería to kill the men and bring back all the women and children. At daybreak of the following day, they came to my camp with 160 souls, among them women and children. They crossed the river with them. Each woman crossed the river swimming with her little ones following in line behind her. All the boys and girls swam like fish. Second Lieutenant Prado Mesa and I raised camp and we came to Mission San José, where the women and children we brought were baptized. The auxiliary Indians told me that they had killed twenty-four men in that ranchería, including the wounded one that had escaped when he crossed the river after his friends were executed.

Esos indios ausiliares eran Moquelemnes, gente muy aguerrida, valiente y fiel, con la que nunca tuve recelo de que me acompañasen en las espednes.

El Alfz. Prado Mesa había indultado en el patíbulo a un alcalde de la misión de Sta. Clara llamado José Jesús. Este indio se comprometió a traerme la caballada que los indios me habían robado. Me alcanzó en el río con 35 caballos, y una indita y un indito que me traía de regalo por el indulto.

José de Jesús Vallejo desaprobó el fusilamto. de los 200 indios al Alfz. Prado Mesa: éste se descargó conmigo.

Vallejo entonces me reclamó a mí, y yo le contesté que "las tortillas sabrosas se comen en la casa, y las amargas en la sierra;" que pues él se jactaba de valiente y de ser capitán con despacho, que tuviera la bondad de venirse con nosotros a la cabeza de la fila. Él respondió que podía disponer de su oficial y tropa. Yo le respondí que no, que él como gefe superior estaba en el deber de marchar al frente de sus soldados. Me replicó que se pondrían dos hombres pa. ver si yo tenía el derecho de obligarlo a salir a la cabeza de la tropa. Vinieron entonces del pueblo de San José el comisionado Luis Peralta y dos ancianos (antiguos militares) Miguel y Bartolo Pacheco. Vallejo habló con Peralta, y éste le respondió que yo, como militar antiguo no tenía réplica; que yo sabía mis obligaciones, y cargaba la cartilla de ordenanzas en mi bolsa, lo cual era verdad; pues siempre llevaba yo conmigo esa cartilla que me había dejado mi difunto y veterano padre. Que no había duda de que el Sr. Vallejo estaba en la obligación de salir con la tropa, lo que le exigió el comisionado, pero el Sr. Vallejo no quiso salir aunque exigía de nosotros que saliéramos a otra espedición. El Sargto. Comisionado Peralta le dijo que nosotros teníamos tanto derecho pa. negarnos a salir como él. El resultado de esta cuestión fue que no salimos. El Sr. José de Jesús Vallejo nunca había salido a campaña con los indios. Yo, molesto, le manifesté que ya que estaba él tan acostumbrado a bofetear indios en la misión, saliera a la sierra en donde las flechas de los indios rompían huesos. Pero nada valió pa. hacerle salir.

Después del año 28 (en mayo) hubo una campaña al río Estanislao, al cargo del alfz. José Anto. Sánchez con 30 soldados y 200 indios ausiliares, moquelemnes y de otras nacls. a un parage llamado La Estacada.

The auxiliary Indians were Moquelemnes, a warrior people, brave and loyal; I never hesitated to have them accompany me in the expeditions.

The Second Lieutenant Prado Mesa had pardoned from the gallows an [Indian] **alcalde** of Mission Santa Clara; his name was José Jesús. This Indian committed himself to bringing me a herd of horses that the Indians had stolen. He found me in the river [and turned over to me] thirty-five horses and a little Indian girl and boy that he brought as a gift for the pardon.

José de Jesús Vallejo told Second Lieutenant Prado Mesa that he did not approve of the execution of the 200 Indians. [Prado Mesa] took it out on me.

Then, Vallejo came to reproach me and I responded: "the tasty tortillas are eaten at home while the bitter ones [are eaten] in the mountains." If he prided himself on being brave and being a captain with the responsibility of the office, he should have the courage to come with us at the front of the troops. He answered that he would assign an officer and troops. I told him that this would not be possible since as a superior officer it was his obligation to lead his soldiers. He replied that two men would be consulted to see if I had a right to force him to go out as head of the troops. From the town of San José came Commissioner Luis Peralta and two old men (ancient soldiers) Miguel and Bartolo Pacheco. Vallejo spoke with Peralta and the latter said that as an old veteran I had no equal, that I knew my obligations, and that I carried my manual of regulations (at all times) in my bag, which was true. I always carried with me such a manual that had been left to me by my deceased veteran father. [Peralta told him] that there was no doubt that Mr. Vallejo had the obligation of leading his troops and the commissioner demanded that he carry it out. Mr. Vallejo, however, did not wish to go, although he continued to insist that we should go out on another expedition. Sergeant Commissioner Peralta told him that we had just as much right to refuse to go out as he did. In the end, we did not go out. Sr. José de Jesús de Vallejo had never been in a campaign against the Indians. I angrily expressed to him that he was only accustomed to hitting Indians from the mission and that he should go to the mountains where the Indians' arrows could break bones. Nothing could convince him to go out.

After 1828 (in May) there was a campaign to the Estanislao River, commanded by the Second Lieutenant José Antonio Sánchez, made up of thirty soldiers and 200 Moquelemne and other nationalities. It was headed to a place called La Estacada.

La espedn. salió el mismo día que yo me casé con mi segunda muger (Josefa Sánchez Ortega de Santa Bárbara). Todos ellos estuvieron en la comida y diversión hasta la tarde en que emprendieron su marcha. Yo era uno de los nombrados pa. salir, pero como era mayordomo de la misión, el alfz. Sánchez por una consideración, me pidió un vaquero pa. arrear la caballada, y me escusó de ir a la espedn. Yo le di instrucciones sobre la manera cómo debía tomar la ranchería que se iba a atacar, por haber cometido muertes de indios cristianos y robado caballada. Los individuos de esa rancha. eran en su mayor parte cristianos. Yo le aconsejé a Sánchez que prendiera fuego al monte todo al derredor pa. que lograra tomar los indios.[14] No lo hizo, pensó haberlos tomado a brazo partido, pero la erró. Salió él de aquella refrega con algunos de sus soldados heridos y sin haber logrado coger ni a siquiera uno de los indios de la rancha. Se retiró a dar cuenta a su gefe. Entonces el alfz. Mariano Guadalupe Vallejo salió de Monterey con su tropa a reunirse con la de San Francisco que mandaba el alfz. Sánchez. Reunidas las tropas (unos 55 hombres) y 200 indios ausiliares, salió la espedn. para La Estacada a vengar la derrota pasada. Los indios de la rancha. tuvieron la precaución de prevenirse para un ataque; habían hecho hoyos en todo el monte que se comunicaban por debajo de tierra. Los hoyos estaban a distancia como de 10 varas unos de otros. Allí se ocultaban los indios y disparaban sus flechas. Habiendo comenzado la acción, Vallejo (como gefe) ordenó al alfz. Sánchez que entrara a batir con la tropa, quedándose él en el campo de la salud, resguardando la pelleja.[15]

---

[14]Es importante observar que aunque José Antonio Sánchez era reconocido como grán guerrero de indios, José María Amador, quien era solamente un soldado común, narra que el le dio instrucciones a Sánxhez sobre como atacar a los indígenas.

[15]José María Amador no le guarda mucho respeto al alférez Mariano Guadalupe Vallejo. Es muy obvio que Amador considera a Vallejo como un cobarde. Se debe mencionar que algunos historiadores han concluido que Vallejo ganó esta batalla. Sin embargo, Amador insiste en aclarar que los indígenas fueron los que le brindaron una derrota desastroza a las fuerzas de Vallejo. Aparentemente, sus derrotas militares no le afectaron la carrera publica de Vallejo. Los escritores Beebe y Senkewics comentan que en los primeros años de la década de 1830, Vallejo sirvió en la Deputación de California y asumió el puesto de comandante militar de San Francisco desde 1831 hasta 1834 (341). Vallejo fue el fundador del pueblo de Sonoma.

The expedition departed on the same day that I married my second wife (Josefa Sánchez Ortega from Santa Bárbara). Everyone from the expedition attended the dinner and the entertainment until dusk, when they started their march. I had been the one chosen to go, but since I was the foreman of the mission, Second Lieutenant Sánchez for some reason excused me from going on this expedition and just asked me to provide a cowboy to take care of the horse herd. I gave him instructions on how he should take possession of the ranchería that he was going to attack for [these Indians] had killed Christianized Indians and stolen a herd of horses. The residents of such ranchería were mostly Christians. I advised Sánchez that he should set fire to the brush all around it so that the Indians could be captured.[14] He did not follow my advice; he thought he could take them by surprise, but he made a mistake. He came out of that skirmish with some soldiers being wounded and without having captured one single Indian from the rancheria. He went to report to his superior. Then, Second Lieutenant Mariano Guadalupe Vallejo left Monterey with his troop to join the one from San Francisco that was commanded by Second Lieutenant Sánchez. Once joined, the troops (some fifty-five men) and 200 Indian auxiliaries left for La Estacada to avenge the previous defeat. The Indians from the ranchería took the precaution of preparing for an attack; they had dug holes throughout the thicket that were connected with underground tunnels. The holes were ten **varas** apart from each other and from there they would hide and shoot their arrows. When the battle began, Vallejo (as commander) ordered Second Lieutenant Sánchez to go with his troop to fight; he stayed behind in safe quarters trying to protect his skin.[15]

---

[14]It is interesting to note that although José Antonio Sánchez was a renowned Indian fighter, Amador, who was merely a common soldier, claims that it was he who gave Sánchez instructions on how to attack the Indians.

[15]José María Amador did not have much respect for Second Lieutenant Mariano Guadalupe Vallejo. In fact, he felt that Vallejo was a coward. It should be noted that several writers have concluded that Vallejo won this battle, yet Amador makes it quite clear that the Indians soundly defeated Vallejo's forces. It appears that the military defeat did not hurt Vallejo's political career. Beebe and Senkewicz note that Vallejo later served in the California Deputation in the early 1830s and became military commander of San Francisco from 1831 to 1834 (341). Vallejo was the founder of Sonoma.

Sánchez obedeció y se entró al bosque con su gente. Los indios empezaron a jarear. Sánchez gritaba a los soldados de Monterey, dándoles golpes con la espada, "¡Avancen, cabrones!" El alférez Sánchez había oído a los de Monterey hacer observaciones denigrantes contra los solds. de la compa. de San Francisco, por el mal resultado de la espedn. ulta., ellos se habían dejado decir cosas insultantes sobre el valor de los de San Francisco, y se jactaban de que ellos (los de Monterey) iban a hacer los otros, que les eran superiores, y que cogerían a los indios hóstiles a mano. Pero cuando llegó la hora de cumplir esa promesa muchos de ellos, esto es, los chachareros, no lo hicieron. Los indios se dieron a conocer por superiores a ellos. Viendo la inutilidad del ataque, por estar minado todo el terreno se retiró el alfz. con su gente afuera del monte. Echó de menos 4 soldados de su compa. Entró con soldados a buscarlos, y hallados sentados, jareados por la cabeza y por todo el cuerpo. Manuel Peña y Lorenzo Pacheco eran sus nombres. A Peña le habían quebrado una muela del lado de la cara por donde le entró la flecha, y otra del lado opuesto por donde salió. Fueron sacados los dos del monte. Volvió Sánchez a entrar con gente en busca de los otros dos. Los indios los habían cogido bebiendo agua, no los mataron sino los escondieron. Se llamaban Andrés Mesa e Ignacio Pacheco. No cogieron los de la espedn. ni siquiera un prisionero. No se supo si la tropa mató o hirió a algunos de los que estaban en los hoyos.

La espedn. entonces marchó a Tahualumes, dejando los heridos con guardia en el campo. [A la]llegada a Tahualumes mataron a algunos enemigos. La mayor parte de estos se salieron por el agua sin ser vistos. La espedn. se volvió en seguida a La Estacada, el día sigte.

La indiada enemiga se había escapado para la sierra. La tropa encontró fuera del monte a Andrés Mesa e Ignacio Pacheco colgados con bejucos de avellano de los testículos a un roble. Los indios los habían colgado y los quemaron vivos. Entonces toda la espedn. se retiró diseminándose cada parte pa. su destino respectivo. Los heridos en esa malhadada campaña fueron: Anto. Soto, cabo, gravemte. en un ojo. La flecha se la estrageron, pero le quedó en la cabeza la piedra. Se volvió loco, y a los ocho días murió, en su casa, en el pueblo. Tomás Espinosa, vecino de San José, por entre el haz de la cuera le metieron la flecha en el ombligo; murió en la misión de San José.

Sánchez obeyed and with his men set off into the thicket. The Indians started shooting [their arrows]. Sánchez shouted at the soldiers from Monterey, hitting them with his sword and saying "Forward **Cabrones**." The second lieutenant had heard those from Monterey make denigrating remarks about the San Francisco Company due to the bad results of the last expedition. They had said insulting things regarding the bravery of those from San Francisco and they boasted that they [those from Monterey] were going to show them that they were superior and that they would capture the hostile Indians with their bare hands. But when the time came to deliver on their promise, many of them, that is the chatterers, could not do it. The Indians proved to be superior to them. After seeing the futility of the attack, since the terrain had been tunneled, the second lieutenant retreated with his men away from the thicket. Four soldiers from his company were missing. He entered with his soldiers to search for them; two were sitting, with arrows in their heads and all over their bodies. The two men were Manuel Peña and Lorenzo Pacheco. Peña had a molar broken on the side of the face where the arrow penetrated and another broken [tooth] where it exited. The two were taken out of the forest. Sánchez went back again in search of the other two. The Indians had captured them while they were drinking water; they did not kill them but hid them. [The two men] were Andrés Mesa and Ignacio Pacheco. The members of the expedition did not get a single prisoner. It was never known whether the troop had killed or wounded some of the men that were in the holes.

The expedition then marched to Tahualumes, leaving behind the wounded at the camp with guards. When they got to Tahualumes, they killed some of the enemy. The majority of them escaped by water without being seen. The expedition returned to the stockade immediately the following day. The Indian enemies had escaped to the mountains. The troop found Andrés Mesa and Ignacio Pacheco outside of the forest hanging from an oak tree, their testicles tied with hazel strips. The Indians had hanged them and burned them alive. Afterwards, the expedition returned, each group scattering to their respective destinations. Among the wounded on this ill-fated expedition was Antonio Soto, a corporal, who was gravely wounded in the eye. The arrow was extracted but the tip remained inside his head; he went crazy and eight days later he died in his house in town. Tomás Espinosa, a resident of San José, had an arrow enter the opening on the side of his leather jacket and penetrated through his navel; he died at Mission San José.

Así es que de la tropa de San Francisco perecieron tres, de la de Monterey creo que no murió ninguno, pero sí tuvo 5 o 6 heridos. El único de que me acuerdo fue José Ma. Villavicencio, uno de los hombres más buenos que había en Monterey.[16] El mismo que más tarde figuró en Cal. como Capitán Villavicencio. Era hombre valiente y de fuerte brazo, al mismo tiempo que de muy buen corazón. Era todo un caballero, aunque en aquel tiempo era soldado raso. Aquí finaliza la hista. de la desgraciada campaña de La Estacada en el río Estanislao que mandó en Jefe Dn. Mariano G. Vallejo.

Advierto aquí que cuando la epidemia de las viruelas en 1839, el Capitán de aquella ranchería, quien se llamaba Estanislao, murió agusanado, con muchos otros de sus compañeros, en la misión de San José.[17]

En una ocasión estuve en una espedn. con el Captn. Luis A. Argüello. No puedo recordar en qué año fue, sé que tuvo lugar antes de que Argüello fuese gobr., de modo que sería antes del año de 1823. Entramos por Napa pa. Santa Rosa. Allí en el arroyo una mañana se nos aproximaron como 200 indios, nosotros estábamos de este lado del riochuelo; nos empezaron a flechas. El Capn. determinó que por ningún motivo hiciéramos armas contra ellos. Él les hablaba por medio del intérprete pa. que se apasiguaran. Al fin se aburrió el Capitán cuando vio que los indios no paraban de dispararnos sus flechas. Nos ordenó que tomáramos carabina en mano (éramos 25 hombres) y diéramos sobre los hóstiles. Se les hizo una descarga únicamente, y cargamos con la lanza en un roblar inmenso, matamos a algunos, hasta que el Capn. nos mandó parar. Seguimos pa. el norte, tomando la sierra y dando vuelta como pa. La Bodega. Los indios nos rodearon a todos lados. Nosotros seguimos la marcha hasta un punto llamado Livantuyolomí.

---

[16]Es muy interesante observar que Amador le demuestra mucho respeto a Villavicencio. Sin embargo, Angustias de la Guerra Jimeno Ord en sus memorias, "Occurrencias de California," llama a Villavicencio "Vill-medio-indio" para demostrar que él no solamente era mestizo, pero que también pertenecía a las clases humildes. Jimeno Ord, dama de sociedad, narra que cuando Villavicencio fue ordenado a conducir a Carlos Carrillo, tió de ella, a Santa Bárbara él no lo trató como prisionero. Al contrario, Villavicencio actuó como si él fuese el sirviente de Carrillo. El buen trato que Villavicencio le dio a Carrillo se puede explicar ya que Carrillo lo crió desde cuando era niño.

[17]Beebe y Senkewicz, 322. Los autores hacen notar que Estanislao era miembro del grupo indígena Lakisamne, que residía a cincuenta millas al este de la misión de San José. Estanislao había sido alcalde en la misión antes que la abandonara en 1828. Él problablemente medía como seis pies de altura y era de piel clara.

From the troops of San Francisco, three were killed; I believe no one died from Monterey, although five or six were wounded. The only one that I remember was José María Villavicencio, one of the best men that lived in Monterey.[16] This same person would later be known in California as Captain Villavicencio. He was a brave man, a strong man, and at the same time, a man who had a good heart. He was a complete gentleman although at that time he was a common soldier. This ends the story of the unfortunate campaign at the stockade on the Estanislao River under the command of Don Mariano G. Vallejo.

I wish to note here that when the small pox epidemic arrived here in 1839, the captain of that ranchería, who was called Estanislao, died infested with worms, along with many of his companions at Mission San José.[17]

On one occasion, I was in an expedition with Captain Luis A. Argüello. I do not remember the year; I do know that it took place before Argüello became governor, so it must have been before 1823. We entered through Napa to reach Santa Rosa. There, at the stream, 200 Indians approached us. We were on this side of the small stream; they attacked us with arrows. The captain ordered that under no circumstances were we to use our weapons against them. Through an interpreter he told them to calm down. After seeing that the Indians did not desist from launching their arrows at us, the annoyed captain ordered us to ready our carbines (we were twenty-five men) and to shoot at the hostiles. We only fired one round and then charged at them through an immense oak grove; we killed some and then the captain commanded us to stop. We continued marching north, going over the mountains and making a turn in the direction of La Bodega. The Indians surrounded us on all sides. We continued our march until we reached a point called Livantuyolomí.

---

[16]It is interesting to observe that Amador demonstrates considerable respect for Villavicencio. In her memoirs, *Occurrences in Hispanic California*, however, Angustias de la Guerra Jimeno Ord, an upper-class woman, called Villavicencio "Villa-half-Indian" to show that he was not only a **mestizo** but also a member of the lower class (Washington: Academy of American Franciscan History, 1956, p. 43). Ord points out that when this officer was ordered to deliver her uncle, Carlos Carrillo, to Santa Bárbara, he did not treat him as a prisoner. Instead Villavicencio acted more like a servant to Carrillo. As it turns out, Villavicencio treated Carrillo well because the latter had raised him while he was a child.

[17]Beebe and Senkewicz, 322. The writers note that Estanislao was a member of the Lakisamne, who lived fifty miles east of Mission San José. He had been an Indian **Alcalde** at the mission before he left it in 1828. Estanislao was supposed to have been about six feet tall and light-skinned.

En esta travesía habíamos logrado coger dos capitanes de la indiada, a quienes recetó Argüello 200 azotes a cada uno para que no volviesen a hacer armas. Aquella espedición llevaba por objeto tranquilizar la indiada toda, pa. que cuando entrase tropa en sus tierras no hicieran oposición ni emplearan sus armas contra nuestros soldados. De allí pasamos al presidio de Ross a hacerle una visita al Comandte. de los rusos.

Estuvimos allí dos días, muy obsequiados por los rusos, y nos retiramos pa. San Francisco.

Invasión de Bouchard

El 2 de nov. de 1818 a las 2 de la mañana, estando yo de centinela en la prevención de San Francisco, llegó un correo estraordinario con el soldado Dolores Cantúa, trayendo la noticia de que dos fragatas piratas armadas al mando de Hipólito Bouchard, habían entrado a Monterey.[18] A las mismas dos de la mañana reunió el Tente. Gabriel Moraga la tropa en el cuartel, y nombró una espedn. pa. Monterey de los soldados que había allí, recogiendo de paso los de las escoltas de las misiones de Sn. Franco., Sta. Clara y Santa Cruz, que fueron reemplazados por los inválidos del pueblo. A mi me tocó ir en la espedn. Salimos lloviendo a torrentes al mando de Dn. José Anto. Sánchez; llegamos al pueblo de San José al oscurecer. Tomamos bastimentos, el que tenía familia la tomó de su casa, y el que no, lo compró. Caminamos toda la noche y llegamos al rancho de la nación aclarando. Encontramos allí al gobr. Solá en una casa del Sargento Miguel Espinosa que estaba encargado del rancho. El Gobr. tenía unas ojeras que llegaban hasta la patilla, causados por la pesadumbre que tenía en sus alma, porqe. Bouchard y sus insurgentes lo habían hecho correr con toda la gente de Monterey. El Sr. Solá se mereció el concepto de ser algo cobarde. Al día sigte. por la mañana llegó el Capn. Dn. Luis Argüello con su escolta al rancho de la nación donde estaba el Gobr. Este le recibió con los brazos abiertos.

---

[18]Beebe y Senkewicz, 318. Los escritores indican que Hipólito Bouchard estaba colaborando con el movimiento independista argentino cuando pasó por California. Después de haber visitado las islas hawaianas y regresando a tierras argentinas, él desembarcó en Monterey y demandó la entrega de las propiedades del rey en nombre de los patriotas americanos. Después de abandonar Monterey, Bouchard también atracó en Santa Bárbara y en San Juan Capistrano.

On this part of the journey we managed to capture two Indian captains for whom Argüello ordered 200 lashes each so that they would never again take up arms. This expedition had as its objective to pacify all Indians so that when the troops entered their territories they would not resist, or use their weapons against our soldiers. From there, we went to Fort Ross to visit the Russian commander.

We stayed there two days, and we were rewarded amply by the Russians, and then we returned to San Francisco.

The Bouchard Invasion

On November 2, 1818, at two o'clock in the morning, when I was serving as a guard at the Presidio of San Francisco, an urgent message was brought by the soldier Dolores Cantúa, with the news that two pirate frigates had entered Monterey, under the command of Hypolite Bouchard.[18] At exactly two o'clock in the morning, Lieutenant Gabriel Moraga gathered the troop at the garrison and organized an expedition to Monterey composed of the soldiers that were there and the guards that were picked up as they passed through missions San Francisco, Santa Clara, and Santa Cruz. The retired soldiers of the town replaced [these guards]. I was chosen to be a part of the expedition. [The expedition], under the command of Don José Antonio Sánchez, left during a heavy downpour and reached San José when it was getting dark. We took supplies; those who had family got them from their homes; those that did not, bought them. We rode all night and arrived at the King's Ranch by daybreak. We found Governor Solá in the house of Sergeant Miguel Espinosa who was in charge of the ranch. The Governor had dark rings under his eyes that reached down to his sideburns; they were caused by the grief he felt in his soul as a result of Bouchard and his insurgents having forced him and all his men to flee Monterey. Mr. Solá deserved to be called somewhat of a coward. On the following day, in the morning, Captain Luis Argüello arrived with his escort at the government ranch where the governor was staying. He welcomed him with open arms.

---

[18]Beebe and Senkewicz, 318. The writers note that Hypolite Bouchard was working for the Argentine Independence movement. After visiting the Hawaiian Islands and while en route back to his home port, he landed at Monterey and demanded the Spanish King's properties in the name of the American patriots. After leaving Monterey, Bouchard also landed at Santa Bárbara and San Juan Capistrano.

Se reunieron allí a otro día las tropas de Monterey, San Francisco, Santa Barba., y algunos hombres de San Diego. Allí se puso la tropa toda sobre las armas para ejercicio por la mañana y por la tarde, bajo las ordenes del Capn. Argüello. Después de estar adiestrada la tropa en 4 días, salimos pa. Mont.

Ahí en el rancho antes de emprender la marcha se averiguó un robo de 20 reales en plata. Los ladrones fueron dos milicianos y un vecino. Los dos primeros se llamaban Antonio Larios y Gracia Larios, el vecino, Andrés García. La tropa se formó en cerco, fueron metidos los ladrones dentro del cerco y a cada uno se le aplicaron 50 palos en las espaldas desnudas por manos de los cabos, y después se les llevó presos a Monterey. En el paso del río pa. pasar a Monterey se nos ahogó un soldado llamado Cayetano Ríos, de la compa. de Monterey. En cinco minutos se ahogó y se perdió, y nunca se encontró el cuerpo. Pasamos a Monterey. Lo encontramos ardiendo, y lo primero que se hizo fue cortar el fuego, después fuimos al castillo. Las fragatas de Bouchard que habían desembarcado una fuerza como de 350 hombres, se habían retirado, después de saquear e incendiar la plaza, fuera de la bahía.

Cuando las fragatas entraron, según supimos, tiraron algunos cañonazos al presidio, los que fueron contestados por el baluarte que tenía a su cargo José de Jesús Vallejo. Éste logró introducir tres balas de a 8 en el costado de la fragata negra que montaba Bouchard. En el calor de la pelea recibió Vallejo orden del Tente. Estudillo que parase el fuego. Esto dio lugar a los buques pa. taponear sus agugeros, retirarse pa. la bahía. Después de eso vinieron las lanchas adelante del castillo e hicieron un desembarque de tropa y marinería, la cual cometió el saqueo e incendio de la plaza.

Las fragatas, después que llegamos a Monterey, hicieron un desembarco de gente en la costa de Monterey. Entonces el Capn. Dn. Luis Argüello destacó 30 hombres a perseguir los insurgentes que habían entrado al pinal. De estos tomamos 21 prisioneros sin tirar un tiro; los demás tomaron las lanchas y se volvieron a sus buques. El Capn. Argüello ordenó que se arreglase todo en el castillo y demás. Nosotros le entregamos la presa y él dispuso de ella, distribuyendo los prisioneros en los diversos presidios. Me acuerdo de los siguientes prisioneros. Acuña (Vicente), hombre muy fuerte, de corta estatura, natural de España.

The next day, the troops from Monterey, San Francisco, Santa Bárbara, and some men from San Diego gathered there. While there, the entire troop was assembled with weapons for exercises in the morning and afternoon, under the leadership of Captain Argüello. After four days of training the troop left for Monterey.

While we were at the ranch, before the start of the march, a robbery of twenty silver **reales** was investigated. The thieves were two militia members and a civilian. The first two were Antonio Larios and Gracia Larios; the civilian was Andrés García. The troop formed itself into a circle, the thieves were placed inside it, and the corporals gave them each fifty blows on their naked backs with a stick, and then they were taken as prisoners to Monterey. While crossing a river on the way to Monterey, a soldier of the Company of Monterey, by the name of Cayetano Ríos, drowned. He drowned in five minutes and we lost sight of him; the body was never found. We arrived in Monterey. We found it burning, and the first thing we did was to put out the fires. Afterwards, we went to the fortress. The frigates of Bouchard, which had landed some 350 men, had retreated outside of the bay after sacking and burning the plaza.

When the frigates entered, we found out they fired off several cannon shots at the presidio; [the volleys] were returned by the bulwark which was under the responsibility of José de Jesús Vallejo. He managed to hit three shots of size eight on the side of a black frigate where Bouchard was aboard. During the heat of the battle, Vallejo received an order from Lieutenant Estudillo to stop fighting. This allowed Bouchard's men to seal the holes of the vessels and leave the bay. Afterwards, the boats came in front of the fortress and unloaded their troops and sailors, and proceeded to sack and burn the plaza.

The frigates, after we arrived in Monterey, disembarked people on the beaches of Monterey. Then Captain Luis Argüello sent thirty men to pursue the insurgents who had entered the pine forest. Of these men, we captured twenty-one [of them] without firing a single shot; the remaining ones got on the boats and returned to their ships. The captain issued orders that the damage should be repaired at the fortress and elsewhere. We turned over the prisoners to him and he distributed them to several presidios. I remember the following prisoners, Acuña (Vicente), a very strong man, very short in stature, a native of Spain.

Francisco ....también español.

Joaquín .... "   id.

Chavarría ....mexicano.

Aguilar ....chileno o peruano.

John Ross ....Escocés.

Un negro Francisco.....Americano

Estuvimos con el Capitán Argüello y el Alfz. Maitorena 3 meses en Monterey, Nov. Dic. 1818 y Eno. de 1819. A ults. de este mes, nos volvimos a nuestras compañías, cambiando las tropas, pues las de Monterey estaban en San Francisco, y la de Sn. Franco. en Monterey.

El Gobr. Solá se había ido del rancho del Rey a la misión de la Soledad, a donde fue a despedirse de el Capn. Argüello.

Cuando se supo en Sta. Cruz de la invasión de Monterey, se esperaban que los insurgentes vendrían allí a saquear, y con tiempo sacaron todo lo de valor de la misión, y lo ocultaron por orden del Gobo. al alcalde de Branciforte. Pero no por esta precaución pudo privar el alcalde de Joaquín Castro que se robasen hasta los baúles de las ropas de los acólitos, y algunos barriles de aguardiente y vino que se bebieron varios particulares, y después que se averiguó todo esto, fueron los hechores enviados a San Francisco. Hasta el Alcalde Castro estuvo detenido en San Francisco por no haber tenido la precaución de haber puesto personas al cuidado de la iglesia. Estuvieron presos todos esos individuos como medio año, se recogieron algunas de las prendas perdidas. Con todo, no dejaron de vestirse algs. particulares calzón corto hecho de paño grana del robado de la misión.

La espedn. de Bouchard estuvo en el rancho de los Ortegas, en Sta. Barba. y últimamte. en San Juan Capistrano, en donde saquearon algunas cosas que se habían dejado en los almacenes. Allí se les desertaron algunos hombres, quienes se presentaron creo que al Sargto. Carlos Anto. Carrillo.

A pocos días de llegar nosotros de Monterey a San Francisco el Alfz. Sánchez y yo fuimos a hacer un paseo al pueblo de San José. En el regreso pa. San Franco., llegamos a San Mateo, que era uno de los ranchos de la misión de San Francisco.

Dormimos allí aquella noche, y se me proporcionó comprar un barril cerrado vacío a un indígena de la misión de San Francisco. Traté el barril delante de Sánchez, y éste me dijo que yo le había llevado la delantera, porque él también

Francisco. . . also Spanish
Joaquín . . . "   "
Chavarría . . ."   "
Aguilar . . ."   "
John Ross . . . Scottish
Francisco, a black man . . . U.S.

We were with Captain Argüello and Second Lieutenant Maitorena for three months in Monterey—November and December of 1818 and January of 1819. On the last days of the last month, we returned to our companies, changing the troops, since the one from Monterey was in San Francisco and the one from San Francisco was stationed in Monterey.

Governor Solá left the King's Ranch to go to Mission Soledad. Captain Argüello went to bid his goodbye from him there.

When the news got to Santa Cruz of the invasion of Monterey, it was expected that the insurgents would go there to sack it. The [town residents], acting on orders from the government to the mayor of Branciforte, had time to take out everything of worth from the mission and hid it. Despite these precautions, the **Alcalde** Joaquín Castro could not prevent the robbery of even the trunks where the clothes of the acolytes were kept and some barrels of **aguardiente** and wine, which were consumed by several individuals. All this was investigated later and the guilty individuals were sent to San Francisco. Even Alcalde Castro was detained in San Francisco for not taking the precautions of stationing people to look after the church. All these people were kept prisoners for about half a year; some of the lost articles were recovered. In the end, some people could not be prevented from dressing with trousers made from the woolen cloth that was stolen from the mission.

The Bouchard expedition went to the Ortega Ranch in Santa Bárbara and lastly to San Juan Capistrano, where they sacked several things that had been left behind in the warehouses. Here, several men deserted who presented themselves to, I believe, Sergeant Carlos Antonio Carrillo.

A few days after arriving in San Francisco from Monterey, Second Lieutenant Sánchez and I took a trip to San José. On our way back to San Francisco, we came to San Mateo, which was one of the ranchos that belonged to Mission San Francisco.

We spent the night there, and an Indian from Mission San Francisco offered to sell me an empty sealed barrel; I made the deal in the presence of Sánchez, and he told me that I had taken advantage of him because he also

quería el barril. En fin, yo pagué por el barril 20 reales, y el mismo alfz. me ayudó a ponerlo sobre el aparejo. Seguimos para el presidio. No sé por qué evento el padre de la misión supo de mi compra del barril, informando que yo lo había robado a la misión. Me demandó por el barril, y me pusieron una barra de grillos a los pies. Me formaron sumaría arreglada a ordenanza, y enseguida me hicieron consejo de guerra. Mi defensor exigió que se presentaran los testigos para probar que yo era un ladrón. Vino entonces el Padre Juan Cabot con el indio que me había vendido el barril, y yo llamé al Alfz. Sánchez para que declarase cómo lo había adquirido yo por compra.[19] Llamaron al indio, y éste dijo que el padre le había obligado a mentir. El padre lo negó, y le dieron al indio 100 azotes. Vino el herrero y me quitó la barra de grillos que tenía doblada en los pies. Entonces me preguntaron cuánto era mi conducta; y yo, por consideración pedí 200$, los cuales me los entregó el Padre Cabot en la mano. Así es que mis 20 reales me dieron de ganancia $197.50, aunque me costó algunos días de tristeza mientras estaba en la prisión con grillos y sometido a consejo de guerra. Con esto concluímos la historia de la invasión de Bouchard.

---

[19]Geiger, 32. El historiador Geiger informa que Juan Cabot nació en Mallorca, España y fue asignado a la misión de San Francisco en 1819 después de haber servido catorce años en varias misiones californianas. A fines de 1820 se mudó a la misión Soledad.

wanted the barrel. In the end, I paid twenty **reales** for the barrel and the same second lieutenant helped me load it on the harness. We proceeded to the presidio. I do not know how the priest of the mission found out about my purchase of the barrel, and he accused me of having robbed the mission. He sued me for the barrel and they put me in leg irons. Adhering to regulations, charges were made against me and I was court martialed; my attorney demanded that the witnesses be presented to prove that I was a thief. Father Juan Cabot came with the Indian that had sold me the barrel and I called on Second Lieutenant Sánchez so that he could testify how I had acquired it through a purchase.[19] The Indian was called and he said that the priest had forced him to lie. The priest denied it and the Indian received 100 lashes. The blacksmith came and he removed the shackles that were locked on my feet. Then, I was asked how much did I seek in compensation; I requested 200 **pesos**, which Father Cabot placed in my hands. Hence, my twenty **reales** gave me the winnings of 197 **pesos** and 50 cents, although it cost me some days of sadness when I was in prison with shackles and given a court martial. With this I conclude the story of the Bouchard Invasion.

---

[19]Geiger, 32. Geiger notes that Juan Cabot was born in Majorca, Spain. After serving fourteen years in several California missions, he was assigned to Mission San Francisco in 1819. In late 1820, he moved to Mission Soledad.

CAPÍTULO 2

LOS RECUERDOS DE LORENZO ASISARA Y JOSÉ MARÍA AMADOR SOBRE LA MUERTE DE El PADRE ANDRÉS QUINTANA

(Aquí suspendemos por un momento las relaciones de Dn. José Ma. Amador pa. tomar la relación del indio Lorenzo Asisara, cantor que fue de la misión de Santa Cruz, y cantor en la actualidad en las iglesias católicas que le ocupan.)

Muerte del Padre Andrés Quintana

La relación que voy a hacer me la comunicó mi señor padre en 1818, fue neófito de la misión de Santa Cruz; uno de los fundadores de ella. Era natural de la ranchería de Asar en la costa del Jarro, adelante de la de Santa Cruz. Se bautizó entre los primeros de la fundación, teniendo él como 20 años de edad. Se llamaba Venancio Azar, y era el hortelano de la misión.

Mi padre presenció todos los hechos. Fue uno de los convidados para matar al Padre, cuando los indios trataron de matar al Padre Quintana. Hicieron una reunión en la casa del hortelano Julián, el mismo que se hizo aparecer enfermo.[1]

---

[1]Geiger, 205. Geiger apunta que el español Andrés Quintana arribó a Monterey en 1805. Aparentemente, Quintana estableció una reputación de ser cruel con los indígenas. En un incidente, él azotó a dos indígenas tan severamente que casi les causó la muerte. El gobernador, sin embargo, prefirió ignorar el lado malo de la personalidad de Quintana y decidió enfocar lo positivo. De Quintana él escribió: "Yo considero que este buen padre excidió no en el castigo a los indios pero en el amor que les tenía. Él agotó todas sus facultades en cuanto a dedicación y trabajo para mejorarlos y avanzarlos."

CHAPTER 2

LORENZO ASISARA AND JOSÉ MARÍA AMADOR'S ACCOUNTS OF THE DEATH OF FATHER ANDRÉS QUINTANA

[Thomas Savage writes:]

At this point, I will suspend for a moment the account of Don José María Amador in order to give the account of the Indian Lorenzo Asisara, a former singer at Mission Santa Cruz and at present a singer for the Catholic churches which employ him.

The Death of Father Andrés Quintana

The narrative that I am going to give was told to me by my father, who was a neophyte of the Mission of Santa Cruz, in 1818. He was one of the original founders. He was a native of the Asar **ranchería** on the Jarro Coast, above Santa Cruz. He was among the first to be baptized during the founding [of the mission], when he was about twenty years old. His name was Venancio Azar, and he was the gardener of the mission.

My father was a witness to all the events; he was one of those who conspired to kill the Father. When the Indians decided to kill Father Quintana, they organized a meeting at the house of the gardener Julián, the same one that pretended to be ill.[1]

---

[1]Geiger, 205. The writer states that the Spanish-born Andrés Quintana arrived in Monterey in 1805. Apparently Quintana had a reputation for being cruel to the Indians. In one flogging incident, two Indians had been so severely beaten that they almost died. Governor Solá, however, preferred not to look at the dark side of Quintana's character. The governor wrote: "I also know that this good Father went to excess, not in punishing his Indians but in the love with which he regarded them. He strained all his faculties as far as zeal and industry carried him in order to improve and advance them."

El hombre que estaba sirviendo adentro de la plaza de la misión, nombrado Donato, fue castigado por el Padre Quintana con una disciplina, pajuelas de alambre. De cada azote le cortaban la nalga. Entonces este mismo Donato pensó vengarse. Él fue quien hizo la reunión de unos 14 hombres y entre ellos el cocinero y los pages del servicio del Padre. El cocinero se llamaba Antonino, el page mayor Lino. Los otros pages se llamaban Vicente y Miguel Antonio. Se juntaron todos en la casa de Julián para ver cómo evitaban los crueles castigos que les imponía el Padre Quintana. Estando allí reunidos Lino, como más hábil y vivo que los demás, dijo: "lo primero ahora pa. que al padre no se le cumplan los deseos de castigar a la gente de ese modo, que no somos animales; él dice en sus sermones que Dios no manda eso, ejemplos y doctrina. Díganme ahora Uds. ¿qué haremos con el Padre? Correrlo no podemos, ni acusarlo ante el juez, porque no sabemos quien le manda a él pa. lo que está haciendo con nosotros." A esto contestó Andrés, padre del page Lino (este Lino era indio puro, pero tan blanco como cualquier español, y hombre de buenas luces naturales.) "Vamos matando al padre mejor, sin que nadie sepa, ni los pages ni ninguno, sino nosotros los que estamos aquí presentes." Dijo entonces Julián el hortelano: "¿Cómo haremos para poderlo matar?" Responde la muger de él: "Tú que siempre te enfermas, sólo así se puede, piénsalo si es bueno así." Lino aprobó, y pidió que todos dijeran sí como él, "y entonces lo haremos mañana en la noche" que era sábado. Es de advertir que el Padre se había propuesto poner a la gente en la plaza el domingo siguiente para probar la nueva cuarta que había hecho con pajuelas de alambre, para ver si salía bien a su gusto.

Todos los concurrentes convinieron en que se hiciese como lo había recomendado Lino.

Efectivamte. en la tarde del sábado como a las 6, día —de —de 1812 le fueron a avisar al Padre que se estaba muriendo el huertero.[2] Ya estaban los indios apostados entre dos árboles de un lado y del otro para coger al Padre al pasar.

[2]Asisara no sabía la fecha de la muerte de Quintana. Sin embargo, el historiador H. H. Bancroft en su obra *California Pastoral* reporta que en el "Registro de Muertes," la muerte del Padre Quintana es dada como el 12 de octubre de 1812 (573).

The man who was working inside the plaza of the mission, by the name of Donato, was punished by Father Quintana with a wire point whip in order to discipline him. With each flogging, the buttocks were cut. Then, the same Donato began planning his revenge. He was the one who held the meeting, attended by fourteen men; among them were the cook and pages at the service of the priest. The cook was named Antonino and the senior page was Lino. The other pages were named Vicente and Miguel Antonio. All of them got together at Julián's house so that they could discuss how to prevent the further cruel punishment that Father Quintana inflicted on them. At the gathering, Lino, as the most able and sharpest individual, said: "The first thing we need to do is to keep the Father from having the desire to punish people in such a manner, as if we were animals. He tells us in his sermons that God does not command this [type of punishment] in his example or doctrine." "Tell me, then, what are we to do with the priest? Run him off, we cannot do, nor can we take him before a judge since we do not know who commands him to do what he does to us." To this, Andrés, who was the father of the page Lino (Lino was a pure Indian but he was as light complexioned as any Spaniard and a man of good looks), responded: "It will be better if we kill the Father, without anyone knowing about it, not even the pages nor anyone else, only those that are here present." Then, Julián, the gardener, said: "What shall we do to kill him?" His wife answered: "You who is always sick, this is the only way, think if this is not the best way." Lino approved [the plan] and asked that everyone answer as he did. "Then, we shall do it tomorrow night," which would be Saturday. It should be noted that the Father had decided to call the people to the plaza on the following Sunday in order to try out a new whip that he had made with metal wire points to see if it had turned out to his satisfaction.

All the participants concurred that Lino's recommendation should be carried out.

In effect, in the afternoon of Saturday, around six p.m._____, of 1812, the Father was informed that the gardener was dying.[2] The Indians had positioned themselves in between two trees, one on one side and the other on the other side so they could get the priest as he went by.

---

[2]Asisara did not know the date of Quintana's death. In *California Pastoral*, H. H. Bancroft, however, reports that the "Registry of Deaths" listed Father Quintana's death on October 12, 1812 (573).

Llegó el Padre a la casa del Julián, que se hacía el agonizante. El Padre lo ausilió creyéndole realmente enfermo y en estado de muerte. Cuando el P. Quintana iba de vuelta pa. su casa, pasó junto a donde estaban apostados los indios. Éstos no tuvieron valor pa. echarle mano y lo dejaron pasar. Ya venía el hortelano moribundo por detrás de él: llegó el Padre a su casa. Dentro de una hora más, subió la muger de Julián a avisarle que estaba acabando su marido. Con esta novedad volvió el Padre a la huerta, precedido de la muger que iba dando gritos y sollozos. Vio que el enfermo estaba acabando. Primeramte. le tomó la mano pa. pulsarle. Lo pulsó, y vio que el enfermo no tenía nada. El pulso no indicaba que Julián tuviese novedad, pero no sabiendo que pudiera ser aquello, volvió a rezar y a ausiliarle. En esto ya era de noche. Cuando salió el Padre, se levantó Julián y se lavó los sacramentos que le había puesto aquel, y se siguió detrás a juntarse con los otros y ver qué era lo que harían sus compañeros. Al llegar al lugar en que éstos estaban situados, volteaba Lino la cabeza a mirar a una y otra parte, y ver si salían a coger al Padre. Se pasó el Padre y no lo tomaron. Llegó a su casa.

Más tarde, estando el Padre a la mesa cenando ya se habían reunido en la casa del fingido moribundo los conspiradores para averiguar por qué no habían apresado al Padre. Quejábase Julián de que el Padre le había echado yerba en los óleos que le había puesto por causa de ellos, y que ahora se iba a morir ya. Entonces la muger dijo, "si no cumplen lo que han prometido, los voy a acusar y no vuelvo más a la casa." Todos le respondieron "Bien, ahora sí, en este viage; vé y háblale al Padre." La muger salió de nuevo en busca del Padre Quintana, estaba éste cenando. Se levantó al momento y acudió a donde se hallaba el supuesto enfermo. Ahora llevaba consigo tres pages; dos que le alumbraban con faroles por delante, y por detrás le resguardaba su mayordomo Lino. Los otros dos eran Vicente y Miguel Antonio. Llegó el Padre a la casa del huertero y lo encontró privado de sentido; ya no hablaba. Le rezó el Padre las últimas oraciones sin ponerle óleos, y le dijo a la muger, "Ya está tu marido dispuesto para vivir o morir, ya no me vayan a buscar más." Entonces se salió el Padre con sus pages de vuelta pa. su casa. Julián le seguía. Llegando al lugar en donde estaban los dos árboles, como no fijaba la vista sino en el camino adelante, Lino le abrazó por detrás, diciéndole estas palabras, "alto aquí, Padre, tienes que

The Father reached the house of Julián, who was pretending to be dying. The Father gave him the last rites, fully convinced that he was really sick and was dying. As Father Quintana was returning to his house, he passed through where the Indians were hiding. These individuals could not build up the courage to capture him and let him pass. Following right behind him was the dying gardener; the Father reached his house. Within an hour, Julián's wife came to tell him that he [her husband] was close to death. With this news, the Father returned to the orchard; he was followed by the woman who was clamoring and crying. He saw that the ailing person was going fast; he took his hand to check his pulse and saw that he did not have any. The pulse did not indicate that Julián's condition had deteriorated, but not knowing what it meant, he started praying and giving him the last rites. While doing this, night fell. When the Father left, Julián got up and he washed off the Sacraments that the Father had put on him and followed him to get together with the others and to see what his companions were going to do. As he came to the place where they were hiding, Lino turned his head to look everywhere, to see if they came out to take the Father. The Father went by and they did not get him. He reached his house.

Later on, as the Father was having dinner, the conspirators had already met at the house of the man who was supposed to be near death to discuss why the Father had not been taken captive. Julián was complaining that the priest had put weeds in the holy oils that he had put on him and because of their fault now he was going to die. Then, his wife said: "If you do not carry out what you promised I am going to inform on you, and I will not come back to the house." Everyone said: "Fine, let's get going on this journey, go and talk to the Father." This woman again went out to look for Father Quintana. He was having his dinner; right away he got up and went to see the alleged sick person. This time, three pages went with him, two in front of him to light the way with lanterns and behind him, to protect him, his foreman, Lino. The other two were Vicente and Miguel Antonio. The Father came to the house of the gardener and he found him unconscious—he could no longer talk. The Father said the last rites without anointing him with the Holy Oils and told the woman, "Your husband is now ready to live or die. Do not call me anymore." Then, the priest left with his two pages to go back to his house. Julián was following him. Coming to the place where the two trees were located, since his eyes were fixed on the road ahead, Lino embraced him from behind, telling him the following words: "Halt, Father, you have to

hablar algún rato." Entonces se voltearon los otros dos pages que llevaban las linternas, y cuando vieron salir a la gente para atacar al Padre, se echaron a huir con sus faroles. El Padre dijo a Lino, "Ay, hijo, ¿Qué me vas a hacer? Contestó Lino, "te lo dirán los que te quieren matar" ¿Qué os he hecho yo, hijos, pa. qe. me vayan a matar?" "Por qué has hecho una cuarta de fierro," le contestó Andrés.

Entonces el Padre replicó, "Ay, hijos! déjenme porque me voy de aquí ahora en este momento." Andrés le preguntó por qué había hecho esa cuarta de fierro. Quintana dijo que era sólo pa. los malos. Entonces varios gritaron, "pues estás en las manos de los malos, acuérdate de Dios. Muchos de los presentes al ver la aflicción del Padre lloraban y se compadecían de su suerte, pero no podían hacer nada en su favor, porqe. estaban comprometidos. Él suplicó mucho prometiendo irse de la misión inmediatamte, que lo dejaran. "Ahora no te vas de aquí a ninga. parte de la tierra, Padre, vas a ir al cielo." Este fue la ulta. contestación del Padre. Algunos qe. no habían podido llegar a tocar al Padre reconvenían a los otros porque hablaban demasiado, exigiendo que lo mataran de una vez. En seguida le taparon la boca con el mismo manto para ahogarlo. Le tenían bien asegurado de los brazos; después que ya se ahogó el Padre le tomaron un grano de los compañeros pa. que no maliciaran que lo habían golpeado, y al momento espiró el Padre.[3] Entonces Lino y los demás lo llevaron a su casa, y lo acostaron en su cama.

Los dos pagecitos Vicente y Miguel Antonio al llegar a la casa, quería el primero ir a dar parte a la guardia, pero el otro le disuadió diciéndole, "no, porque matarán a tu padre y madre y a todos los demás, y a tí mismo, y a mí. Así déjalos que hagan lo que quieran." Se escondieron los dos. Después que pusieron los indios al Padre en su cama, Lino buscó a los otros dos pages, y los halló escondidos. Desnudaron el cuerpo del Padre Quintana y lo acostaron como quien va a dormir. Todos los malhechores, incluso la muger de Julián, estaban presentes.

Andrés pidió a Lino las llaves del almacén. Él les preguntó "¿qué querían?" Y ellos dijeron que plata y avalorios. Entre la partida de los convidados había tres indios de la misión de Santa Clara. Estos propusieron que

---

[3]Amador usa la palabra "compañeros" para referirse a los testículos masculinos.

talk for a little while." At that moment, the two pages with the lanterns looked back, and when they saw the people come out to attack the priest, they fled with their lanterns. The Father told Lino: "Oh, my son, what are you going to do to me?" Lino answered: "The ones that want to kill you will tell you." "What have I done to you, my sons, that you may want to kill me?" "Because you have made a metal whip," answered Andrés.

Then, the Father replied: "Oh, my sons, let me go and I will leave here this very moment." Andrés asked him why he had made the metal whip, and Quintana said it was only for the bad people. Then, several shouted, "Well, you are in the hands of the bad people. Be thinking of God." Many of those who were present became saddened by the priest's predicament, and they cried and took pity for his fate but they could not do anything on his behalf since they were committed [to achieving their objective]. Promising that he would leave the mission immediately, he repeatedly begged them to let him go. "You are not going to any place on this earth, Father, you are going to Heaven." These were the last words of the priest. Some who had not been able to get close to the priest admonished the others for talking too much and demanded that he be killed right away. Immediately, they covered his mouth with the same cloth of his robe to suffocate him. They made certain that his arms were secured. After he had suffocated, they squeezed one "grain" of his **compañeros** so that there would be no evidence that he had been beaten.[3] At that moment, the Father expired. Then, Lino and the others took him to his house, and they put him on his bed.

When the two little pages, Vicente and Miguel Antonio, got to the house, the first one wanted to notify the guard. But the other [one] discouraged him, telling him, "Do not [do it], because they will kill your father and mother, and everyone else, you, and me. Let them do whatever they want." Both of them went to hide themselves. After the Indians put the priest in his bed, Lino searched for the other two pages and found them hiding. They took off the clothes of the body of Father Quintana and put him to bed as if he were asleep. All the evildoers, including Julián's wife, were present.

Andrés asked Lino for the keys to the warehouse. He asked them: "What do you want?" And they said silver and things of value. Among the party of the invited were three Indians from Mission Santa Clara. They proposed that

---

[3]Asisara uses **compañeros** to refer to a man's testicles.

se averiguara cuánto dinero había. Lino abrió la caja y les enseñó el oro y plata acuñada que había. Los tres indios clareños tomaron una parte bastante pesada pa. llevarla a su misión. No sé qué habían de hacer con esa moneda. Los otros tomaron su parte como pudieron. Entonces pidieron las llaves del convento, o monjerío. Lino entregó a uno de ellos la llave del Jayunte, o cuartel de los indios solteros pa. sacarlos y juntarlos con las solteras abajo en la huerta, pa. que no sintieran en la plaza o ranchería ni en la guardia. Los solteros salieron sin hacer ningún ruido pa. la huerta al mismo lugar donde fue asesinado el padre. Allí estaba uno instándoles que no hiciesen ruido, que iban a pasar un buen rato. Al poco llegaron las monjas para pasar la noche allí. Se juntaron jóvenes de los dos sexos y tuvieron su diversión. A media noche, estando Lino en la sala con una de las muchachas del monjerío, se entró al cuarto del Padre para ver si estaba realmente muerto. Lo encontró reviviendo, ya estaba a punto de levantarse. Lino fue a buscar a sus cómplices pa. avisarles que el Padre estaba volviendo en sí. Vinieron los otros, y le magullaron el otro grano o testículo al Padre. Esta ulta. operación que puso fin a la vida del padre Quintana, la hizo Donato el azotado, quien andaba con las disciplinas en la mano diciendo, "yo las enterraré en los comunes."

Donato le dijo a Lino que cerrasen el arca. Con estas palabras, "Cierra el baúl de la plata colorada (así llamaban los indios al oro) y vamos a ver dónde lo enterramos." Bajaron con él ocho hombres a la huerta y lo enterraron, sin que lo sintieran los demás. Como escondidos.

Como a las 2 de la mañana volvieron las monjas a su convento, y los solteros a su jayunte. Sin hacer ningún ruido. Los asesinos se reunieron después de todo para oír la disposición de Lino y Donato. Unos querían huirse, y otros decían "por qué nadie sabe más que nosotros." Lino les preguntó qué querían tomar, azúcar, panocha, miel o qué otra cosa pa. llevar a sus casas, y acostarse a dormir un poco, pues ya todo estaba listo. Donato propuso volver a donde el Padre y ver cómo estaba. Lo encontraron no sólo muerto, sino perfectamte. frío y tieso. Lino entonces les enseñó la cuarta que se iba a estrenar al sigte. día, asegurándoles que ya no se usaría. Los mandó a sus casas a descansar, quedándose solo en la casa con las llaves. Les encargó mucho que no hiciesen ruido, arregló el cuarto y

it should be found out how much money there was. Lino opened the chest and he showed them the gold and silver bullion. The three Santa Claran Indians took a real heavy share back to their mission. They did not know what to do with the money. The others took their share in whatever way they could carry it. Then, they asked for the keys to the convent, or the nunnery. Lino gave one of them the keys to the **jayunte** or the dormitories for the bachelors so that they could be taken out and gotten together with the single girls down at the orchard, so that no one in the plaza, the **ranchería**, or at guard quarters would take notice. The bachelors came out without making a single sound on their way to the orchard, the same place where the priest had been killed. Once there, someone was urging them not to make noises, that they were going to have a good time. In a short time, the nuns arrived to spend the night there. The youth of both sexes got together and they had their entertainment. At midnight, when Lino was in the reception room with one of the girls from the nunnery, he went into the priest's room to see if he really was dead. He found him trying to regain consciousness and was about to awaken. Lino went to find his accomplices to notify them that the Father was about to wake up. The others came and they squeezed the other grain, or testicle, of the priest. Donato, the one that had been flogged, made this last operation that ended the life of Father Quintana. With the [priest's] testicles in his hand, he said: "I will bury them with those of the commoners."

Donato told Lino to close the coffer with these words: "Close the chest with the reddish silver (that is what the Indians called gold) and let's go find a place to bury it." Eight men went with him down to the orchard, and they buried it with no one detecting them. They did so as if they were in hiding.

Around two o'clock in the morning the nuns returned to their convent and the single men to their **jayunte** without making noise. The assassins, then, got together to listen to Lino and Donato's plans. Some wanted to flee while others asked: "Why? No one else but only us know." Lino asked them what they wanted to take—sugar, **panocha**, honey, or some other things—to their homes, and sleep a little since everything had been arranged. Donato proposed to go back to the priest's room to check on his condition; they not only found him dead but perfectly cold and stiff. Then, Lino showed them the whip that [the priest] was going to use for the first time on the following day, assuring them that it would no longer be used. He told them to go to their houses to rest and he remained by himself, with the keys, in the house. He greatly cautioned them not to make any noise, [as he proceeded to] fix the room and

el libro todo como acostumbraba el Padre hacer pa. acostarse, diciéndoles
que él no tocaría las campanas en esa mañana hasta que viniesen el mayordomo y el cabo de la escolta, y el hablaría con ellos. Todos se fueron por la
huerta con mucho sigilo.

Aquella misma mañana (Domingo) se debía tocar la campana como a las
8, pues a esa hora comenzaba a llegar la gente de la villa de Branciforte pa.
asistir a la misa. Visto esto por el mayordomo fue a ver a Lino que era el 1er.
asistente del Padre, a preguntarle por qué no había mandado el padre tocar.

Él estaba en la sala haciéndose el inocente y contestó que él no podía
decirle nada al Padre, porqe. éste estaba adentro todavía durmiendo o rezan-
do, y debía aguardar a que él le hablase primero. Se volvió el mayordomo pa.
su casa. A poco rato vino el cabo de la escolta, y Lino le dijo lo mismo que
al mayordomo. Volvió el mayordomo a terciar en la conversación,
resolvieron aguardar otro rato. Finalmte. Lino les dijo que en presencia de
ellos tocaría a la puerta del cuarto, observando, "Si él se enoja, Uds. volverán
por mí." Así se hizo, llamando al Padre, y como no se oyó ruido dentro, el
mayordomo y el cabo le pidieron a Lino que hiciese el primer toque, y él se
negó. Se retiraron encargándole que al cabo de algún tiempo volviera a llamar al Padre, porque ya se hacía muy tarde. Todos los sirvientes estaban en
sus trabajos como todos los días. Así es que no había señal que causara
ninguna sospecha. Volvió el mayordomo ya después de las 10, y pidió a Lino
que le gritase al Padre pa. ver qué tenía. Lino, con las llaves en la bolsa, le
tocaba al Padre. Al fin el mayordomo insistió en que Lino entrase al cuarto
y él se escusaba. En esto llegó de nuevo el cabo, que era el viejo Nazario
Galindo (el mayordomo era Carlos Castro). Lino (aunque tenía la llave del
cuarto en la bolsa) dijo, "pues voy a ver cómo abro la puerta," y pretendió ir
a buscar una llave con qué abrir. Volvió con un mazo de llaves y no encontró ninga. que le viniese a la cerradura. Se salieron el mayordomo y el cabo
pa. hablar con unos hombres que estaban allí. Despues Lino sacó la misma
llave de la puerta diciendo que era de la cocina. Abrió otra puerta que caía a
la plaza (llave que abría 3 puertas) y por allí entró.

the book as the Father was accustomed to do before going to bed. He told them that he would not ring the bells in the morning until the foreman and the corporal of the guard had arrived. He would talk to them [the foreman and corporal]. Everyone left through the orchard, in great secrecy.

On that same morning (Sunday), the bells should have been rung around eight since at that hour the people from the Villa of Branciforte started arriving for mass. After observing this, the foreman went to see Lino, who was the first assistant of the priest, and asked him why the Father had not ordered the sounding of the bells.

He was in the reception room, and looking innocent he answered that he could not say anything to the priest because he was still inside his room either sleeping or praying, and he had to wait until [the priest] talked to him first. The foreman went back to his house. In a short while the corporal of the guard came, and Lino told him the same thing he had said to the foreman. The foreman came to join the conversation; they resolved to wait awhile. Finally, Lino told them that in their presence he would knock on the door, warning them, "If he gets angry, will you speak on my behalf?" They both agreed. He called on the priest, and since no sounds were heard inside his room, the foreman and the corporal asked Lino to knock on the door; he refused to do so. They left and asked the corporal to call on the priest after a short time since it was getting very late. All the servants were performing their chores, as they were accustomed to do everyday; hence, there was nothing that could arouse suspicion. The foreman came back after ten o'clock and he asked Lino to shout at the priest to see if anything was wrong with him. Lino, with the keys in his pockets, was knocking on the priest's door. Finally, the foreman insisted that Lino go into the room and that he [the foreman] would assume responsibility. At this point, the corporal returned; he was the old man, Nazario Galindo (the foreman was Carlos Castro). Lino (although he had the room key in his pocket) said, "Well, I am going to see if I can open the door," and he pretended to go and find a key that would open the door. He came back with a bunch of keys but none fitted the door lock. The foreman and the corporal left the house to talk to some of the men that were outside. Afterwards, Lino took out the room's key claiming that it was for the kitchen. He opened another door that led to the plaza (the key opened three doors), and he entered through there.

Entonces abrió por dentro la puerta principal a la cual estaban los otros. Salió Lino sollozando y llorando, haciendo una gran gritería que el padre estaba muerto. Le preguntaron si era eso cierto y el respondió "como esta luz que nos alumbra, por Dios, voy a tocar los clamores." Entraron los tres: cabo, mayordomo y él. No dejó entrar a nadie más. El cabo y el mayordomo y las demás gentes escribieron a las demás misiones y a Monterey al P. Marcelino Marquínez.[4] (Este Marquínez era gran ginete y buen amigo.) Los pobres neófitos viejos y muchos otros indígenas que no sospechaban que el P. había sido matado, sino creían que había muerto de repente, lloraban amargamte. Lino daba unos bramidos dentro de la casa como un oso.

Vinieron los P.P. de Sta. Clara, y de otras misiones y se le hicieron los funerales, creídos todos que había muerto de muerte natural, pero no antes que hubieran examinado el cadáver en la sala y le hubiesen abierto el estómago pa. cerciorarse de que no había muerto envenenado. Asistieron a esos actos oficiales, sargentos y muchos otros. Nada se descubrió. Finalmente por casualidad alguno de los presentes notó que tenía embotados los compañeros y se convencieron de que allí había estado la causa de la muerte. Por suerte no descubrieron, y le dieron sepultura al cadáver todos convencidos de que había sido natural la muerte.

Pasados algunos años de la muerte, entonces Emiliana, la muger de Lino, y María Tata, la muger del cocinero Antonino, tuvieron sus celos: ellas eran costureras y estaban en sus trabajos. Esto fue como en agosto cuando la cosecha de la lenteja.

Carlos Castro estaba con su gente en la milpa cuidando. Antes de las once se vino pa. su casa a la comida. Era hombre que entendía bien la lengua de los indios. Viniendo de la milpa paso detrás de una muralla de una plaza en donde estaban cosiendo esas mugeres, y oyó a una decirle a la otra que comía panocha a escondidas. Se detuvo Castro, y oyó que la segunda muger respondió a la primera "¿Cómo es que tú tienes tanto dinero?" La 1a. replicó, "tú también tienes, porque tu marido mató al padre."

---

[4]Geiger, 146. El historiador Geiger dice que el misionero Marcelino Marquínez nació en España y llegó a la misión de San Francisco en 1810. Según Geiger, Marquínez logró forjar una reputación de ser un excelente administrador y de tener cierta aptitud para la medicina.

Then, he opened from the inside the main door leading to where all the others were waiting. Lino came out sobbing and crying, screaming loudly that the priest was dead. They asked him if it was really true that the priest was dead, and he responded, "As this light that shines, by God, I am going to sound the news." The three—the corporal, foreman, and himself—went in [into the priest's room]; he did not allow anyone else. The corporal and the foreman and others wrote to the other missions and to Monterey to Father Marcelino Marquínez.[4] (This Marquínez was a great rider and a good friend.) The poor old neophytes and many other Indians, who did not suspect that the priest had been killed since they believed that he had died suddenly, cried with much sorrow. Lino bellowed inside the house like a bear.

The priests from Santa Clara and the other missions came. The funeral was held with everyone believing that he had died a natural death but not before the body was examined in the reception room and his stomach was cut open to make sure that he had not been poisoned to death. Those attending these inquests were the officers, sergeants and many others. Nothing was discovered. Finally, by sheer accident, one of those who were present detected that he had a bluntness on the testicles and concluded that this had been the cause of his death. Fortunately, they did not discover [the actual causes of the priest's death] and they buried the body; all were convinced that he had a natural death.

Some years had passed since his death when Emiliana, Lino's wife, and María Tata, the wife of Antonino, the cook, had a case of jealousy while they were engaged in their work as seamstresses. This was around August during the lentil harvest.

Carlos Castro was overseeing his men in the fields and before eleven o'clock in the morning he returned to his house to have his meal. He was a man that understood well the language of the Indians. Coming from the fields, he passed behind a wall in the plaza where the two women were sewing and he heard one telling the other, that she was secretly eating **panocha**. Castro stopped and heard the second woman answer the first one, "How is it that you have so much money?" The first woman responded, "you also have [it] because your husband killed the priest."

---

[4]Marcelino Marquínez was born in Spain and reached San Francisco in 1810 (Geiger, 146). He developed a reputation for being an excellent administrator and possessing an aptitude for medicine.

Entonces la segunda acusó al marido de la 1a. del mismo delito. Siguió la guerra de palabras, y Castro se convenció que el P. Quintana había sido asesinado, y fue a darle parte al P. Ramón Olbes que era a la sazón el misionero en Santa Cruz.[5] El P. Ramón fue a avisar al P. Marquínez. Este ult. mandó a uno de sus pages a la huerta para hacer saber a Julián y sus cómplices que se fugaran porque si no los iban a coger. Al medio día ya pa. hora de comer el Padre Olbes habló a Lino que mandara por su mujer a comer allí y para que cortase algunas piezas de ropa. Vino la Emiliana, y el P. Olbes la metió en un cuarto en que había ropa, y le entregó unas tijeras pa. cortar algunas piezas diciéndole aquí comerás. Después mandó con un page a traer a la María Tata pa. sacar ropa sucia de la iglesia pa. lavar. El mayordomo estaba presenciando las maniobras del Padre.

Hizo éste a la María Tata detenerse allí pa. comer. La metió en otro cuarto pa. qe. cortase unos vestidos pa. los pages. El mayordomo y los dos Padres se fueron a comer. Después de la comida, y que ya habían comido también las dos mugeres, el Padre Olbes le dijo a la Emiliana "¿sabes tú quién come mucha azúcar blanca?" Ella contestó que la María Tata "porque su marido había matado al P. Quintana." El Padre la hizo volver al cuarto, e hizo venir a la María Tata. El Padre le preguntó, "díme si sabes quiénes fueron los que mataron al P. Quintana; díme la verdad que nada te sucederá." En esto comían Lino y el Antonino con mucha frescura en la cocina. La María Tata respondía, "Lino, Padre." El P. Olbes entonces las despachó a sus casas a descansar ofreciéndoles un regalo. Entonces mandó el Padre por el Cabo Nazario Galindo pa. apresar a los asesinos. Empezaron con los huerteros y el cocinero, sin decirles por qué se les arrestaba. Antonino fue el 1er. preso. Puesto en el calaboso le preguntaron quién era su compañero. Dijo quien era, y éste fue arrestado, y preguntado le daba el nombre de su compañero. De este modo fueron arrestados todos, menos Lino, a quien se temía por hombre valiente y de mucha fuerza. Él fue tomado con engaño por su mismo Compadre Carlos Castro, quien le pasó un cuchillo pa. tusar unas

---

[5]Geiger, 167. Según Geiger, Ramón Olbes era originario de Zaragoza, España. Este misionero había servido en las misiones de Santa Inés y Santa Bárbara hasta que fue trasladado a la misión de Santa Cruz en 1818. Es muy probable que el padre Olbes sufría de ataques de locura que eran provocados por su mal estado de salud. Aparte de maltratar a los indígenas también regañaba a los vecinos del pueblo de Branciforte al igual que a las autoridades de California.

Then, the second woman accused the husband of the first woman of committing the same crime. The war of words continued and Castro became convinced that Father Quintana had been killed, and he went to inform Ramón Olbes, who was at that time the missionary of Santa Cruz.[5] Father Ramón went and told Father Marquínez. The latter sent one of his pages to the orchard to let Julián and accomplices know that they had to flee, otherwise they were going to get captured. At noon, just before lunch, Father Olbes talked to Lino to send for his wife so that she could come and eat there and to cut some pieces of cloth. Emiliana came and Father Olbes put her in a room where the cloth was kept and he gave her some scissors with which to make the cuts. He told her that she would eat there. Afterwards, he sent a page to bring María Tata to take out the dirty clothes from the Church so that they could be washed. The foreman was observing the maneuverings of the priest.

He [the priest] made María Tata stop there so that she could eat; he put her in another room so that she could cut some clothes for the pages. The foreman and the two priests went to eat. After their meal and after the two women had eaten, Father Olbes asked Emiliana, "Do you know who eats a lot of white sugar?" She answered that María Tata was the one "because her husband had killed Father Quintana." The Father made her go back to the room and called on María Tata. The Father asked her: "Tell me if you know who were the ones that killed Father Quintana. Tell me the truth and nothing will happen to you." Around this time, Lino and Antonino were calmly eating in the kitchen. María Tata responded: "Lino, Father." Father Olbes then sent them to their houses to rest, offering them a gift. Then the priest sent for Corporal Nazario Galindo so that he could arrest the assassins. They started with the gardeners and the cook, without telling them why they were being arrested. Antonino was the first one to be arrested and put in a jail cell; he was asked who was his accomplice. He told them who he was and when this one was arrested he then would be asked who was his accomplice and he would give his accomplice's name. In this manner, everyone was arrested with the exception of Lino, who was feared for he was a brave man and very powerful. He was taken through deceit by his own **compadre** Carlos Castro, who gave him a knife, and told him to cut the

---

[5]Geiger, 167. According to Geiger, Ramón Olbes was born in Zaragoza, Spain. Geiger also notes that Olbes served at Missions Santa Inés and Santa Bárbara before going to Mission Santa Cruz in 1818. Seemingly, Olbes experienced bouts of insanity, which were triggered by poor health. In addition to his mistreatment of Indians, he often scolded the residents of Branciforte and the provincial authorities.

yeguas negras y blancas pa. hacer una jaquima galana pa. la bestia del Padre. Maliciando Lino le dijo a Castro, "Compadre, ¿por qué me estás engañando, yo sé que me vas aprenhender." Ya estaban dos soldados escondidos detrás del corral, "Tenga su cuchillo, compadre; lo que yo pensé ya está hecho.

Voy a pagarlo, y si yo hubiera querido, los acabo en la misma noche que maté al Padre, a soldados, mayordomo y cuantos más había."

El resultado de todo [fue] que los acusados y cómplices fueron llevados a San Francisco, entre ellos iba mi padre. Allí los juzgaron y los que mataron al Padre fueron sentenciados a recibir un novenario de 50 azotes cada uno, y a servir en obras públicas en San Diego.[6] Los demás, incluso mi padre, fueron dados libres, porque habían servido de testigos, y no se les probó que habían tomado parte en el asesinato.

Todos volvieron después de muchos años a su misión.

Los Padres españoles eran muy crueles con los indios. Los maltrataban mucho, los tenían mal comidos, mal vestidos, y los hacían trabajar como esclavos. Yo alcancé un poco de esa vida cruel. Los Padres no practicaban lo que predicaban en el púlpito. El mismo Padre Olbes por sus crueldades fue una vez apedreado por los indios.

Rancho de San Andrés de Sta. Cruz.
Jurisdicción de Watsonville
Julio 10 de 1877
Lorenzo Asisara
[Firmado]

Yo, José Ma. Amador, fui comisionado con Jesús Mesa para llevar los presos en la causa de la muerte del P. Quintana, de Santa Cruz al presidio de San Francisco. Llevamos 16 atados de los dedos pulgares de la mano y con una vara pasada por el cogote. Me los entregaron engrillados, pero yo rehusé recibirlos así, y entonces me autorizaron pa. llevarlos como me pareciera. Yo les hice quitar los grillos.

---

[6]Bancroft, 593. Bancroft encontró documentos en el archivo "Provincial State Papers" que demuestran que el gobernador de Solá condenó a los asesinos del Padre Quintana en marzo de 1816. A Lino, Antonino, Quirico, Julián se les castigó con 200 latigazos cada uno. También a Lino y a Antonino se les fijó una sentencia de diez años de prisión formal mientras que a Quirico y Julián se les dictó una de seis años a cada uno.

manes of some black and white mares in order to make an elegant head-stall for the Father's horse. Cursing, Lino told Castro: "**Compadre**, why are you trying to deceive me, I know that you are going to arrest me." There were two soldiers hiding behind the corral. "Here is your knife, **Compadre**: What I planned is already done.

I am going to pay for it. And if I had wanted to, I could have killed you all on the same night that I killed the Father—the soldiers, the foreman, and whomever else."

The result was that all the accused and their accomplices were taken to San Francisco. Among them was my father. While there, they were tried and those that killed the Father were sentenced to fifty lashes each for nine days and they had to serve [their sentence by] performing public works in San Diego.[6] The others, including my father, were set free because they had served as witnesses and it could not be proven that they had taken part in the killing. After many years, they all came back to their mission.

The Spanish priests were very cruel with the Indians: they mistreated them a lot, they kept them poorly fed, ill clothed, and they made them work like slaves. I managed to experience some of that cruel life. The priests did not practice what they preached at the pulpit. For his cruelty, Father Olbes himself was one time stoned by the Indians.

Rancho de San Andrés de Santa Cruz
Jurisdiction of Watsonville
July 10, 1877
Lorenzo Asisara
(Signature)

I, José María Amador, along with Jesús Mesa, was commissioned to take the prisoners who were charged with the death of Father Quintana from Santa Cruz to the Presidio of San Francisco. We took sixteen [of them] tied from the thumbs to a stick that ran across the back of their necks. They gave them to me shackled but I refused to receive them in that manner and then I was authorized to take them whichever way I desired. I made them take off the irons.

---

[6]Bancroft, 593. Bancroft found documents in the Provincial State Papers indicating that Governor Solá sentenced the murderers of Father Quintana in March 1816. Lino, Antonino, Quirico, and Julián received 200 lashes each; in addition, Lino and Antonino received a ten-year prison sentence while Quirico and Julián were given six-year terms.

Hablando de castigos a indios, una vez siendo yo mayordomo de la misión de San José, un indio lazó a otro indio por el pescuezo y lo arrastró como una milla dejándolo por muerto después de haberle quitado la frazada y la camisa. Yo mandé a mis acreditados Moquelemnes para que lo persiguieran por el camino de Sta. Cruz y el pueblo de San José. Aquellos indios eran más lijeros que los caballos, sin exageración ninguna. Lo alcanzaron al malhechor en Gilroy y me lo volvieron a la misión. Le puse un par de grillos y le mandé dar 300 azotes para salvarle de la pena capital a que se había hecho acreedor. El indio arrastrado no murió.

El azotado era sirviente de José Martínez, quien me lo reclamó después de castigado, y yo le respondí que se aviniese él a recibir 50 azotes, y entonces le entregaría el sirviente para que fueran emparejados amo y criado. Yo hice curar con cuidado al indio, pero lo tenía preso. Cuando llegó el día de entregar yo la administración, vino él con sus grillos, y me suplicó que no lo dejase preso en manos de otro. Que lo pusiera en libertad pa. irse. Yo accedí a su súplica y él se marchó. Estuvo preso como 3 meses.

Talking about punishment inflicted on the Indians, one day when I was the foreman at Mission San José, an Indian roped another Indian by the neck and dragged him about a mile, leaving him for dead after he took his blanket and shirt. I sent my Moquelemne associates to chase him on the road from Santa Cruz to San José. Without exaggerating, these Indians were swifter than horses. They caught up to the culprit in Gilroy and they brought him to me at the Mission. I put on him a pair of shackles and I ordered that he be given 300 lashes to save him from getting the capital punishment sentence that he had earned for himself. The Indian who was dragged did not die.

The Indian who was whipped was a servant of José Martínez, who reclaimed him after he received his punishment. I told him [Martínez] to come and receive fifty lashes and then I would return to him his servant so that master and servant would be paired together. I ordered that the Indian be cured with great care, but I kept him as a prisoner. When the day came to surrender my position as mission administrator, he came to see me in shackles and begged me not to hand him over as a prisoner to anyone else, and asked me to set him free so that he could leave. I accepted his plea and he left; he was kept prisoner for about three months.

José María Amador. Courtesy of the Amador County Archives.

"The Reception of Jean-François de la Perouse at Mission Carmel in 1786, California," by Jose Cardero (1791–1792). Reprinted by permission of The Bancroft Library, Berkeley, California.

"California Vaqueros, Returned from the Chase," by Harrison Eastman (ca. 1854). Reprinted by permission of The Bancroft Library, Berkeley, California.

"Danse des Californiens (at Mission San Francisco de Assis, California)," by Ludwig Choris of the Kotzebue Expedition (ca.1815). Reprinted by permission of The Bancroft Library, Berkeley, California.

"Horse Market in Sonora, California," by Francis Samuel Marryat (1855). Reprinted by permission of The Bancroft Library, Berkeley, California.

"Northern Valley Yukut Indians Hunting on the Bay of San Francisco, California," by Ludwig Choris of the Kotzebue Expedition (1822). Reprinted by permission of The Bancroft Library, Berkeley, California.

"Mission San Jose, Alameda County, California," by unknown artist (1800s). Reprinted by permission of The Bancroft Library, Berkeley, California.

"Vue du Presidio San. Francisco," by Ludovik [Louis] Choris, 1822. Courtesy of California Historical Society, FN-25092.

"Indian Encampment on the Banks of Feather River, California," by Fritz Wikersheim (1845–1851). Reprinted by permission of The Bancroft Library, Berkeley, California.

"California Gold Rush Gambling," by unknown artist (ca. 1850). Reprinted by permission of The Bancroft Library, Berkeley, California.

"San José from City Hall," by Levi Goodrich (1858). Reprinted by permission of The Bancroft Library, Berkeley, California.

"Native Californians Lassoing a Steer," by Auguste Ferra (no date). Reprinted by permission of The Bancroft Library, Berkeley, California.

CAPÍTULO 3

LOS RECUERDOS DE LORENZO ASISARA Y JOSÉ MARÍA AMADOR SOBRE LA VIDA EN CALIFORNIA DURANTE El RÉGIMEN MEXICANO, 1822–1846

Me acuerdo de cuando en el año de 1821 se enarboló la bandera de la independa. en Cal. Vino un comisionado especial de la regencia del imperio de México a efectuar el cambio. Era Gobr. todavía Dn. Pablo Vicente de Solá quien juró la independencia, y la hizo jurar a las tropas y al pueblo. Yo me hallaba a la sazón sirviendo en la campa. de cuera de San Francisco, cuando llegó la orden de Monterey de hacer la pira del nuevo orden de cosas. Recibió la orden el Capn. Argüello quien desde luego le dio cumplimto. Se reunió la tropa como a las 9 de la mañana, y también en la tarde después de las 3. Se hicieron las evoluciones correspondtes. y descargas de fusilería, y en el castillo, arreglado a ordenanza se dispararon 21 cañonazos al tiempo de enarbolar la bandera nueva. Cuando Solá vino a la visita, como un mes más tarde, se repitió todo el ceremonial. Solá quiso mandar en persona las evoluciones y no pudo hacerlo, y tuvo el Capn. Argüello que dar las órdenes. La verdad es que nosotros estabamos hechos a Argüello y no a Solá.

El Capn. Argüello era hombre muy querido de la tropa por su benignidad con ella sin faltar a la disciplina.

Una peculiaridad de él. Si a un soldado en formación se le caía una bota, el sombrero o alguna otra prenda, quedaba esta caída, y Argüello la recogía y se la ponía al soldado con sus propias manos, acompañando las palabras siguientes, "Oh, costal de azumbres descuidado!" Esta era la única represión.

Después de la salva general mandó Solá al Capn. Argüello que pusiera la tropa en acto de guerra, y que tomara el bastón cuando el arma estuviera preparada para cargar, y la tirara de una punta a la otra de la fila para ver si estaba bien alineada. Solá se quedó admirado de la perfección que había adquerido la tropa de San Francisco, debida a la pericia y consta. del Capn. Argüello. Poco después, por invitación del Gobr.

CHAPTER 3

AMADOR AND ASISARA'S VIEWS OF LIFE IN CALIFORNIA DURING THE MEXICAN REPUBLIC

I remember that in 1821 the flag of Independence was raised in California. A special commissioner of the regency of the Mexican Empire came to make the change [of government]. Don Pablo Vicente de Solá was still the governor and he supported Independence and made the troops and people take the oath of loyalty to it. At that time, I was serving in the **soldado de cuera** company of San Francisco when the order came from Monterey to implement the new order of things. Captain Argüello received the order and he immediately carried it out. The troops were gathered at nine o'clock in the morning and again in the afternoon, after three PM. The proper corresponding drills were performed, there was a gun fusillade, and at the fortress there was a discharge of twenty-one cannon rounds at the moment that the new flag was being raised. When Solá came to visit, about a month later, the ceremony was repeated. Solá, in person, tried to lead the drills but he could not do it so Captain Argüello had to issue the orders. The truth is we were conditioned [to follow] Argüello and not Solá.

Captain Argüello was a man who was well liked by the troops for his kindness yet without weakening discipline.

One of his idiosyncrasies was that if a soldier in formation lost his boot, a hat, or any other clothing item, it would remain on the ground until he picked it up. [He, then, would] put it back on the soldier with his own hands while saying the following words, "careless sack of **azumbre**." This would be the only reprimand [he would give them].

After the general salute of firearms, Solá ordered Captain Argüello to put the troops in battle ready status and to take the staff of command. When the weapons were ready to be loaded, [he was to] throw it from one end of the line to the other end to see if the troops were well aligned. Solá was impressed by the perfection that the San Francisco troops had acquired due to the expertise and firmness of Captain Argüello. Shortly thereafter, at the invitation of Governor

Solá, 30 hombres de nuestra compa. (yo entre ellos, como que era el asistente del Capitán) con Argüello pasamos a Monterey, y llegamos allí la antevíspera del día de Corpus Christi. El Gobr. mandó a Estudillo, comandte. de la Compa. de Monterey, examinar su tropa, y pasamos a la misión a hacer los honores de la fiesta del Corpus. Argüello puso sus 30 hombres a las órdenes de Estudillo para que éste mandase las evoluciones de las tropas reunidas. Solá se puso con Argüello fuera de la formación pa. marchar en la procesión. En la 2a. ermita empezó Estudillo a darle palos a los soldados de su compa. porqe. no conocían sus deberes. Solá le habló, y entonces puso al Capn. Argüello a mandar las evoluciones. Argüello entrevesó la tropa poniendo un soldado de Monterey entre dos de San Francisco pa. que aquel en la marcha y demás hiciese lo que éstos. Este arreglo tuvo el éxito deseado, y ya no hubo necesidad de dar bejucazos a los soldados. Solá manifestó mucho regocijo de esto.

En esas ceremonias del cambio de bandera si mal no recuerdo, los Padres de la misión, como españoles rancios que eran, se negaron a tomar parte por creerlo atentatorio contra los derechos del Rey de España. Así tuvieron que oficiar el Canónigo Comisionado Dn. Valentín Fernández de San Vicente y un capellán clérigo que venía con él.[1]

Después que nos retiramos de la función del Corpus a Monterey, ordenó el Gobr. a Dn. Luis Argüello que nombráse las dos compas. reunidas pa. hacer la salva general dentro de la plaza con todas las evoluciones de la ordenanza. Salió Dn. Luis con toda la tropa fuera de la plaza, como a 6 a.m. y después del desayuno formó la tropa en la plaza en batalla. En las evoluciones iba haciendo la salva de fusilería, hasta que concluyó. Salió a esto Solá y en voz alta delante de toda la tropa y concurrencia, dijo: "Gracias a Dios que conozco un oficial que enseña bien a la tropa sus deberes, que veo una tropa tan honrada e instruida como la de San Francisco. Quisiera que todas las demás compañías se pusiesen bajo el mismo pie." Este cumplido nos hizo el Gobr. a nuestro Capitán y a nosotros. Volvimos a paso oblicuo al cuartel. Ordenó Solá dar $3. [pesos] a cada soldado. Permanecimos 8 días paseándonos hasta que nos volvimos con nuestro gefe a San Francisco.

---

[1]Beebe y Senkewicz, 323. Los escritores creen que Fernández de San Vicente fue enviado a Alta California por el emperador Agustín de Iturbide para preparar el cambio de gobierno de las autoridades de España a México. Beebe y Senkewicz piensan que Fernández de San Vicente fue el responsable del nombramiento de Argüello como gobernador.

Solá, thirty men from our company (I among them since I was the assistant to the captain) went with Argüello to Monterey; we got there on the evening before Corpus Christi day. The governor sent Estudillo, the commander of the Company of Monterey, to examine the troops, and then we went to the mission to serve as the honor guard for the Feast of the Corpus. Argüello put his thirty men under the command of Estudillo so that he could direct the drills of all the troops that had been gathered. Solá, with Argüello, placed himself outside of the formation that would march in the procession. In the second **ermita**, Estudillo started to hit the soldiers of his own company with a stick because they did not know their own responsibilities. Solá talked with him and then he put Captain Argüello to command the drills. Argüello mixed the troops, putting one soldier from Monterey in between two from San Francisco in order that he and the others would march in the same way as the other two. This arrangement had the desired effect and there was no longer any need to beat the soldiers. Solá expressed much joy with this success.

In these ceremonies of the changing of the flag, if I remember correctly, the priests, rancid Spaniards that they were, refused to participate [in them], believing that they would be violating the rights of the Spanish King. This is why the Canon Commissioner Don Valentín Fernández de San Vicente and a clerical chaplain that was accompanying him had to officiate.[1]

After the celebration of Corpus and we retired to Monterey, the governor ordered Don Luis Argüello to name two of the companies that had gathered there to conduct the general salute of firearms in the plaza with all obligatory drills. Don Luis left the plaza with the entire troop and around six in the morning, after breakfast, he regrouped the troops in the plaza in battle-ready formation. Throughout the drills and until they concluded, the troops discharged their weapons. Solá came out and in a loud voice, in front of the troops and the crowd, said, "Thank God that I know an officer who well instructs the troops their responsibilities. I have not seen troops that are as honest and well instructed as those from San Francisco. I would like to see that all the other companies achieve the same level." The governor offered this compliment to our captain and to us. We came back to the barracks in an indirect way. Solá commanded that each soldier be given three **pesos**. We stayed eight days, enjoying ourselves until we went with our commanding officer back to San Francisco.

---

[1]Beebe and Senkewicz, 323. The authors believe that Fernández de San Vicente was sent to Alta California by Emperor Agustín de Iturbide to manage the change of government from Spain to México. The writers believe that Fernández de San Vicente would later arrange the appointment of Argüello as governor.

El año de 1823 en sus principios se marchó el Gobr. Solá pa. Méx. por haber sido electo por la Junta Provincial diputado por Californias a las Cortes del imperio. El Capn. Dn. Luis Argüello, como oficial mexicano más antiguo en el servicio, fue llamado por la Junta con la anuencia del Comisionado imperial, a ocupar el puesto de Gobr. interinamte.

Cuando marchó Solá pa. México, lo cual hizo embarcándose en San Diego le pusieron dos o tres o cuatro soldados que le acompañasen hasta Guadalajara. Recuerdo que uno de ellos se llamaba Vicente Cantúa, quien volvió algún tiempo después. Los demás se quedaron en Méx.

Durante el Gobo. de Argüello se entraron a Monterey un navío y un bergantín españoles para rendirse. No puedo dar razón de las causas ni de lo que ocurrió en Monterey con ese motivo, porque yo estaba en San Francisco, que en aquel tiempo distaba de Monterey mucho más que hoy día, pues no había las facilidades de comunicación. Pero sí recuerdo haber ido a San Francisco a alga. diligencia, y haber visto el navío Asia allí, que era el buque más grande que jamás habíamos visto.

En 1825 vino de México el Tente. Coronel de ingenieros Dn. José Ma. de Echeandía con el carácter de gefe político y Comandte. Gen. de Cal. Este señor se hizo cargo del mando, y fijó su residencia en San Diego.[2]

Poco vivió en la parte del Norte, a donde solo hacía visitas de cuando en cuando. Apenas me acuerdo de haberlo visto una vez estando yo en la fundación de Sonoma, o más bien, de la misión de San Francisco Solano.

Este Señor Echeandía fue el que dio las primeras disposiciones conducentes a la secularización de las misiones, y a principios del 1831 espidió un decreto pa. llevar a efecto dicha secularización; pero a esto vino su relevo, reemplazándole en el mando el Teniente Coronel Dn. Manuel Victoria.

Antes de pasar a ocuparme de la admon. de Victoria, debo hacer mención de las revueltas militares que ocurrieron en la de Echeandía.

---

[2]Beebe y Senkewicz, 322. Los escritores opinan que Echeandía decidió establecerse en San Diego porque le disgustaba el frío y la neblina del norte de California. Según Rosaura Sánchez, Echeandía era un liberal yorkino que profundamente influyó la juventud de San Diego y Monterey (117). Como resultado de la tutela de Echeandía, Juan B. Alvarado, Salvador Vallejo, José Fernández, José de Jesús Vallejo, y Mariano Guadalupe Vallejo se volvieron grandes conocedores de la política nacional mexicana. Sin duda alguna, estos jóvenes se daban cuenta del antagonismo que existía entre los yorkinos y escocés, entre liberales y conservadores, y entre monarquistas y republicanos. Sánchez también cree que otros mexicanos del centro del país como José María Padrés y el gobernador José Figueroa sirvieron de maestros de la política liberal para estos jóvenes californianos.

In the beginning of 1823, Governor Solá left for México because he had been elected by the Provincial Junta to be the deputy for the Californias at the **Cortes** of the [Mexican] Empire. Captain Luis Argüello, as the Mexican officer with the longest record of service, was called by the Junta, with the consent of the Imperial Commissioner, to occupy the post of Interim Governor.

When Solá left for México, which he did by boarding [a ship] in San Diego, he was assigned two, three, or four soldiers to accompany him all the way to Guadalajara. I remember that one of them was Vicente Cantúa, who came back some time later. The rest stayed in México.

During the Argüello administration, a Spanish ship and brigantine entered Monterey to surrender. I can not give the reasons why they did so, nor what happened in Monterey when they entered it because I was in San Francisco, and at that time the distance to Monterey was much greater than today, since there were no means of communication. I do remember going to San Francisco on some business matter and having seen the vessel *Asia* there, which was the largest vessel that we had ever seen.

In 1825, Lieutenant Colonel of Engineers, José María de Echeandía, came from México with the title of Political Chief and General Commander of the Californias. This man assumed command [of the territory] and located his residence in San Diego.[2]

He spent very little time in the northern part [of the territory], where he made only occasional visits. I barely remember having seen him only one time when I went to the founding of Sonoma, to be more precise, the founding of the Mission of San Francisco Solano.

This Señor Echeandía was the person who took the first steps leading to the secularization of the mission; at the start of 1831 he issued a decree to implement such secularization but soon thereafter his replacement arrived. He was relieved of his command by Lieutenant Colonel Don Manuel Victoria.

Before I go on to discuss the administration of Victoria, I should make mention of the military rebellions that took place under Echeandía.

---

[2]Beebe and Senkewicz, 322. The authors believe that Echeandía chose to stay in San Diego because he disliked the chilly and foggy climate of northern California. According to Rosaura Sánchez (117), Echeandía was a Yorkino liberal who profoundly influenced the youth of San Diego and Monterey. As a result of his tutelage, individuals such as Juan B. Alvarado, Salvador Vallejo, José Fernandez, José de Jesús Vallejo, and Mariano Guadalupe Vallejo became well-versed in the national politics of México. Hence, these young men were aware of the antagonism that existed between Yorkinos and Escocés, between liberals and conservatives, and between monarchists and republicans. Sánchez also believes that other Mexicans from the center of the country, José María Padrés and Governor José Figueroa, also served as liberal political mentors for these young Californios.

Era tal abandono en que Echeandía tenía a la tropa, que carecía ésta de casi todas las cosas más necesarias a la vida, hasta los víveres les faltaron varias veces. De aquí resultó un descontento muy marcado que reventó al fin en la tropa de Monterey en 1828. La tropa tomó sus armas, abandonó el presidio y sus oficiales, y se echó a andar por los campos , buscando cada uno su modo de vivir. Al oír Echendía de esto hizo llamar a los soldados mediante un indulto que les ofreció. Unos aceptaron desde luego y volvieron al servicio; otros se mantenieron renuentes por mucho tiempo, y al fin re-ingresaron a servir.

En fines de 1829 se levantó la tropa de Monterey otra vez, debido a la misma causa, el abandono en que se le tenía. El destacamto. de artilla. y los soldados de cuera se apoderaron de los oficiales y los metieron en un calabozo.

Después mandaron buscar a Joaquín Solís desde su rancho para que los capitaneara. Él vivía en el rancho de Mariano Castro.

Solís era un mexicano que vino en calidad de presidario a Cal.[3]

Después de nombrar una guarnición de 10 o 20 hombres (no me acuerdo bien cuantos) salieron Solís y los amotinados (entre cuyos cabecillas recuerdo a Raymundo de la Torre y Pablo Béjar; los nombres de los demás se me han olvidado) para tomar el presidio de San Francisco. Pasaron por el pueblo de San José, en donde tuvieron por la noche una gran función de baile y comilona, sin que faltara el aguardte. Yo en ese tiempo estaba en la misión de San José de mayordomo bajo el Padre ministro, por lo que no vi lo que relató sobre estos puntos; pero como cosa notoria supe que se trató por el alcalde y vecindario de atraparlos a todos, y que no se llevó a efecto el plan porque todos eran paisanos y parientes, y los del pueblo veían que aquella revoln. no pararía en nada, sino en que se disolvería la fuerza, pues veían ya los elementos de disolución en la falta de respeto y subordinación al gefe superior y sus subalternos. Pasaron los insurrectos a San Francisco y después de muchas salvas, y demás se les unió la guarnición del presidio. De allí partió la fuerza insurrecta al mando de Solís con dirección a Sta.

---

[3]Beebe y Senkewicz, 338. Los escritores informan que Joaquín Solís luchó durante le guerra de independencia de México. Más tarde se entregó a una vida criminal, y después de ser capturado fue senteciado en 1825 a residir en California.

The troops were so abandoned by Echeandía that they lacked almost all the things that were necessary for survival; even basic provisions were lacking on several occasions. Consequently, there arose a marked discontent that finally exploded among the troops of Monterey in 1828. The troops picked up their weapons and abandoned the presidio and their officers, and they started wandering about in the country, each one trying to find a way to survive. Upon hearing this, Echeandía called upon the soldiers to return [to the barracks], offering them a general amnesty. Some of them accepted [the offer] right away and returned to service. Others remained intractable for a very long time but in the end returned to serve again.

At the end of 1829, the troops of Monterey rebelled again due to the same cause: the general state of abandonment that they were in. The artillery detachment and the leatherjacket soldiers took the officers captive and put them in the jail.

Afterwards, they contacted Joaquín Solís at his ranch so that he could lead them. He lived at the ranch of Mariano Castro.

Solís was a Mexican who came to California as a presidial soldier.[3]

After naming a garrison of ten to twenty men (I do not remember how many), Solís and the mutineers (among the leaders I remember Raymundo [Savage spells this name Raymundo and Raimundo] de la Torre and Pablo Béjar; the names of the others I have forgotten) left to capture the presidio of San Francisco. They went to the town of San José where at night they had a grand dance and a great meal; aguardiente was abundant. At that time I was a foreman at Mission San José, under the supervision of the Father Minister. Hence, I did not see what actually transpired but because it was so notable I found out that the town's **alcalde** and the residents sought to capture all of them but the plan was not carried out because they were all fellow countrymen and relatives. The town residents also knew that the revolution would go nowhere and that the rebel force would disband since they could already see signs of it breaking up, manifested in the lack of respect for and insubordination to their commander and his officers. The rebels went to San Francisco and after many salvos, the garrison of the presidio joined them. From there, the rebel force, under the command of Solís, departed in the direction of Santa

---

[3]Beebe and Senkewicz, 338. The authors note that Joaquín Solís fought in the Mexican War of Independence. After turning to a life of crime, he was sentenced to reside in California in 1825.

Bárbara pa. ver que se les uniese también aquella guarnición. En el camino hicieron emprestitos de las misiones, y fueron provistos de bastimentos y demás en San Buenaventura por el P. Luis Martínez.[4]

Mas antes de llegar a Sta. Bárbara se había establecido ya la disolución, y la mayor parte de la tropa se había desertado, pasándose al Comandte. Gen. Echeandía (que ya estaba en Sta. Barbra.), quedando con Solís únicamente los cabecillas más comprometidos. Se volvieron atrás pa. Monterey, pero antes de llegar allí supieron que los oficiales presos se habían embarcado para San Diego, y que la guarnición se había pronunciado en favor del gobo. legítimo. En vista de esto cada uno de ellos tomó el camino que le pareció, y Solís se marchó pa. su rancho, en donde poco después lo arrestaron, y le condujeron a Monterey. La misma suerte cupo a los demás cabecillas. Después de formarles sumaria, se les acusó de haber atentado en unión del P. Luis Martínez y otros, volver a enarbolar la bandera espa. sobre este territorio. Con este pretesto (y realmente no pasó de ser un pretesto) los mandaron a todos a Méx. pa. ser allá sometidos a consejo de guerra. Nada les sucedió, sino el ser detenidos. Sé que dos o tres volvieron a Cal. después de 1847. Recuerdo que Raimundo de la Torre y Pablo Béjar fueron de los que retornaron a su país. A Béjar lo vi, y me contó de la manera como se habían desertado de México, mas no me acuerdo de las circunstancias.

(Antes de entrar a ocuparnos de la Admon. del Coronel Victoria, se pondrá aquí una relación sobre la vida de misión bajo el punto de vista de un indio, que participó del régimen que tenían los frailes españoles. Este indio, Lorenzo Asisara, era hijo de uno de los indios fundadores de la misión de Sta. Cruz, y fue criado para page y cantor de la iglesia.)

---

[4]Geiger, 150. Según Geiger, Luis Martínez, quien era originario de España, se pasó la mayor parte de su vida sirviendo en la misión de Santa Bárbara. Rosaura Sánchez comenta que mientras Martínez apoyaba la rebelión de Solís, los jóvenes de California respaldaban a Echeandía. Sánchez escribe que el llamado de Solís para que un californio gobernara su tierra natal era simplemente una estrategia del padre Martínez para lograr la salida del gobierno liberal de Echeandía e izar de nuevo en California la bandera de España. En 1830, el gobernador Echeandía arrestó a Martínez. Después un tribunal militar lo declaró culpable de fomentar la rebelión de Solís y fue expulsado del territorio. De esa manera, Martínez regresó a su tierra natal.

Bárbara to get the detachment stationed there to join them. On the way, they obtained loans from the missions and they received supplies and other things from Father Luis Martínez at San Buenaventura.[4]

Even before they reached Santa Bárbara the process of dissolution was already beginning to set in; the largest part of the troops had deserted and had joined Commander General Echeandía (who had already arrived at Santa Bárbara) and the only ones who remained with Solís were the most compromised leaders. They went back to Monterey but before arriving there they found that the imprisoned officers had boarded [a ship] bound for San Diego and that the local garrison had pronounced themselves in favor of the legitimate government. In view of this, each one of them went his own way and Solís parted for his ranch where, a little later, he was arrested and taken to Monterey. The other leaders suffered the same fate. After being charged, they were accused, along with Father Martínez and others, of trying to raise the Spanish flag over the territory. Under this pretext (in reality it was nothing but a pretext), all of them were sent to México so that there they could get court-martialed. Despite being arrested, nothing happened to them. I am aware that two or three of them came back to California after 1847; I remember that Raimundo [sic] de la Torre and Pablo Béjar were among the ones who returned to their homeland. I saw Béjar and he recounted to me the way that they had escaped from México. I, however, do not remember the circumstances.

[**Amador interjects**] Before proceeding to discuss the administration of Colonel Victoria, I will give an account of life in the missions from the point of view of an Indian who experienced the regimen that was established by the Spanish friars. This Indian, Lorenzo Asisara, was the son of one of the founding Indians of Mission Santa Cruz and was raised to be a page and a singer for the church.

---

[4]Geiger, 150. According to Geiger, Spanish-born Luis Martínez arrived at Mission Santa Bárbara and spent his entire missionary life there. Rosaura Sánchez writes that while the young Californios supported Governor Echeandía, Martínez backed the Solís revolt (236). She notes that Solís' call for a Californio to govern their homeland was merely a ploy by Father Martínez to overthrow the liberal government of Echeandía and raise the Spanish flag anew in Alta California. In 1830, Governor Echeandía had Martínez arrested; after a military trial, the judges convicted him of fomenting the Solís revolt and he was expelled from the territory. Martínez returned to Spain.

Después de la muerte del P. Quintana en 1812, estuvo el P. Olbes de ministro de la misión, como dije en otra ocasión. Era hombre muy desconfiado y muy malo, tomó en su propia mano la llave del jayunte, una noche, para encerrar a los solteros. Iba con él el cabo de la escolta pa. resguardar su persona. El cabo era Ignacio Peralta. Tomó lista de todos los que estaban adentro del jayunte para saber si alguno faltaba y quien era. Le faltó uno llamado Dámaso, que era muy dado a jugar a la baraja, y que se le dilató en conseguir algn. alimento pa. irse a su cuartel. Ya le esperaban el P. Olbes y el cabo por algunos minutos, menos de media hora. Llegó Dámaso, y el Padre le preguntó con aspereza en dónde había estado. Contestó el indio que estaba esperando por un bocado que le darían sus parientes. Los alcaldes dieron parte que él había faltado de mediodía a la tarde del trabajo para ir a ocuparse del juego.[5] El padre le preguntó si esto era verdad, y Dámaso respondió que sí, que había faltado, que había ido en busca de un poco de leña pa. traer a la casa en donde le daban la comida. "Ahora te voy a castigar (dijo el P. Olbes) no en el culo, sino en la barriga." Dámaso contestó, "No, Padre, eso no está en razón, que me castiguen la barriga, fui a buscar un poco de leña para la gente que me mantiene; no he cometido otra falta." El Padre mandó que los alcaldes le agarraran pa. castigarle. El Indio se resistió alegando que no tenía delito. El Padre insistía en que fuese castigado. Los demás que estaban en el jayunte le gritaban en indio a Dámaso, "no te dejes agarrar ni castigar." El P. volteaba a mirar, para ver lo que decían los indios.

Ordenó que a la fuerza cogieran a Dámaso; éste se resistía, y les decía a los alcaldes, "déjenme, que me agarre el Padre, y que me castigue él mismo." Pero el P. insistía en que lo hiciesen los alcaldes, y éstos, como entendían lo que se gritaba en el jayunte, no se atrevían a obedecer al Padre; entonces un indio llamado Crisanto, tío de Dámaso, le gritó "no te dejes." El P. Olbes entonces ordenó a los alcaldes "Apéenme a aquél también," agarrando a los alcaldes y empujándolos para que fueran a traer a Crisanto. Los alcaldes tenían miedo del motín de los indios contra el P. y ellos. A esto el cabo desenvainó la espada para irlo a tomarlo [cuando] el mismo Crisanto se apeó diciendo, "Ch! vamos a matar a éstos." Se levantaron todos los del jayunte, y se apearon, para atacar

---

[5]El cargo de alcalde indígena era el más alto que un neófita lograra obtener en la jerarquía de las misiones. Se supone que los alcaldes eran electos a sus puestos por la población neófita pero lo más seguro es que ellos eran escogidos por los propios misioneros. Las responsabilidades de los alcaldes consistían en supervisar a los neófitas al igual que mantener el orden e imponer castigos.

[**Asisara narrates**] After the death of Father Quintana in 1812, Father Olbes served as minister at the mission, as I earlier stated. He was a very suspicious man and very mean. One night, he decided to take the key of the dormitory in order to lock in the single men; accompanying him was the corporal of the guard to protect him. The corporal, Ignacio Peralta, took roll call of everyone who was in the dormitory to see if anyone was missing and find out who this person was. One individual, by the name of Dámaso, was missing; he was in the habit of playing cards and he was late because he wanted to get some food before going to the dormitory. Father Olbes and the corporal waited for him for a few minutes, less than thirty minutes. When Dámaso came back, the Father harshly asked him to tell him where he had been. The Indian responded that he had been waiting for a meal that his relatives were going to give him. The [Indian] Alcaldes reported that he had been missing from work from noon until the evening because he had gone to play cards.[5] The priest asked him if this was true and Dámaso responded affirmatively, that he had been missing but that he had gone in search of wood to bring to the house where he was being fed. "I am now going to punish you," Father Olbes said, "not on your ass, but on your belly." Dámaso responded: "No, Father, there is no reason for you to punish me in the belly. I went to find some wood for the people that feed me; I have not committed any other offense." The Father ordered the Alcaldes to grab him in order to punish him; the Indian resisted, claiming that he had done nothing wrong. The priest insisted that he be punished. The others who were in the dormitory shouted to Dámaso in the Indian language, "Do not let yourself be caught, nor punished." The Father turned around to see what the Indians were saying.

He ordered that Dámaso be caught through the use of force but [the latter] resisted, telling the alcaldes, "Let the Father catch me, and let him punish me himself." The Father, however, insisted that the alcaldes do the punishment, but they, since they understood what those in the **jayunte** were saying, did not dare to obey the priest. Then, an Indian called Crisanto, the uncle of Dámaso, shouted at him, "do not let them." Father Olbes, then, ordered the alcaldes, "get that one, also." He grabbed the alcaldes and pushed them to go and get Crisanto. The alcaldes were afraid of an insurrection of the Indians against the Father and themselves. At this point, the corporal unsheathed his sword in order to get Crisanto but he [the latter] got away, saying "F——! Let's kill them." Everyone from the jayunte got up and got ready to attack

---

[5]Indian *alcaldes* were the highest-ranking neophytes in the mission hierarchy. They were supposed to have been elected to the position by the neophytes but most likely they were chosen by the missionaries. The alcaldes possessed the authority to supervise Indians and maintain order and carry out punishments.

al cabo, Padre y alcaldes. Empezaron a coger tejas el padre arrancó por un lado; el cabo tiró la espada y echó a huir, a pesar de los clamores el Reverendo, "Cabo!" " Cabo!" Pero éste era más cobarde que el diablo y huía a más correr. Los alcaldes buscaron su salvación también. Los indios les tiraban tejas al cabo y a los alcaldes, pero ninguna piedra se le tiró al Padre ni a los otros mas que para asustarlos, no para lastimarlos. Muchas pedradas se le tiraron a las campanas. El P. Olbes con el grito de Cabo! a cada minuto corría de duro y no paró hasta entrar en su casa.

Los indios querían meterle miedo pa. que no diera tantos azotes, porq. Olbes era muy aficionado a azotar cruelmente. Nunca se conformaba con recetar menos de 50 azotes, unas veces en las nalgas, y muy a menudo en la barriga. Esto le gustaba mucho.

Aún a los niños chicos de 8 a 10 años les mandaba dar 25 azotes por mano de un hombre fuerte en las nalgas o en la barriga, como le entraba el capricho.

Después de la fuga del Padre Olbes, y sus defensores, los indios solteros se entraron al jayunte a dormir, diciendo "vamos a dormir, que mañana es seguro el castigo." A la mañana sigte. volvió el Padre con el cabo a preguntar que quién había pensado eso de apedrearlos. Nadie le contestó. El Padre les sermoneó, de allí fueron a misa a la iglesia, todos ya perdonados del castigo. Como a fines de aquel año, allá por Dic., (ahora que me acuerdo fue el día 8, día de la Purísima) el P. Olbes les hizo a los indios un regalo consistente de un barril de miel y como eso de 100 quesos partidos en dos. Les empezó a dar ración de todo eso a cada uno después de la misa porque si bien Olbes era cruel en los castigos, por otro lado era cuidadoso de tener bien alimentada y vestida a la gente. Concluyó con repartir la ración de los mismos artículos a las mugeres. Vió que habían dos de estas rasguñadas en las caras porque habían estado peleando por celos. Las desapartó para averiguar por qué se habían arañado. Una era estéril, y la otra tenía hijos. Cuando el Padre se informó de la causa de la pendencia, él preguntó a la estéril por qué era que no paría? Mandó buscar al marido a quien le preguntó: ¿por qué no paría su muger? El indio apuntaba

the corporal, the priest, and the alcaldes. They started to pick up roof tiles and the Father took off running in one direction; the corporal dropped his sword and fled despite the clamor of the Reverend, "Corporal! Corporal!" But this one, who was more cowardly than the devil, was fleeing as fast as he could; the alcaldes also [ran] seeking their safety. The Indians were throwing tiles at the corporal and the alcaldes but no rock was thrown at the priest or the others to hurt them, only to scare them. A lot of rocks were thrown at the bells. Father Olbes kept shouting, "Corporal!" at every instant while running hard and did not stop until he reached his house.

The Indians wanted to instill fear in him so that he would not resort to so many floggings because Father Olbes was a firm believer in giving cruel lashings. He was never satisfied with prescribing fewer than fifty lashes, sometimes on the buttocks, and quite frequently on the belly. This, he enjoyed very much.

Even children between the ages of eight to ten, he would order that they receive twenty-five lashes at the hands of a strong man, on the buttocks or the belly, according to his fancy of the moment.

After the flight of Father Olbes and his defenders, the Indian bachelors went to their jayunte to sleep, saying, "Let's go to sleep, for tomorrow it is certain that we will be punished." On the following morning, the Father and the corporal came back and asked about who came up with the idea of stoning them. No one answered him. The Father gave them a lecture and then they went to hear mass at the church; everyone was now forgiven from punishment. At the end of the year, around December (I now remember that it was the 8th—the Day of La Purisíma), Father Olbes gave the Indians gifts that consisted of a barrel of honey and about 100 cheeses cut in halves. After mass, he started distributing these rations to every one. Father Olbes was cruel in his punishment yet, on the other hand, he took care to keep his people well clothed and well fed. He finished by distributing the same articles to the women. He saw that two of them had scratched faces because they had been fighting due to jealousy. He separated them in order to find out why they had scratched each other. One was sterile and the other had children. When the Father found out what had caused the quarrel, he asked the sterile one why she did not give birth. He ordered that the husband be brought to him and asked him why his wife did not give birth. The Indian pointed

pa. el cielo (no sabía hablar español) como pa. significar que sólo Dios sabía la causa. Trajeron un intérprete. Éste repitió al indio la pregunta del Padre, y aquél contestó que le preguntase a Dios. El P. preguntó por conducto del intérprete si él no dormía con su muger, a lo que el indio dijo que sí.

Entonces el Padre los metió en un cuarto pa. emparejarlos, esto es, para que hiciesen el coito en su presencia. El indio se negó, pero lo obligaron por fuerza a enseñar su miembro para cerciorarse si lo tenía en buen orden. Después el Padre tomó la muger y la metió en el cuarto. Al marido lo destinó al cuerpo de guardia con un par de grillos. El intérprete por orden del Padre, le preguntó a ella cómo era que tenía la cara rasguñada. Ella respondió que otra muger se lo había hecho por celos. Preguntó el Padre si su marido andaba con la otra muger; ella dijo que sí. Entonces, se le volvió a preguntar: ¿por qué no paría como las otras mugeres? Le preguntó el P. Olbes si su marido dormía con ella, y ella contestó que sí. El P. reiteró su pregunta: "¿por qué no pares?" "¿Quién sabe?" contestó la india. La hizo entrar a otro cuarto para registrarle su parte pudenda. Ella se resistió, y agarró del cordón al Padre. Hubo una lucha fuerte y larga entre los dos que estaban solos en aquel cuarto. Ella trató de meterle los dientes en el brazo, pero sólo le agarró el hábito. Gritó el P. Olbes, y entraron el intérprete y el alcalde a socorrerle. Entonces Olbes mandó que la llevasen de las manos y le diesen 50 azotes. Después de asotada le hizo poner grillos y la encerró en el monjerío. Acabado esto, mandó el P. Olbes hacer un muñeco de madera, como una criatura recién nacida; se lo llevó a la mujer azotada ordenándole que tomara aquel muñeco por hijo, y lo cargara 9 días, delante de toda la gente. La obligó a presentarse en la puerta del templo con aquello como si fuera su hijo, hasta cumplir los 9 días.

Con estas cosas todas las mugeres que eran estériles se alarmaron mucho.

Al marido de aquella muger le hizo el malvado fraile poner cuernos de res en la cabeza asegurados con baqueta. Al mismo tiempo lo tenía engrillado. Así lo traían diariamte. a misa desde la cárcel, y los otros indios se mofaban de él y lo toreaban. Vuelto a la cárcel le quitaban los cuernos.

towards heaven (the Indian did not know Spanish) as if he was indicating that only God knew why. They brought an interpreter. This person repeated to the Indian the question that the priest had asked, and he [the latter] answered that God should be asked. The Father asked through the interpreter if he slept with his wife, and the Indian answered yes.

Then, the Father put them in a room in order to "level" them out, in other words, to have them perform coitus in his presence. The Indian [male] refused but he was forced to show his member [penis] in order to make certain that it was functioning properly. Then, the priest took the woman and put her in a room; the husband was sent to the guards with a pair of shackles. The interpreter, on orders from the priest, asked her how her face had been scratched and she responded that the other woman had done it due to jealousy. The Father asked if her husband was involved with the other woman; she said yes. Then, she was asked again, why she did not give birth like other women. Father Olbes asked her whether her husband slept with her and she answered yes. The Father reiterated his question: "why can't you give birth?" "I do not know," answered the Indian woman. She was made to go to another room in order to check her private parts. She resisted and grabbed the Father's cord. There was a vigorous, long struggle between the two, who were alone in the room. She tried to sink her teeth into his arm but only managed to bite his habit. Father Olbes yelled out and the interpreter and the alcalde came to his aid. Then, Father Olbes ordered that she be taken, by the arms, outside and that she be given fifty lashes. After being punished, he ordered that she be shackled and locked up in the nunnery. After this was done, Father Olbes ordered that a wooden doll be made in the shape of a newly born baby, and took it to the flogged woman, and ordered her to take the doll as her child, and that she should carry it for nine days in the presence of the people. He forced her to present herself at the door of the Church with the doll as if it were her son until she completed the nine days.

As a result of these occurrences, the sterile women became highly alarmed.

The wicked priest had cattle horns placed on the head of the woman's husband, and they [horns] were secured with a leather cord. At the same time, he had him shackled. In this condition, they would bring him daily to Mass from jail. The other Indians would mock him and bullfight him. After returning him to his cell, they would take off the horns.

Por fin P. Olbes pidió su relevo y fue destinado a Sonoma. Le sucedió el P. Luis Gil Taboada.[6] Este Padre por la noche solía quitarse los hábitos y disfrazarse para ir a coger los juegos en las rancherías. Muchas veces lo hizo sin ser descubierto ni por los que le conocían bien. Se metía a los juegos pa. quitar las barajas. Antes de todo observaba bien quienes eran los jugadores, después de ésto metía la mano en el centro y apuntaba tanta cantidad sobre alga. carta. Tan luego como los jugadores veían la mano blanca de un soplo apagaban la luz. Él entonces llamaba por sus nombres a los que conocía y les ordenaba encender la luz; después les exigía que entregasen los naipes. Ellos querían entregar naipes viejos, pero nunca lo pudieron embaucar, siempre les sacaba toda las barajas que tenían. Así iba visitando los juegos de las diversas naciones que había en su misión. Los había del río de San Joaquín, de los Tulares, y de estas mismas inmeds. Los tulareños eran los que jugaban el peón, juego de escondidos. Eran dos huesos como de 2 pulgs. de largo, uno negro y otro blanco. El blanco era el que valía.

Allí se sentaba el Padre disfrazado una hora o dos mirando el juego. Él les ponía abalono por dinero, y ellos le apostaban con plata. Después de ganar o perder se retiraba pa. su casa. Bajo el cuidado del P. Taboada descansó la gente mucho de los castigos. La trataba muy bien. Era muy enamorado, abrazaba y besaba a las indias y tenía contacto con ellas hasta que tuvo gálico y le salieron encordios. (A Dn. José Ma. Amador le constó esto, y como eran muy amigos, Amador a menudo le daba medicinas para curarlo.) Hallándose en esta situación decía misa sentado en su casa. No podía muchas veces decirla parado porque estaba todo llagado. Aún así salía a ausiliar a los enfermos graves; finalmte., después de mucho cuidado, logró sanarse, estando el tío de Amador de cabo de la escolta.

Taboada llegó a ser muy querido de los indios todos, particularmte. de los Tulareños cuya lengua entendía él algo. Era muy alocado y muy alegre y salía a divertirse con los indios y a jugar el peón con ellos.

[6]Geiger, 106. Geiger hace la anotación que a diferencia de los otros misioneros del colegio de San Fernando que habían nacido en España, el padre Luis Gil y Taboada provenía de Guanajuato, México. Antes de radicarse en la misión de Santa Cruz en 1818, el padre Gil y Taboada había servido en las misiones de San Francisco y San José. Aparentemente, Gil y Taboada era bien conocido por ser apostador y mujeriego. El histodiador Geiger comenta que Gil y Taboada no negaba su conducta y cita una carta que Gil y Taboada escribió a José M. Herrera, oficial de aduana, con fecha del 26 de abril de 1826: "Yo nunca he atentado de defraudar a nadien en ninguna forma, menos a la nación." Geiger piensa que los superiores del padre Gil y Taboada sabían de relaciones que él tenía con mujeres pero preferían ignorarlas.

Finally, Father Olbes asked that he be relieved and was sent to Sonoma. Luis Gil Taboada replaced him.[6] At night this Father would tend to take off his habit and disguise himself in order to catch those that were gambling in the **rancherías**. He did this many times yet he was not discovered, not even by those who knew him well. He would play games to take away the cards. Before playing, he would take note of who the players were and then he would put his hand in the center and he would bet a sum of money on a specific card. As soon as the players saw the white hand, with a single blow of breath they would put out the light. He, then, would call by their names those he knew and ordered them to light [the candle], then he would demand that they give him the cards; they would want to give him the old cards, but they could never deceive him. He would always find all the cards that they had. In this way, he would visit the games of the diverse peoples that lived in the [jurisdiction of his] mission; they were from the San Joaquín River, the Tulares, and from this area [Watsonville]. The Tulareans were the ones who played **peon**, a game of hidden objects; there were two pieces of bones about two inches long: one black and the other white. The white one was the one of value.

The disguised Father would sit for one or two hours observing the game. He would put abalone as money and they would use silver [coins]. After winning or losing he would retire to his house. Under the tenure of Father Taboada, the people rested a lot from punishment; he treated them very well. He was easily infatuated and he would embrace and kiss the Indian women and he would have relations with them until he caught syphilis and lesions erupted on his skin. (Don José María Amador can verify this since they were very good friends. Amador frequently gave him medicine so that he could get cured.) In this condition, he would celebrate mass sitting down at his own home. Many times he was incapable of saying mass standing since his entire body was covered with wounds. Even then, he would go out to help those who were gravely ill. Finally, after a lot of care, he was able to heal. At that time, the uncle of Amador was the corporal of the guard.

Taboada came to be beloved by all the Indians, particularly the **Tulareños**, whose language he partly understood. He was a foolish, very happy person who would go and enjoy himself with Indians and play **peon** with them.

---

[6]Geiger, 106. Geiger notes that unlike the other missionaries of the College of San Fernando, who were born in Spain, Father Luis Gil y Taboada was from Guanajuato, México. Gil y Taboada had served at Missions San Francisco and San José before being moved to Mission Santa Cruz in 1818. Apparently, he had a well-known reputation as a gambler and a womanizer, and he did not deny this behavior. Geiger writes: "Concerning the charge of gambling, he [Gil y Taboada] wrote to José M. Herrera, a customs officer on April 26, 1826: "I have never attempted to defraud anyone, much less the nation in any way." Geiger believes that Gil y Taboada's superiors were aware of his relations with women but preferred to ignore them.

Rara vez castigaba. Era preciso que fuese muy grave la culpa y aún entonces no pasaba el castigo de 12 o 15 azotes cuando más. Él me enseñó a leer, escribir, y música. Él fue quien empezó a dar instrucción en la escuela a los inditos. Hizo que se enseñase a los indios las oraciones y demás cosas de iglesia en su propia lengua para que las comprendiesen bien.

Trataba muy bien a la indiada, dándole de comer bastante, teniéndola vestida, y no haciéndola trabajar con esceso.

El P. Taboada estuvo de ministro en la misión de Sta. Cruz hasta que lo relevó el P. Anto. Jimeno.[7] Este Padre duro en la misión apenas dos años. Fue muy bueno y cuidadoso, castigando únicamte. a los que verdaderos culpables, y aún a ésos sin ningún rigor. Mas cuando entró, estuvo celoso, y se agarró a flechazos con el P. Taboada para obligar a éste a que saliera de la misión inmediatamte. Ya los indios habían curado a Taboada, quien salió de la misión a media noche. Ya tenía yo unos 13 o 14 años o más en ese tiempo. Después de Jimeno vino el P. Juan Moreno, hombre muy de a caballo, que salía con sus vaqueros a lazar animales, osos.[8] Llegó a lazar un día a una osa parida del primer tiro, y muchos lo atestiguaron. El estuvo en la misión como tres años y trataba a los indios con el mayor cariño. A menudo se quedaba a comer con ellos en sus rancherías. Le sucedió el P. José Jimeno, hermano de Antonio, buen ministro.[9] Duró hasta que vinieron los Padres Zacatecanos. El P. Anto. Real fue el que relevó al P. José Jimeno. Este Real era ranchero, más bien lo había sido, montaba muy bien a caballo y jugaba con un toro como el mejor vaquero.[10] Lo mismo era su hermano José María.

---

[7]Beebe y Senkewicz, 328. Según los autores, Antonio Jimeno Casarín nació en México y acompañando a su hermano José Joaquín llegó a California en 1827. Su hermano, Manuel Jimeno Casarín, quien se casó con Angustias de la Guerra, logró consagrarse como una importante figura política en California durante los años que México gobernó ese territorio.
[8]Geiger, 150. Geiger menciona que Juan Moreno nació en España en 1799 y junto con los hermanos Jimeno Casarín, fueron los últimos reclutas del colegio de San Fernando que llegaran a California.
[9]Geiger, 131. Según Geiger, José Joaquín Jimeno, quien nació en 1804, sirvió en la misón de Santa Cruz desde los últimos meses de 1830 hasta principios de 1833. Geiger comenta que José Jimeno llegó a pensar durante la secularización que las riquezas de las misiones fuesen distribuidas entre los indígenas que residían en ellas pero que también se les debería requerir que trabajaran en ellas para que no se volvieran vagabundos.
[10]Geiger, 284. Geiger menciona que Antonio Súarez del Real nació en México. Según el historiador H. H. Bancroft tenía muchos malos vicios ya que se le acusaba de emborracharse en tavernas públicas y de juntarse con las clases populares en las fiestas que ellos organizaban.

Only rarely would he punish. He would always make sure that the offense was a serious one and even then the punishment was never more than twelve to fifteen lashes at most. He taught me reading, writing, and music. He was the one who started teaching Indian children in school. He was the one that ordered that Indians be taught prayers and other things of the church in their own language so that they could understand them well.

He would treat Indians very well, giving them plenty of food, kept them clothed, and did not make them work in excess.

Father Taboada served as Minister at Mission Santa Cruz until he was relieved, by Father Antonio Jimeno.[7] This Father [Jimeno] stayed at the mission only two years and he was very kind and caring, only punishing those who were truly guilty and even then not with much rigor. Yet, when he arrived, he was jealous, and he got into an arrow fight with Father Taboada to force the latter to leave the mission immediately. By then, the Indians had cured Father Taboada, who left the mission in the middle of the night. I was thirteen or fourteen years old, or more at that time. After Jimeno, Father Juan Moreno came [to the mission]; he was an expert horseman who would go out with his cowboys to rope livestock and bears.[8] One day he managed to rope with the first throw a female bear that had just given birth. Many people witnessed it. He was at the mission about three years and he treated the Indians with great warmth. Frequently, he would stay to eat with them in the **rancherías**. Father José Jimeno, the brother of Antonio, replaced him.[9] [Father José Jimeno] was a good minister; he lasted until the arrival of the priests from Zacatecas. Father Antonio [Suárez] del Real was a **ranchero,** or perhaps it is better to say he had been; he rode on horseback very well and he would play with a bull as would the best cowboy.[10] His brother was the same way.

---

[7]According to Beebe and Senkewicz, Antonio Jimeno Casarín was born in México (328). He, along with his brother José Joaquín, came to California in 1827. His brother Manuel Jimeno Casarín married Angustias de la Guerra and he also became a leading political figure in California during the Mexican period.

[8]Geiger, 150. Geiger states that Juan Moreno was born in Spain in 1799. Moreno and the two Jimeno brothers were the last recruits who came to California from the College of San Fernando.

[9]According to Geiger, José Joaquín Jimeno was born in 1804 (131). He served at Mission Santa Cruz from late 1830 to early 1833. Geiger notes that José Jimeno believed that with secularization under way the missions' assets should be distributed amongst the Indians but that they should be required to work lest they become vagrants.

[10]Geiger states that Antonio Súarez del Real was born in México (284). In addition, Geiger points out that H. H. Bancroft perceived Father Antonio as having many vices. He was accused of getting drunk in public taverns and joining the lower classes in their fiestas.

P. Anto. Real estuvo muchos años en la misión hasta mucho después de la secularizn.

Recuerdo que estando este Padre de ministro, y yo era sacristán encargado del cuidado de la iglesia y sus pertenencias, vino el General José Figueroa de visita, procedente de San Francisco.[11] Le acompañaban los Capitanes Nicolás Gutiérrez y Agustín V. Zamorano, Eugenio Montenegro, Tente. Navarrete, y varios otros de comitiva, militares y paisanos. Se le recibió al Gen. con mucha pompa. El P. revestido de capa, con palio y cruz alta recibió al Genl. como a dista. de 200 varas de la iglesia, y le acompañó hasta entrar a ésta, en donde se le cantó un Te Deum. Fuera se le hicieron salvas de artilla. y fusilería; se quemaron cohetes ta. En una palabra, se le recibió con entusiasmo y regocijo y con los honores debidos a su alto cargo.

El P. Anto. Real siempre trató a los indios con la mayor liberalidad, rara vez castigaba, y sólo a muy malos. Era muy paseador, divertido, y dado a la buena vida. Tenía muy bien vestidos a todos los indios cada uno en su clase. Abrió los fardos que había en la misión de seda, pana, baño ta, y les dio a los indios de todo. Ya él sabía que las misiones se secularizarían. Estuvo el Gen. Figueroa como 10 días en la misión revisando lo que ésta poseía. Después se marchó a la capital. Un mes después me envió el P. Real y a 4 muchachos más, a Monterey a cargo del Sargto. Estrada para aprender allí a tocar el clarinete. Ya yo tenía nociones de la flauta, y en 6 meses aprendí lo bastante y volví a la misión.

Así como su hermano, José María, fue inclinado a los vicios, especialmte. a las mugeres.[12] Anto. por el contrario, era moderado y moral en su conducta. Si alga. vez tuvo desliz, de que yo no tengo noticia, lo supo ocultar bien de la vista pública.

---

[11]Beebe y Senkewicz, 324. Los escritores comentan que el gobernador José Figueroa, quien nació en 1792, era nativo de Jonatepec, Nueva España. El luchó con los líderes del movimiento independencista, como José María Morelos y Vicente Guerrero. En 1824, Figueroa fue designado comandante militar para Sonora y Sinaloa, en donde subyugó a rebeldes mayos y yaquis. En 1833, Figueroa llegó a la Alta California cuando fue nombrado su gobernador y desempeñó su puesto hasta su muerte en 1835.

[12]Geiger, 250. Geiger anota que al igual que su hermano Antonio, José María Suárez del Real era bien conocido por ser mujeriego. Geiger indica que H.H. Bancroft localizó una carta escrita por el padre Doroteo Ambriz en donde menciona que José María tenía relaciones sexuales con tres mujeres. Estas mujeres eran conocidas como las mujeres "Real" y los hijos de ellas se les llamaban los hijos "Real." El padre José María también tuvo encuentros sexuales con otras mujeres. Entre 1846 a 1851, el padre José María tuvo enfrentamientos con las nuevas autoridades norteamericanas que habían asumido el control sobre California.

Father Antonio Real stayed at the mission for many years, long after the secularization.

I remember that when this Father was Minister, and I was the sacristan in charge of caring for the church and its belongings, General José de Figueroa came to visit from San Francisco.[11] Accompanying him were Captains Nicolás Gutiérrez, Agustín V. Zamorano, and Eugenio Montenegro, Lieutenant Navarrete, and various others in his party that were either military officers or countrymen. The general was received with much pomp. The Father, wearing a cape and cloak and holding a high cross, received the general at a distance of 200 **varas** from the church, and he accompanied him until entering the church; a Te Deum Mass was sung in his honor. Outside [the Church] shots of the artillery and a fusillade of firearms was made while fireworks were also burned. In short, he was received with much enthusiasm and joy and with the respective honors due to his high office.

Father Antonio Real always treated the Indians with the greatest laxity; rarely would he punish and only those who were truly bad. He was a pleasure-seeker who liked to enjoy himself and was given to the good life. He kept the Indians well clothed, each according to his class. He opened the bundles of silk that were at the mission, those of corduroy, and also **paño**, and he gave the Indians some of everything. He already knew that the missions were going to be secularized. General Figueroa spent about ten days in the mission investigating its possessions; then, he left for the capital. One month later, Father Real sent me and another four boys, under the supervision of Sergeant Estrada, to Monterey to learn to play the clarinet. I already had an idea of [how to play] the flute and in six months I had learned enough and went back to the mission.

Like his brother, José María was inclined to vices, especially women.[12] Antonio, in contrast, was moderate and moral in his conduct. If ever he had a weakness, I am not aware of it because he was able to hide it very well from the public eye.

---

[11]Beebe and Senkewicz note that José Figueroa was born in Jonatepec, New Spain, in 1792 (324). He fought with José María Morelos and Vicente Guerrero during the Mexican War of Independence. In 1824, he was appointed military commander of Sonora and Sinaloa, where he subdued Yaqui and Mayo Indian rebellions. Figueroa came to serve as governor of California in 1833; he remained in office until he died in 1835.

[12]Geiger, 250. Geiger states that just like his brother Antonio, José María Suárez del Real had a reputation as a womanizer. Geiger also notes that H. H. Bancroft found a letter written by Father Doroteo Ambriz stating that José María had had sexual relations with three women. These women were known as the "Real" women and their children were the "Real" children. He also had sexual liaisons with other women. Between 1846 and 1851, José María had confrontations with the U.S. authorities that were in control of California.

Finalmte., se secularizó la misión viniendo a efectuarlo Dn. Ignacio del Valle, quien entró a la sala arrastrando la espada y pidiendo la llave del cuarto donde se iba a hospedar.[13] Era hora de cenar, y el Padre lo convidaba a ello, pero él no aceptó. Entonces el Padre le entregó la llave pa. que se fuera a su cuarto. Me dio a mi orden de facilitar al Sr. Valle todo lo que pidiera y así lo hice.

El Sr. Valle me preguntó si yo era el mayordomo y llavero, le contesté que sí, y me dijo que pusiera cuidado con lo que hiciera el Padre esa noche, pues él había venido a recibir la misión. Yo fui a mi cuarto, tomé mis cobijas, y las tendí a un lado de la puerta de la sala, en la parte de adentro. Allí me acosté a vigilar.

Como dos horas después salió el Padre a ver si los muchachos estaban dormidos para él hacer su negocio, y sacar de la misión todo lo que pudiera. Me encontró acostado y me hacía el dormido y roncaba. Él se asustó y me dijo pelado, qué estás haciendo aquí?

No me tocó y yo no me di por entendido.

Tenía él un muchacho llamado José Aguilar (español) que había traído de San Luis Rey, estaba dormido. El Padre lo despertó a la fuerza, y el muchacho se levantó muy asustado. El P. lo mandó a llamar a sus amigos que tenía allí. Juan González, el mayordomo, y su familia vinieron. Yo seguí roncando. Ellos entraron al cuarto del Padre y sacaron porción de efectos de los de más valor, incluso moneda de oro y plata, vajillas ta. Visto esto por mí a la 3a. vuelta que dieron entre su casa y la del padre con sus nudos y cargas, una muger de las mismas que estaban allí, llamada Ma. Gracia Rodríguez, que era la asistenta del padre, salió con un envoltorio de géneros de seda en la mano, y otro debajo del brazo. Yo me incorporé y le pregunté qué llevaba, ella quedito muy asustada, me dijo, "anda dentro con el Padre" y se fue con sus envoltorios. A poco salieron Juan González y su muger cargados. Yo estaba sentado pa. ver a los demás. Nada me dijeron y salieron volviendo a entrar

---

[13]Beebe y Senkewicz, 340. Según los escritores, Ignacio del Valle acompañó al gobernador José María Echeandía a California. Después, del Valle estuvo involucrado en varias rebeliones militares. En 1831, él se opuso al gobernador Manuel Victoria y un año más tarde al gobernador Agustín Vicente Zamorano. En 1836, del Valle respaldó al gobernador NicolásGutiérrez en su lucha contra Juan Bautista Alvarado. Con el triunfo de Alvarado, del Valle se fue a un breve exilio. Después de la muerte de su padre, del Valle se retiró a vivir al rancho de la familia pero siguió sirviendo en varios puestos públicos.

Finally, the mission was secularized and Don Ignacio del Valle, the person in charge of carrying it out, entered the reception room, dragging his sword and asking for the key to the room where he was going to stay.[13] It was dinnertime and the Father invited him [to have dinner] but he did not accept. Then, the Father gave him the key so that he could go to his room. He gave me the order to assist Sr. Valle with all the things that he asked for and so I did.

Sr. Valle asked me if I was the foreman and the key keeper, and I said yes. He told me to watch what the Father did that night since he had come to receive the mission. I went to my room, picked up my blankets and I laid them down on one side of the door of the reception room, on the inside. Then, I lay down to keep watch.

About two hours later, the Father came out to see if the boys were asleep so that he could do his business and take out from the mission as much as he could. He found me lying down and I pretended to be asleep and snoring. He got frightened, called me a **pelado** and he asked, "What are you doing?"

He did not touch me, and I pretended that I was not aware of his presence.

He had a boy by the name of José Aguilar (Spaniard) that he had brought from San Luis Rey, who was asleep. The Father violently woke him up and then the boy got up very scared. The Father ordered him to go and call on the friends that he had there. Juan González, the foreman, and his family came. I continued snoring and they entered the Father's room and brought out some items of greater value, including gold and silver coins and also silverware. After seeing this, on the third trip that they had made between their house and the Father's house with their bolts [of cloth] and loads of goods, a woman, one of the people that were there, named María Gracia Rodríguez, who was the Father's assistant, came out with a bundle of silk fabric in her hands, and another one under her arm. I got up and asked her what it was she was carrying and she, frightened, in a very low voice told me to "go inside to the Father," and she left with her bundles. A little later, Juan González and his wife came out loaded [with things]. I was now sitting down and looking at them. They did not say anything to me and left but came back

[13]According to Beebe and Senkewicz, Ignacio del Valle came to California with Governor José María de Echeandía (340). It appears that he was involved in several military rebellions. In 1831, he opposed Governor Manuel Victoria and, one year later, Governor Agustín Vicente Zamorano. In 1836, del Valle supported Governor Nicolás Gutiérrez, who was trying to subdue a rebellion by Juan Bautista Alvarado. After the triumph of Alvarado, del Valle went into a brief exile. After the death of his father, del Valle lived in the family rancho while holding several public offices.

inmediate. sin los envoltorios. Presumo que le dijeron al Padre que yo estaba mirando. El Padre vino a donde mí, y yo me había envuelto cabeza y todo en las cobijas y acostado me llamó y me dijo que fuera adentro. Yo obedecí. Entonces me dijo él, "aquí tienes 40$ en puro oro, y un cajón de abalono pa. tu padre." Esto fue pa. qe. yo no los acusara. Me prometió, además, un vestido desde los pies hasta la cabeza. Sacó una botella y un vaso, y me dio a beber medio vaso de brandy. El Padre bebía mucho licor y vino continuamente aunque no se embriagaba. Me mandó que esa misma noche llevara el cajón de abalono a mi padre para que nadie lo supiese.

Así lo hice. Mientras yo estuve ausente, supongo que ellos concluyeron su negocio, pues cuando retorné estaba cerrada la puerta, y el Padre se paseaba en la sala aguardándome. Luego que llegué me dijo, "Qué te dijo Dn. Ignacio?" Yo le informé. Entonces me dijo "ven acá." Nos fuimos pa. adentro, me entregó los 40$ [pesos] en oro, sacó dos vasos (era casi de madrugada) uno pa. él y otro para mí. Me sirvió el licor y tomó él también. Después me encargó diciéndome, "Como hombre, te callas sobre lo que has visto." Yo le contesté, "Padre, ¿cómo ha de ser eso, que mi padre ha de tomar sólo un cajón de abulón, cuando todo el interés de la misión es de la comunidad?" Me contestó, "te pido ahora por este momento que mañana no hables con Dn. Ignacio Valle," hablando estas palabras Valle vino, tocó la puerta, que se le abrió. Y el Padre me mandó ir a tocar el alba, cuando todavía no era tiempo de eso. Valle tenía su espada a la cintura, y le dijo "Padre, quiero las llaves de la misión." Yo no fui a tocar porque me detuvo Valle. El Padre le contestó que tiempo había para que recibiera la misión y los intereses. Entonces me mandó Valle a dormir. Ellos se quedaron allá arreglando su negocio y bebiendo. Como a la media hora, estando yo en mi primer sueño, vino el Padre y me cogió de las manos diciendo "oh, pelado, ya estás durmiendo." Él y Valle ya estaban convenidos. Me mandó el Padre ir por Juanillo González el mayordomo, pa. qe. viniera. Así lo hice. Vino Juanillo. Lo presentó el Padre a Valle como amigo, se dieron las manos él y Dn. Ignacio. El Padre me hizo traer queso, panecitos, y el frasco de licor de su cuarto. Los tres tomaron. Yo no quise tomar, haciéndome el que no sabía beber. El Padre estaba ya alegre y lo mismo Dn. Ignacio, que era también aficionado al licor, y me mandaron tocar el alba.

right away without the bundles. I presume that they told the Father that I was watching them and the Father came to see me. I had covered my head and my entire body with my blankets and while lying down he called me and told me to go inside. I obeyed him. Then, he told me, "Here is forty **pesos** in pure gold and a box of abalone for your father." This was so I did not accuse them. In addition, he promised me a set of clothes from head to toe. He took out a bottle and a glass and he gave me a half a glass of brandy. The Father drank a lot of liquor and wine continuously but never got drunk. He ordered me to take the box of abalone to my father that very night so that nobody would find out.

I did what he told me. During the time I was away, I suppose that they had finished their business since when I came back the door was locked and the Father was walking back and forth in the reception room awaiting my return. After I got there, he asked me, "What did Don Ignacio tell you?" I told him. Then, he said: "Come with me." We went inside. He gave me forty **pesos** in gold and took out two glasses (it was almost dawn), one for him and one for me and he served me liquor and he also drank as well. Then, he entrusted me: "As a man you will keep quiet on what you have seen." I answered him, "Father, why is it that my father has only taken one box of abalone, when everything belongs to the community?" He answered: "For now, I beg you that tomorrow you say nothing to Dn. Ignacio Valle." As he was saying these words, Valle arrived. He knocked on the door, and it was opened. The Father ordered me to sound daybreak, when it was not yet time. Valle had his sword on his waist, and he told him: "Father, I want the keys of the mission." I did not go sound daybreak because Valle stopped me. The Father told him that there was plenty of time for him to receive the mission and its assets. Then, Valle ordered me to go to sleep. They stayed to settle their business and drinking. About half an hour later, while I was in my first sleep, the Father came in and he grabbed me by my arms, telling me: "Oh, **pelado**, you are already sleeping." He and Valle had already reached an agreement. The Father told me to go get Juanillo González, the foreman, and I did what I was told. Juanillo came and the Father introduced him to Valle as a friend and he and Don Ignacio shook hands. The Father ordered me to get some cheese, sweet bread, and a jar of liquor from his room. The three drank. I did not drink; I was pretending that I did not know how. The Father was now happy and so was Don Ignacio, who also had an affinity for drinking; they told me to sound daybreak.

Volví a ver si el Padre quería decir misa, pero ya él no podía, estaba demasiado embriagado. Valle tenía ya las llaves de la misión. Pasamos a los almacenes el Padre con nosotros pa. hacer la entrega. De cuando en cuando me hacía señas el Padre para que no hablara. Yo me mantuve muy callado. Valle preguntó si en aquellos almacenes estaba todo lo que poseía la misión en efectos, manifestando duda de que fuese así, porque a la verdad los fondos todos presentaban el aspecto de haber sido saqueados; no habían tenido el Padre y sus amigos tiempo de arreglar las cosas. Si yo no le hubiera hablado a la María Gracia Rodríguez, mucho más habrían sacado de los almacenes. Dn. Ignacio, sin embargo, se dio por entregado. Nos retiramos, de allí me llevó Dn. Igno. pa. su cuarto, me amenazó con la espada mandándome que le dijese la pura verdad. Yo le dije que nada había visto fuera del orden. Entonces él me contestó, "allá se compongan Uds. Esto es todo de Uds; yo venía a recibir para darlo a Uds." Él sí repartió los efectos todos a los indios de la misión, pero lo que es dinero no lo vieron los indios. Eso lo arreglaron allá entre los dos, sin duda.

El Padre entregó, además, a Valle 5000 cabezas ganado mayor, una gran cantidad de borregada en 7 ranchos, once manadas de bestias caballares, 3 manadas de yeguas aburradas. La correspondte. cantidad de bueyes, caballos de servicio ta. La misión tenía abundancia de todo. Acabó este comisionado Valle con casi todo, gobernando el Sr. Alvarado. Después vino Francisco Soto de Amor y él concluyó con lo restante, hasta las tejas se llevó con sus borracheras. Después quiso mandar a los indios como en tiempo de la misión a palos y a patadas.

Se sublevaron los indios una tarde que estaba él medio ebrio y lo agarraron, le hicieron entender que si seguía haciendo eso no viviría muchos días. Entonces pasó a Monterey y trajo a Joaqn. Soto, su hermano, y a Vicente Cantúa su cuñado pa. que le hicieran compañía. Franco. Soto era Tente. o Alférez de cívicos. Llegó el tiempo de que los Robles (Nicolás, Avelino, Secundino, y otro que llamaban el Chato) por alga. causa de que no me acuerdo, los hizo prender Soto, quien quiso ponerles soga al pescuezo como se había hecho con los indios, ellos se resistieron. El Avelino era el más valiente y el que más desobedecía. Soto se paseaba algo borracho, tenía soldaditos consigo.[14] Con su borrachera dio orden a los soldados que le dispararan sus

---

[14]Asisara usó este término en una forma denigrante y burlona para indicar que estos supuestos soldados carecían las cualidades para ser verdaderos soldados.

I came back to inquire if the Father wished to celebrate mass, but he no longer was able to; he was too drunk.

Valle now had the keys of the mission. We went to the warehouses; the Father came along with us to make the transfer. From time to time, the Father would make signs to me not to talk. I kept very quiet. Valle asked if in those warehouses were kept all that the mission owned, doubting this was the case, because, in fact, all their interiors demonstrated evidence that they had been sacked. The Father and his friends had not had time to fix things. If I had not talked to María Gracia Rodríguez, they would have taken out much more from the warehouses. Don Ignacio, however, appeared to be resigned. We left. From there, Don Ignacio took me to his room and he threatened me with his sword, ordering me to tell him the entire truth. I told him that I had not seen anything out of the ordinary. Then he told me, "You people will come to regret it; all this belongs to you. I came to receive it to give it all to you." He actually did distribute all the goods from the mission to the Indians, but regarding the money, the Indians did not see any of it. Without a doubt, the two reached some understanding regarding it.

In addition, the Father turned over to Valle, 5000 head of cattle, a great number of sheep kept on seven ranches, eleven herds of horses, three herds of mules, a corresponding number of bullocks and also service horses. The mission had an abundance of everything. This commissioner Valle finished almost everything during the governorship of Alvarado. Francisco Soto de Amor came afterwards to finish the rest. Even the roof tile was taken during his bouts of drunkenness. Afterwards, he wanted to treat Indians as during the mission days, with kicks and sticks.

The Indians rebelled one afternoon when he was half drunk. They got him and made him understand that if he continued committing [his cruelties] he would not live very long. Then, he went to Monterey and brought Joaquín Soto, his brother, and Vicente Cantúa, his brother-in-law, to keep him company. Francisco Soto was a lieutenant or a second lieutenant in the militia. The time came when Soto arrested the Robles brothers (Nicolás, Abelino, Secundino, another one called El Chato) for some reason, which I do not recall, and he tried to put a rope around their necks as had been done with Indians. They resisted. Abelino was the bravest and the most disobedient of them. Soto was walking around somewhat drunk and had some **soldaditos** with him.[14] In his drunkenness, he issued orders to the soldiers to discharge their

---

[14]Asisara uses the term in denigrating way, to indicate that these individuals were ill-fit to be real soldiers.

fusiles a Avelino. Éste se separó de sus hermanos y descansando contra una pared, dijo que allí le tenían y podían matarle, pero que no se dejaría poner cuerda al pescuezo. Los soldados apuntaron a Avelino, dispararon la mayor parte a los lados y uno de los tiros (disparado por Pantaleón Higuera) dio a Avelino en la región de la ingle, de cuya herida murió a los dos o tres días.

Por este hecho anduvo la viuda de Avelino Robles disfrazada de hombre con un puñal acechando la ocasión de matar a Francisco Soto. Sus amigos y compañeros lo persuadieron que se fuera de Santa Cruz para que pudiera escapar de la furia de aquella muger y del padre y hermanos del difunto. Él de noche cruzó el río crecido, y pasó a Monterey. Ya no volvió más. Por unos días quedaron en el establecimto. Joaqn. Soto y Vicente Cantúa.

Después entró a administrar la finca José Anto. Bolcoff. [Yo entré de alcalde de indios entonces.]

Él era juez también de la villa de Branciforte. Éste repartió a los indios los bienes sencovientes que quedaban, esto es, yeguas viejas que ya no parían, borregos viejísimos retirados del servicio; tomó para si algunos animales por su trabajo. Él desenterró las cesiones de tierras que Figueroa había hecho a los indios, cuyos docs. los habían tenido ocultos Valle y Juan González. Me los enseñó, se les dio las tierras a los indios, pero de nada les sirvieron. Vino la peste de viruelas y acabó con la indiada.

Bolcoff, no hallando otra cosa que apropiarse, se llevó pa. su rancho los adobes, ladrillos, tejas, morillos, vigas viejas ta. de la misión. Así fenecieron los bienes de la misión. Las tierras estaban repartidas a los indios; los que vivieron vendieron sus partes por licor. Los que murieron dejaron sus ter-renos y otros se apoderaron de ellos

Lorenzo Asisara

(Sigue la relación del Sr. Amador)

En los años de 1818 y 1819 habían parado los situados. Ya no venían de Méx. Las tropas y toda la poblacn. estaban en la mayor miseria por lo tocante a vestuario y otras cosas necesarias. El alimento sí abundaba y aún el cacao pa. hacer chocolate, porque si bien no lo mandaba el Gobr. desde Méx., entraban buques particulares que lo traían, y nosotros lo comprábamos a cambio de dinero o semillas.

weapons at Abelino. This one separated himself from his brothers and while resting himself on the wall he told them that they had him and they could kill him but that he would not allow them to put a cord on his neck. The soldiers pointed [the weapons] at Abelino and they fired at him, mostly at the sides but one of the shots (fired by Pantaleón Higuera) hit Abelino in the groin area, from which injury he died two or three days later.

Because of this action, the widow of Abelino Robles disguised herself as a man, and carrying a dagger, awaited the chance to kill Francisco Soto. His friends and fellow soldiers convinced him to leave Santa Cruz so that he could escape the fury of the woman and of the father and brothers of the deceased person. During the night he crossed the swollen river and went to Monterey. He never came back again. For a few days longer Joaquín Soto and Vicente Cantúa remained there.

Afterward, José Antonio Bolcoff came to administer the property (I started to serve as **alcalde** of the Indians at this time).

He also was the judge of the Villa of Branciforte. He distributed to the Indians the remaining assets, that is, old mares that no longer gave birth, extremely old rams that were retired from service; he took for his own use some animals as payment for his work. He uncovered the land cessions that Figueroa had made to the Indians, whose titles Valle and Juan González had hidden. He showed them to me, [which indicated that] land had been given to Indians, but they would have been of little use to them. The smallpox epidemic came and finished off the Indians.

Not finding anything else to appropriate, Bolcoff took to his ranch the adobes, bricks, roof tile, timbers, and old beams also belonging to the mission. This is how the belongings of the mission came to vanish. The lands had been distributed to the Indians; those who survived sold their properties for liquor; those who died abandoned their lots and others took possession of them.

Lorenzo Asisara

The account of Sr. Amador continues . . .

In 1818 and 1819, the appropriations stopped coming; they no longer came from México. The troops and the entire population were experiencing the worst misery in regards to clothing and other necessities. Food was abundant, even cacao to make chocolate, since even if the government of México was no longer sending it, private vessels would bring it and we would buy it with money or grains.

El café no se conocía aquí hasta 1828. Yo mismo hice un contrabando de efectos de todas clases, valor de unos 1500$ que pagué en dinero y pieles. Entre los efectos venía una tercerola de café en grano. Todo me salió muy barato porque no se pagaron derechos. El mismo Capitán, francés de nacimto., me enseñó la manera de preparar el café pa. tomarlo. Té sí teníamos, pues lo sembrábamos en nuestros jardines. Mi madre siempre lo tenía en la huerta. Las papas fueron también desconocidas aquí hasta que vinieron de Columbia u Oregón.

El régimen alimenticio que había en mi casa, en la que había comodidades, era el sigte.

Desayuno de 6 a 7:

un día chocolate, otro atole
de pinole con dulce hecho en
leche. (En mi casa se ordeñaban
60 vacas diarias pa. hacer queso ta.
Yo y mis hermanos de ambos sexos
éramos los trabajadores, en Sn.
Franco. primo. y más tarde en San José.)

Almuerzo como una hora después del desayuno:

Carne guisada, frijoles guisados al
estilo Mexicano, unas veces pan, otras,
tortilla de maíz.

Al Medio Día: Se empezaba tomando mis hermanas de mano de la mamá un vasito de vino cada una. La comida corriente era sopa de arroz o fideos, olla de carne cocida con verduras, frijoles. A veces un postre de queso o panecitos dulces. Concluída la comida nosotros los varones tomábamos una copita de aguardte. de España.

Ese era el modo de vivir de casi todas las familias que tenían posibilidades.

Cena:

Frijoles y un guisado de carne con chile, un
poco de vino, de 8½ a 9 de la noche.

Coffee was not known here until 1828. I myself smuggled things of various classes, in the amount of 1500 pesos that I paid with money and some hides.

Among the things was a **tercerola** of coffee beans; I bought everything very cheaply since no import duties were paid. The captain, a Frenchman by birth, taught me how to prepare the coffee to drink it. We had tea, since we planted it in our gardens. My mother always had it in the orchard. Potatoes were also unknown here until they were brought from Columbia or Oregon.

The basic food regimen in my house, which was one of means, was the following:

Desayuno [light breakfast] from six to seven:

One day, chocolate, another day sweetened **atole**
de pinole made with
milk. (In my house we would also milk
sixty cows daily to make cheese.
My siblings and I, of both genders,
were the workers: first in San
Francisco, and later in San José.)

Almuerzo [Main Breakfast] [This meal took place] about an hour after [the light] breakfast.

Cooked beef and cooked
Mexican-style beans. Sometimes we had bread, and other times
corn tortillas.

Noon Meal: Each of my sisters would get a small glass of wine from my mother. The main dish was rice or noodle soup, a pot of boiled beef with vegetables, and beans. Sometimes we got dessert cheese or sweet breads for dessert. After our meal, the males would get a small glass of **aguardiente** from Spain.

This was the way of living of almost every family of means.

Supper:

Beans and beef cooked in a chile sauce.
A little wine. [This meal] was had between eight and nine o'clock at night.

Los pobres se componían como podían. En las poblaciones, antes de ir a ordeñar las vacas los muchachos de 8 años pa. arriba hacían una estaca con punta, y tomaban una mazorca de maíz blanco muy blando, y con la púa esa la asaban al fuego, desgranaban la mazorca en una gícara de leche de la 1a. vaca que se ordeñaba, y se lo tomaban. Ese era el desayuno y almuerzo común del pobrerío. Otras veces tomaban pinole, o calabaza cocida en leche. A la hora de comer cada uno tomábase platillo colorado hecho por los alfareros de aquí. Sus cubiertos eran más curiosos que los nuestros, los de posibles. que los usaban unos de plata y otros de algn. otro metal. Esos cubiertos eran la misma tortilla y el plato a la mano, no había mesa, así es que a cada bocado se tenía cuchara nueva. El asiento era el puro suelo, o algún hueso de ballena, o algún cacaste hecho de madera. Esa comida consistía de carne, leche, frijoles y tortilla. En lugar de sopa solían hervir maíz o trigo hasta que reventara, y con agua caliente, un poco de manteca, sal y chile lo guisaban. Para postre los más usaban queso, y algunas veces asaderas con panocha, el qe. tuviera panocha.

A la noche guisado de carne, o carne asada, frijoles, atole de maíz, o migas, que eran un atole con manteca medio quebrajado el maíz.

Vino ni aguardte. no tenían porqe. eran artículos muy caros, especialmte. el ulto.

Pero volviendo ahora a los sufrimtos. de las tropas y vecinos por falta de ropa ta. en 1818–20.

Los Sres. oficiales que eran los de más posibilidad usaban cuello y pechera de ropa blanca con un ojal para abrochar la pretina del pantalón por dentro, y su chaleco. La espalda del chaleco iba al ras con la piel, porque no había camisa. Con mis ojos lo he visto eso.

Los soldados, muchos portaban gerga de camisa hecha en las misiones. Otros llevaban su camisa remendada o hilachenta. Se puede decir que la tropa estaba casi desnuda, casi toda descalza. Muchas veces montaron guardia gran número de ellos con los pies descalzos, y el cuerpo envuelto en una frazada. Sin embargo, hacían el servicio contentos por el cariño que le tenían a sus oficiales. Esto de que hablo era en San Francisco; la misma desnudez

The poor would eat whatever they could. In the towns, before going to milk the cows, boys who were eight years or older would make a pointed stake and they would get young ears of very soft white corn. With the point [inserted through the cob], they would toast them on an open fire, and then they would thresh the kernels into a container and, with milk from the first cow that they had milked, drank them. This was the common breakfast and **almuerzo** of poor people. Other days, they would have **pinole** or pumpkin cooked in milk. At the noon meal, each one got their red plates made by the local potters. Their eating utensils were much more curious than those of the people of means, some of whom used silver [utensils], while others used some made from other metals. [The poor's] utensils were the very same tortillas and they would hold their plates in their hands because there were no tables; hence, after every mouthful, they would make a new spoon. The seat would be the bare floor, whalebone, or a box made from wood. This meal would consist of meat, milk, beans, and tortillas. Instead of soup, they would boil corn or wheat until it burst and with hot water, a little lard, salt, and chilies, they would cook it. For dessert, the most they would have was cheese and, on some occasions, **asaderas** with **panocha,** those who could afford [to buy] **panocha.**

At night they would have cooked meat or roasted meat, beans, corn **atole**, or **migas**, which was a type of **atole** cooked in lard with the corn partly cracked.

They had neither wine nor **aguardiente** because these were articles that were very expensive, especially the last one.

But let's return to the suffering of the troops and the civilians due to the lack of clothing from 1818 to 1820.

The officers, who were the ones that had the most [financial] means, used a collar and a stomacher with eyelets to secure to the **pretina** from the inside; they also wore a vest. The back of the vest made contact with the [wearer's] skin because there was no shirt. I saw this with my own eyes.

Many of the soldiers wore shirts of cloth made in the missions. Others wore shirts that were mended or frayed. It can be said that the troops were almost naked, and almost always shoeless. Many times, a great number of them assumed guard duty barefoot and with only blankets to cover their bodies. Yet, they served happily due to the fondness that they had for their officers. All of what I am saying took place in San Francisco, yet the same nakedness

y sufrimto. existieron en los demás presidios. Los paisanos pasaban la misma miseria. Las mugeres se cubrían con gerga. Alga. que otra vez lograban ponerse camisa de manta, pero la nagua era de gerga. Las señoras de los oficiales y otras de posibilidad fueron pasando con indiana y carga. De zapato usaban chinela de coletilla o de paño cuando hallaban. Pero en medio de tanta miseria las pobres mugeres manifestaron mucha conformidad.

Durante el tiempo de miseria la tropa se llenó de piojos. El cuartel estaba infectado de ese insecto asqueroso.

El soldado que estaba de escolta en alga. de las misiones y venía al presidio de Sn. Franco. de correo, de pasar solamte. por el portón de la guardia se llenaba de piojos porque el aire los levantaba, y los descargaba sobre él. Para deshacernos de este tormento no nos quedaba mas remedio que echarnos en el mar, y poner la ropa a hervir con agua, pa. que se muriera el insecto. Así lográbamos algn. poco de descanso por unos cuantos días, hasta que se hacía necesario repetir esas operaciones. Esto duró hasta que se inauguró el comercio de los rusos de Sitka con San Francisco, fue esto del año 19 al 20. Los rusos traían efectos de todas clases, géneros, paños, azúcar ta ta, que cambiaban por trigo, maíz y otras semillas, y reses en pie para salar carne. Después ya se estableció el comercio con los ingles[es] y americanos, y más tarde los franceses y otros, que traían sus efectos y llevaban esquilmos del país, esto es, cueros, pieles de castor, oso, nutrias, venados, ta semillas, carne seca, sebo y manteca, que al principio valían 20 rs. la arroba cada cosa, y más tarde se pusieron a 2$ [pesos].

cueros . . . . $2. cada uno
trigo. . . . . $3. la fanega
maíz . . . . $1.50 " "
frijol . . . . $2.50 " "
lenteja . . . . $3 " "
garbanzo . . . . $3. " "
chícharo . . . . $3 " "
habas . . . . $1.50 " "
pieles de castor . . $7 la libra, bien curada; la piel de nutria de agua dulce, lo mismo que el castor. [la piel de nutria] de agua salada, siendo buena de 7 a 9 cuartos, $100; corrientes $80.

Esos precios rigieron desde 1821 hasta que el país cayó en manos de los Estados Unidos.

and suffering also existed in the other presidios. Our [civilian] countrymen went through the same misery. The women would cover themselves with **gerga**; once in a while they managed to wear a shirt made of **manta** [coarse cotton cloth] but the skirt was made from **gerga.** The wives of the officers, and others of [economic] possibilities, got by with printed calico and other cloth. The shoes that were worn were homemade from **chinela de coletilla** or **paño** when it could be found. But despite living amidst such misery, the poor women expressed much conformity.

During this time of misery, the troops became infested with lice. The quarters were infected with that filthy insect.

The soldier who was stationed in one of the missions and came to the presidio of San Francisco to bring mail would, just by entering the gate of the guard, become plagued with lice because the wind would lift them up and would unload them on him. In order to rid ourselves of this torment, we had no other remedy but to throw ourselves into the ocean and put the clothes to boil in water in order to kill the insects. This is how we managed to rest for a few days until it was again necessary to repeat this operation. This lasted until commerce began between the Russians of Sitka and San Francisco. This was in the years 1819 and 1820. The Russians brought goods of all classes and types, woolen cloth, and also sugar, which they traded for wheat, corn, and other grains, and live cattle to be used to make salted meat. Afterwards, commerce was also established with the English, Americans, and later on, the French and others who brought their goods and would take local products, such as cattle hides and beaver, bear, seal, and deer pelts; also they would take grains, dried meat, tallow, and lard. At the beginning [these products were] worth twenty **reales** per **arroba** and later went up to two pesos.

Cattle hides   . . . . . .2 pesos   each
Wheat 3   per **fanega** [1½ bushels]
Corn . . . . .1.50   "   "
Beans . . . . .2.50   "   "
Lentils   . . . . .3.00   "   "
Garbanzo beans . . .3.00   "   "
Peas   . . . . .3.00   "   "
Fava beans   . . . . . .1.50   "   "
Beaver Pelt . . . . . . .7.00 pesos per pound—the well-cured; pelts of fresh water otters were at the same price as for beaver pelts. Salt water otter [pelts] if they were of good [quality], from seven to nine **cuartos** [in length], 100 pesos; ordinary [pelts], 80 pesos.

These prices prevailed from 1821 until the country fell to the United States.

El año de 1827 estaba yo de mayordomo y cabo de la escolta de la misión de Sn. Francisco Solano. Llegó a mi noticia que a los milicianos que estaban agregados a la compa. permanente de cuera, los hiban a sacar. Yo me valí de este pretesto pa. salir del servicio pues ya tenía 10 años y 5 meses en la compa. de cuera. El Comandte. accidental de la Compa. me dió licencia pa. ir a Monterey en donde se hallaba mi Capitán Dn. Luis Argüello. Me le presenté reclamando mi licencia absoluta. Al principio no me la quiso dar, y llegó a ofrecerme una gineta de sargento pa. que siguiera en el servicio. Yo la rehusé diciéndole que no se me había favorecido en tiempo oportuno ni siquiera haciéndome cabo ni sargento a pesar de ser hijo de oficial y de haber cumplido fielmte. con mis deberes. Que toda la consideración que me había merecido era la de Soldado Distinguido me tocaba por derecho, aunque debía confesar que él me la había convidado varias veces, cuando era yo su asistente, a tomar vino con él vaso por vaso.

La ventaja que teníamos en la compa. los soldados distinguidos (que además de mí, eran Joaquín Moraga, Guadalupe Moraga y Marcos Amador, mi hermano. Había habido otro distinguido nombrado Domingo Sal, hermano de la muger de Dn. Luis Argüello, e hijo del Tente. Hermenegildo Sal. Domingo murió jóven) era que no teníamos obligación de hacer nada de mecánica, sino únicamte. el servicio en las filas y en la guardia. Cuando se nos mandaba cosa de mecánica, y la aceptábamos, nos tenían que pagar 10 reales por el día (aparte del prest. ordino.) adelantados. Y cuando nos decían que no había dinero rotundamente. nos negábamos a llevar las cargas o hacer lo que nos ordenaban. Sin embargo de que teníamos ese derecho, el Capn. Dn. Luis muchas veces nos puso en el cepo, al ras del suelo, sin cabecera, y batiéndonos el sol y el aire en el corredor. Esto lo llamaba el Pena Arbitraria, y nos la imponía alegando que dábamos mal ejemplo a la tropa con negarnos a cargar las mulas y conducirlas desde Santa Cruz al presidio. Pero tan pronto como Da. Rafaela Sal, su esposa, nos veía en el cepo insistía en que se nos pusiese en libertad. Muchas veces vino ella misma y hacía que el cabo de la guardia nos sacara. Yo me figuro que el Capn. y ella estaban de acuerdo porque un día en presencia del mismo Capitán y del oficial de la guardia ella levantó el cepo y nos puso en libertad después de obtener el permiso del oficial. El Capitán no hizo más que reirse, llamándonos, como acostumbraba, "costales de azumbre."

In 1827, I was serving as foreman and corporal of the guard at Mission San Francisco de Solano. The news came that the militiamen, who had been attached to the permanent company of leatherjacket soldiers, were going to be discharged. I used this pretext to leave the service since I had already served ten years and five months in the leatherjacket company. The temporary commander of the company gave me license to go to Monterey where my captain, Don Luis Argüello, was stationed. I presented myself to him requesting my complete discharge. In the beginning he refused to give it to me and instead he offered me the post of sergeant so that I would continue in the service. I refused it, telling him that he had not favored me at the time when I wanted to remain, not even by making me either corporal or sergeant in spite of being the son of an officer and faithfully having carried out my obligations. The only consideration that I had received from him was being recognized as a distinguished soldier, but that I had earned a right to be one. Nonetheless, I have to confess that he had invited me several times, when I was his assistant to drink wine with him. I drank a glass of wine for every one of his.

The advantage that we, the most distinguished soldiers (in addition to myself, they were Joaquín Moraga, Guadalupe Moraga, and Marcos Amador, my brother. There was another distinguished one by the name of Domingo Sal, brother of the wife of Don Luis Argüello and son of Lieutenant Hermegildo Sal; Domingo died young), had in the company was that we had no responsibility for mechanical work. [We] only had the duties of drilling and guarding. Whenever we were ordered to perform a mechanical task, and we accepted it, they had to pay us ten **reales** per day in advance (in addition to our regular pay). And, when they told us that there was no money we would categorically refuse to carry out those orders or refuse to comply with them. In spite of this right, Captain Luis Argüello put us in stocks many times; we were [sitting] at ground level and without back support, and battled the sun and the wind in the corridor. This he called "Arbitrary Punishment" and would impose it on us, arguing that we were setting a bad example for the rest of the troops when we refused to load the mules and take them from Santa Cruz to the presidio. Yet, as soon as Doña Rafaela Sal, his wife, saw us in the stocks, she insisted that we be set free. Many times she herself came and made the corporal of the guard release us. I believe that she and the captain had come to an agreement [to set them free] because one day in the presence of the captain and the officer of the guard she lifted the stocks and set us free after she got permission from the officer. The Captain merely laughed, and as usual he would call us "sacks of **azumbre**."

Voy a ocuparme de la admin. del Tente. Coronel Victoria.[15]

Este Señor se hizo cargó de los dos mandos en los primeros meses de 1831, y se apresuró a deshacer lo que había dispuesto su antecesor Echeandía sobre secularizn. de las misiones, providenciando que quedasen éstas como estaban antes. Muy pronto se hizo amigo de los Padres misioneros, quienes le manifestaron muy buena voluntad, y le facilitaron recursos pecuniarios.

Hizo sus visitas oficiales por el Territorio, pero fijó su residencia en Monterey.

Durante el mando de Echeandía los robos se habían hecho muy comunes, lo mismo otros delitos. Todo debido a la desidia del gefe. Victoria juró que cualquiera había de poder arrojar su pañuelo o cualqa. prenda en la plaza o camino público, sin que nadie se atreviera a levantarlo pa. apropíarselo. Publicó un bando que todo el que robase valor de 20 reales pa. arriba, fuese inmediatamente fusilado, cuando se le comprobase el delito. Muy pronto se le presentaron ocasiones de probar que su bando no era letra muerta. Dos sirvientes de la misión de San Carlos, ayudados por un muchacho indio, page de los misioneros, cometieron varios robos en el almacén, facilitándoles el page las llaves.

Justificado el delito, después de la consulta del Asesor Licdo. Rafael Gómez, fueron los dos ladrones fusilados en Monterey, sin que les valiera las fervorosas súplicas del padre misionero de San Carlos que vino a Monterey y se echó a los pies de Victoria y le abrazó las piernas pidiendo que se les perdonase la vida.[16] Al page indio lo acribillaron a azotes.

Más tarde un indio muy joven, de menos de 20 años, se robó unos botones militares de la habilitación y se fue a jugar con los demás muchachos, perdió los botones. Se averiguó que él los había sacado. Se le formó causa, y avaluado el robo en 20 reales, se le condenó a muerte, sentencia que firmaron el Asesor Gómez y el Sr. Victoria, y se llevó la debida ejecución en Monterey.

---

[15]Beebe y Senkewicz, 342. Los autores mencionan que Manuel Victoria, un oficial de infantería, había nacido en Tecpan, Nueva España. Victoria pudo retener el puesto de gobernador de Alta California solamente unos cuantos meses. Después de haber sido herido durante una batalla con insurrectos en Cahuenga en diciembre de 1831, Victoria abandonó California y regresó a México en enero de 1832.

[16]Beebe y Senkewicz, 325. Según estos autores, Rafael Gómez era oriundo de México y con la profesión de abogado, llegó a California en 1830 a servir como asesor legal. Gómez sirvió en el ayuntamiento de Monterey en 1835 y año más tarde fue miembro de la Diputación de California. Él murió en un accidente de un caballo en su rancho Los Tularcitos a final de la década de 1830.

I am now going to focus on the administration of Lieutenant Colonel [Manuel] Victoria.[15]

This person took charge of two offices [civil and military] in the first months of 1831, and he proceeded to undo what had been ordered by his predecessor Echeandía on the secularization of the missions, ruling that they remain as they were before. Very quickly, he became a friend of the missionaries, who manifested much good will to him, and they made available to him financial resources.

He made official visits throughout the territory, but he established his residency in Monterey.

During Echeandía's rule, robberies as well as other crimes had become very common due to the laziness of the governor. Victoria promised that anyone would be able to drop a handkerchief or any other item in the plaza or public road without anyone being so bold as to pick it up and appropriate it for himself. He published an edict stating that anyone who stole any item worth more than twenty **reales** would be immediately executed, if he was found guilty of the crime. Very quickly the occasion presented itself to show that his edict was not a dead letter. Two servants from Mission San Carlos—helped by a young Indian boy, a page of one of the missionaries—committed several robberies in the warehouse when they got the keys from the page.

After being found guilty of the crime, and upon consulting the [Government's] legal advisor, **Licenciado** Rafael Gómez, the robbers were executed despite the fervent petitions of the priest of Mission San Carlos.[16] [He] came to Monterey and kneeled at Victoria's feet, and while embracing his legs, he asked that their lives be spared. The Indian page received a severe whipping.

Later on, a young Indian, under twenty years old, stole some military buttons from the military store and he went to play with the rest of the boys and lost them. It was discovered that he had taken them. He was tried and the robbery was valued at twenty **reales** and [he] was condemned to death. Legal Assessor Gómez and Sr. Victoria signed the sentence and the corresponding execution was carried out in Monterey.

---

[15]Beebe and Senkewicz note that Manuel Victoria, an infantry officer, was born in Tecpan, New Spain (342). He remained in the governorship of California only a few months. After being wounded during a battle with insurrectionists at Cahuenga (December 1831), he left for México in January 1832.

[16]Beebe and Senkwicz, 325. According to these authors, Rafael Gómez was born in México. As a lawyer, he came to California in 1830 where he served as legal adviser for the state government. He served in the Monterey town council in 1835 and one year later became a member of the California Deputation. He was killed by a horse on his Rancho Los Tularcitos in the late 1830s.

En ese mismo año de 1831 un indio se introdujo como a las 6 de la tarde por la parte del Polin. Ahí tomó una niña y un niño, hijos de mi medio hermano Venancio Galindo y Ramona Sánchez. El niño varón echó a huir, y el indio violó la niña y después la mató, dejándola en el sitio. La niña no la pudieron encontrar hasta el día sigte. en la mañanita, que la hallaron muerta, y fue conducido el cuerpo a la casa de sus padres. Por la palabra del niño que decía que el Coyote había cogido a su hermanita, vino a resultar que poco después arrestaron al soldado de cuera Franco. Rubio, a quien daban el apodo de Coyote, creyéndole el autor de aquellos crímenes.

Se le formó causa y cosejo de guerra, y depués de la consulta del Asesor Gómez aprobando la sentencia de muerte que recayó contra el preso, firmó la condena el Comandte. Gen. Victoria, y fue Rubio fusilado en San Francisco, sin que las pruebas realmente estuviesen convincentes.

Muchos esfuerzos hicieron los Alfres. Ma. Guadalupe Vallejo y José Anto. Sánchez, la esposa de éste y varios otros para salvar la vida de Rubio, porqe. no le creían el autor de los crímenes que se le imputaban en la causa. Rubio clamaba que era inocente, el padre ministro que le ausiliaba, hizo también cuanto pudo por él. Nada valió, y Rubio fue llevado al patíbulo, desde el cual habló al público que moría inocente de aquel crimen, y sufriría la muerte por Dios. A los primeros tiros no murió, se bajó la cabeza sobre el banquillo, entonces le dispararon un tiro en la sien, y quedó muerto.

Algún tiempo después se hizo evidente que Rubio no cometió esos crímenes. El indio malhechor que los perpetró fue denunciado, cogido, y puesto en un calabozo en San Francisco. Estaba este indio podrido de gálico y murió en el calabozo antes de concluirse la causa.

Victoria, además de esos actos que le grangearon la reputación de déspota (y en verdad que lo era, por muchas razones) se puso mal con los hombres principales del país que deseaban la secularizn. de las misiones, pa. poderse ellos hacerse de tierras propias. Se indispuso con los miembros de la Diputación rehusando convocarla en la época que prescribía la ley.

Sobre esto de secularizn. me dijo el mismo Victoria en San José, en donde permaneció 20 o 30 días alojado en la casa de los padres, que él había suspendido la secularizn. porqe. no tenía órdenes del Gobo. para efectuarla. Que más adelante podrían emanciparse los indígenas, y se les repartirían las tierras y los bienes. Pero que de la manera que había providenciado su antecesor no cogerían los neófitos nada.

In the same year of 1831, an Indian entered around six PM by the side of the Polin [a water spring in San Francisco] and took a little girl and boy. They were the children of my half-brother Venancio Galindo and Ramona Sánchez. The boy managed to get away and the Indian raped the girl and later killed her, leaving [her body] on the site. The girl was not found until the following morning; they found her dead and her body was taken to the home of her parents. Going by the word of the boy who said that Coyote had taken his little sister, in a short time, the leatherjacket soldier Francisco Rubio was arrested since he had the nickname of Coyote, and therefore was considered the one responsible for those crimes.

He was charged, court-martialed, and after consultation with the Legal Assessor Gómez, who approved it, the death sentenced was given to the prisoner. The sentence was signed by Commander General Victoria and Rubio was executed in San Francisco, in spite of the evidence not being very compelling.

Many attempts were made to save the life of Rubio by Second Lieutenants José María Guadalupe Vallejo and José Antonio Sánchez, his wife, and various others because they did not believe he was guilty of the crimes he was accused of committing. Rubio claimed that he was innocent and the priest who was aiding him did whatever he could for him, but it came to naught. Rubio was taken to the execution yard, where he told the public that he was going to die innocent of having committed such a crime and that he would suffer death for God. Since he did not die from the first shots, his head was placed on the stool and a shot was fired into his temple and he died.

Sometime later, it became clear that Rubio had not committed those crimes. The Indian wrongdoer who committed them was charged, arrested, and thrown into a dungeon in San Francisco. This Indian was rotting from syphilis and died in prison before his case was completed.

Victoria, in addition to these actions that earned him the reputation of being a despot (in reality he was a despot for many reasons), created ill-will among the leading men of the territory who desired the secularization of the missions so that they could appropriate the mission lands for themselves. He did not make himself available to the members of the Deputation by refusing to convoke it, as prescribed by law.

Victoria personally told me when he stayed for twenty or thirty days in the priests' house in San José, that he suspended the secularization because he did not have orders from the government to carry it out. He noted that in the future, when the Indians were emancipated, the lands and other resources would be distributed to them. He felt that with the way his predecessor had implemented it [secularization], the neophytes would not get anything.

Le conté yo al Comandte. Gen. Victoria un caso que sucedió en San Luis Obispo, con el P. Luis Martínez, y el P. Tapis cuando era Vicario Foráneo. Era una noche muy silenciosa con luna muy clara. Estaba yo sentado con un español. Discutían los dos Padres sobre la naturaleza de la luna; uno de ellos llamó al español viejo que estaba conmigo, y le preguntó su parecer sobre la luna. El español le respondió, "tierra no puede ser; agua tampoco; bosques menos; porque si tierra fuera, borregas habría allá arriba. Porque cuando Vuestras Paternidades ven a algún pobre vecino que pide un terreno pa. colocar en él sus bienes de campo y ganarse la vida, informan al gobo. que no se le puede dar, porque la misión lo necesita para sus borregas." Con la mayor frescura les echó eso a la cara; los Padres se echaron el capillo sobre el rostro, y se metieron en sus celdas. Eso lo presencié yo. El español les había dicho la pura verdad. Nosotros nos quedamos riendo de la ocurrencia. Yo había ido a San Luis Obispo escoltando al P. Tapis, junto con otro soldado llamado Tiburcio López.

El Sr. Victoria se rió mucho con este caso reconociendo también que al español, a pesar de ser paisano de los Padres, les había dicho una verdad dura.

Es un hecho que los P.P. misioneros no toleraban que nadie poseyese terrenos. Todos los que habían los reclamaban como pertenecientes a las misiones, hacían que cada misión cesara en donde empezaba la otra. Esto tenía exasperados a los Californios, quienes ansiaban ver otro régimen establecido.

Victoria era tan despótico con sus subalternos, como lo había sido el Gobr. Solá. Sin embargo yo había tenido la buena suerte de ser bien mirado por Solá quien me guardaba alga. considn. Una vez que se le presentó el Alcalde de San José, Rafael Galindo pa. pedirle que se le diera un peso de cigarros de la Habilitación, se arrimó mucho a Galindo, y le dijo, "¿Quién es Ud? Contestó Galindo, "Alcalde de San José." "Ola! Con qué V. alcalde de San José, el pueblo libre, y Ud. paseando!" Galindo trató de esplicar, pero Solá le dijo, "no se me pegue V. mucho, parece que es como sanguijuela. Salga V. inmediatamte. pa. su destino." Otros viejos que aguardaban a la puerta se burlaban de Rafael Galindo, quién estaba muy corrido.

Voy a relatar, antes que se me olvide, una anécdota sobre lo que ocurrió entre el Gob. Solá y el soldado Pedro Chabolla en la misión de Sta. Cruz.

Estaba Chabolla de escolta a mis órdenes. Esto fue ya cuando se sabía en Cal. que la dominación española sobre México había concluido. Todos los nativos Californios, soldados y paisanos, estaban por la independencia, aunque muy solapadamente. A pesar de todas las ocultaciones del Gobo.,

I told Commander General Victoria about a case that took place in San Luis Obispo between Father Luis Martínez and Father Tapis when he was Visiting Vicar. It was a very quiet night with a very clear moon and I was sitting with a Spaniard. The two priests were discussing the composition of the moon. One of them called the old Spaniard that was with me and asked him his views about the moon. The Spaniard answered, "Land it could not be and neither could it be water, forest even less because if it were land, there would be sheep up there. When Your Excellencies see a poor fellow who requests property to graze his animals and earn a living, you inform the government that it can not give it to him because the mission needs it for its sheep." With great frankness, he told them that to their faces; the priests covered their faces with their cowls and went inside their cells. I personally witnessed this. The Spaniard had told them the absolute truth. We remained there laughing at this occurrence. I had gone to San Luis Obispo to escort Father Tapis with another soldier by the name of Tiburcio López.

Sr. Victoria laughed a lot about this story, acknowledging that the Spaniard, although a countryman of the priests, had told them the plain truth.

There is no doubt that the missionary priests did not tolerate anyone else possessing property; they would claim all the property as belonging to the missions. They would claim that every mission ended where another began. This situation exasperated Californios, who desired to implant a new regime.

Victoria was despotic toward his officials, as Governor Solá had been. Yet, I had the good fortune of being well liked by Solá, who treated me with some consideration. One day when the alcalde of San José, Rafael Galindo, presented himself before him [Solá] to ask him to give him a peso's worth of cigarettes from the military store, he approached very close to Galindo and asked him, "Who are you?" Galindo responded: "The alcalde of San José." "Aha! so you are the alcalde of San José, the free pueblo, and you are on an outing!" Galindo tried to explain but Solá told him, "Do not get so close to me, you are like a leech. Leave immediately for your destination." Other old people who were by the door were making fun of Rafael Galindo, who left hurriedly.

I am going to recount, before I forget, an anecdote regarding what took place between Governor Solá and the soldier Pedro Chabolla at Mission Santa Cruz.

Chabolla was serving as a guard under my command. This was during the time when it was already known in California that Spanish domination over México had ended. All native Californios, soldiers as well as civilians, favored Independence, although very discreetly. Despite all the government's

había entrado al país una cartilla que esplicaba todo el sistema federal de gobo. republicano, la división de los poderes en ejecutivo, legislativo, y judicial ta.

Ya todos estaban imbuídos en las ideas republicanas, y aunque nadie se movía, no dejaban de haber sus combinaciones para unirnos al resto de la nación Mexicana que ya sabíamos había conquistado al fin su independa.

Vino el Gobr. Solá como a las 9 de la mañana de la casa del padre a la guardia. Yo le formé la tropa, como era de ordenanza, y salí al frente de mis seis hombres a darle parte de las ocurrencias del día. Le dí los buenos días. "Buenos días, Señor Gobr., ¿está buena Su Señoría?" "Bueno estoy, Sr. Amador, y ¿Ud. cómo está? Bueno, a Dios gracias." Entonces me ordenó que retirase la guardia y yo lo hice. Revisó las armas en el banco, y me preguntó si esa era la tropa que tenía yo a mi cargo. Respondí, "Sí, Señor, a disposición de Su Señoría." Se dirigió él a tomar la banqueta del corredor. Estaban mis hermanas allí cerca cosiendo ropa de la iglesia; se pararon a saludar al Sr. Gobernador, y él con mucha política las tomó de los brazos y las hizo sentar. Siguió él entonces hacia una zanjita de agua (habían como 40 varas desde la puerta de la guardia a la zanjita). En esto se me acercó Pedro Chabolla y me dijo que quería hablar con el Gobr. pa. pedir su licencia. Yo traté de disuadirle esplicándole que la concesión de licencias era cosa que se hacía por turnos, pero no quiso escuchar y se fue a donde estaba el gobr. cerca de la zanja. (Chabolla no era nada tonto.) Dirijiéndose al Gobr. se cuadró militarmente con el sombrero quitado le dijo: "Sor Gobr. quiero que Ud. me dispense la inprudencia de venirle a pedir mi licencia absoluta, porqe. tengo 18 años de servisio, y no logro mi licencia todavía."

Estaba el Gobr. parado con su bastón de mando y le contestó, "Señor Militar, no le han leído a Ud. la ordenanza? Todo militar la debe saber." Llámome el Sr. Gobr. "Cabo de guardia." "Mande su Senoría." "!Tiene Ud. la cartilla de ordenanza?" "Sí, Señor, la tengo." (Siempre la llevaba yo en la bolsa, la misma que me dejó [mi] Señor Padre. Estaba como nueva.) "Hágame Ud. el favor de pasármela," dijo Solá. Obedecí. Solá leyó a Chabolla las prevenciones de la ordenanza sobre la manera de pedir los soldados la licencia a un gefe Superior. Le dijo a Chabolla, "tiene Ud. cabo y sargento, alférez, teniente y capitán, se dirije Ud. a mí directamente, teniendo su cabo presente?

measures to conceal [news and information from the Californios], a manifesto entered the territory, which explained the federal system of Republican government and also the division of power among the executive, legislative, and judiciary.

Everyone was imbued with republican ideas and although no one acted, there was much agreement that we should unite ourselves with the rest of the Mexican nation that we already knew had finally won her Independence.

Governor Solá came around nine o'clock in the morning from the Fathers' house to the guard station. I formed the troops for him, as was required by regulations, and in front of my six men I went to give him my daily report. I wished him a good day. "Good day, **Sr. Gobernador!** Are you well, Your Excellency?" "I am fine, **Sr.** Amador, and how are you?" "Fine, thank God." Then, he ordered me to withdraw the guard, which I did. He approached the guard and checked the weapons in the armory, and asked me if these were the troops under my command. I answered, "Yes, Sir, they are at the disposal of Your Excellency." He then headed for the walkway of the corridor. My sisters were sewing clothes there for the church; they got up to greet the governor, and he with much politeness took them by the arms and sat them down. Then, he headed for a small ditch (it was about forty **varas** from the guard's door to the little ditch). At this moment, Pedro Chabolla approached me and told me that he wanted to talk to the governor to request a discharge. I tried to dissuade him from doing so by explaining to him that petitions for a discharge could only be done by rotation but he refused to listen to me and went to where the governor was standing, near the ditch. (Chabolla was no fool.) As he was about to address the governor, he adopted a military stance and with his hat off, he told him: "Sr. **Gobernador**, I wish that you pardon me for my lack of prudence in asking you to give me my permanent discharge because I have eighteen years of service, and I still have not obtained my discharge."

The governor was standing with his cane of authority and responded: "Sr. soldier, have they not read the regulations to you? All military personnel should know them." The governor called me. "Corporal of the guard!" "At your command, Your Excellency," I said. "Do you have your regulation manual?" he asked. "Yes, Sir, I have it." (I always carried it in my pocket, the same one that my Sr. father left me; it was almost like new.) "Please hand it over to me," Solá said. I complied. Solá read Chabolla the provisions of the ordinance on the manner that soldiers can request a discharge from a superior officer. He told Chabolla, "You have a corporal, a sergeant, a second lieutenant, lieutenant, and captain and you address me directly, even while having a corporal present?"

Concluyó el Gobr. diciendo a Chabolla que no había abierto la boca, sino al contrario estaba cortado. "Ud. es un Sor. bachiller atrevido que no se rije por la ordenanza, aunque se le han leído y re-leído muchas veces." A esto Solá le pegó en la cara con el puño cerrado, y le hirió con la uña del dedo pulgar en la barba. y me mandó ponerle en arresto. Tuve que hacerlo. Solá después de eso se fue para la casa de los padres. Fui a darle parte de haber cumplido su órden. Solá me mandó que dentro de una hora pusiera a Chabolla en libertad, y le dijera que fuese a presentársele. Chabolla no quería ir porqe. era soberbio y le quemaba la bofetada del Gobr., pero lo persuadí que fuese. Salió Solá al corredor de los Padres; Chabolla se acercó, se cuadró militarmente muy tieso con el sombrero sobre el muslo. Solá le prometió hablarle al Capitán pa. que le extendiese su licencia, metió mano a la bolsa y le dio 5$. Chabolla los recibió, y cuando el Gobr. le dijo que podía retirarse, hizo al giro correspondte. y se volvió a la guardia más colorado que un camarón.

Chabolla era hijo de Español nacido en Jalisco, vino de niño de pecho a California, y siempre hablaba como español cerrado. Era buen soldado, muy aseado y cumplido, pero aquella vez se olvidó de la ordenanza y pasó una desazón. Vino, todavía después de la últa. entrevista con el Gobr. Solá, diciendo, "El Sr. Gobr. me insultó, y si hubiera sido uno de mi clase, lo mataba, pero me ha pagado la bofetada con 5$. Yo le di las gracias con buena gana— 5$. Dios se los pague."

Chabolla sentía mucho más que la bofetada el haber sido llamado "Sor. Bachiller," esto era horrible. Mucha chacota le dieron mis hermanas y otros; pero todo lo sobrellevó con muy buen humor. Chabolla era valiente y nada tonto, pero no podía hacer otra cosa que resignarse. Algn. tiempo después en San Francisco, pocos días antes de recibir Chabolla su liciencia, estaba de centinela Gervacio Soto. Dentro del cuerpo de guardia tuvieron Chabolla y Soto sus razones. Soto se arrimó al banco de armas, dejó allí su arma de fuego, tomó una lanza y le dio a Chabolla dos lanzadas una en cada muslo. El cabo de la guardia estaba dormido, lo despertaron; puso él a Soto en el calabozo con un par de grillos. Chabolla obtuvo su licencia antes de haber sanado de sus heridas.

The governor concluded by telling Chabolla, who not only had not opened his mouth but was now tongue-tied. "You are a Mr. Babbler, bold enough not to abide by regulations even though they have been read and re-read to you many times." Then, Solá punched him in the face with a closed fist, and cut [Chabolla's] chin with his thumb. [The governor] ordered me to arrest him [Chabolla]. I had to do it. After this, Solá went to the Fathers' house. I went to inform him that I had complied with his order. Solá commanded me to set Chabolla free in one hour and to tell him to present himself before him. Chabolla did not want to go because he was very proud and the governor's punch was still stinging him. I persuaded him to go. Solá came out to the priests' corridor and Chabolla approached him and squared himself militarily, very stiffly, and with his hat on his thigh. Solá promised him that he would talk to the captain so that he could grant him a discharge; he then put his hand in his pocket and gave him five pesos. Chabolla took them and when the governor told him he could leave, he made the corresponding turn and returned to the guardhouse redder than a shrimp.

Chabolla was the son of a Spaniard who was born in Jalisco and had been brought to California while he was still nursing; he always talked like a Spaniard. He was a good soldier, very clean, and always knew his duties. On that occasion, he had forgotten the regulations and the unpleasant incident took place. After the last meeting with the governor, he came to me and said, "The governor insulted me and if he were one of my own status, I would kill him. But he has paid me the punch with five pesos and I sincerely thanked him for the 5 pesos. May God repay them to you."

Much more than the punch, Chabolla was bothered by being called "Mr. Babbler"; this was horrible. My sisters and others made fun of him but he handled himself with a good sense of humor. Chabolla was brave and not dumb, yet he had no choice but to resign himself [to continued military service]. Some time later in San Francisco, a few days before he was discharged, Gervacio Soto was on guard duty. While serving as members of the guard, Chabolla and Soto had built animosity towards each other. Soto went to the armory, and after leaving his firearm there and getting a spear, he returned and speared Chabolla twice, once on each thigh. The corporal of the guard was asleep and he was awakened. He put Soto in the dungeon with a pair of shackles. Chabolla obtained his discharge before his wounds were able to heal.

Por fin, en fines del año mismo de 1831, le hicieron una revolución al Comandte. Gen. Victoria en San Diego, secundada en Los Angeles.[17]

Acudió allí Victoria acompañado del Capn. Romualdo Pacheco; las fuerzas de Victoria lo abandonaron pasándose a los pronunciados. Hubo una lucha personal enfrente de Cahuenga,entre Victoria y José Ma. Ávila, según me relató mi suegro Francisco Alviso que estuvo presente. Acudió otro individuo cuyo nombre no recuerdo, éste mató al Capn. Pacheco.[18] Ávila clavó la lanza a Victoria, éste sacó la pistola. Ávila le tiró otra lanzada que lo arrancó del caballo y lo tiró al suelo. Victoria caído, disparó en pistoletazo y Ávila lo tiró del caballo muerto. Alviso me dijo que él estaba a 6 varas de dista. de los combatientes. Finalmente recojieron a Victoria y lo llevaron malherido como estaba, creo que a San Gabriel. Los pronunciados habían puesto al ex-Comandte. Genl. Echeandía al frente del movimto. Cuando estuvo ya en disposición de movérsele lo embarcaron en la fraga. "Pocahontas" pa. un puerto de México. A mi me dijeron que él rehusó [ceder] el mando de las armas, diciendo que sólo muerto lo entregaba. Lo creo bien porque Victoria era hombre de mucho valor, muy militar, lo cual no era Echeandía. Quedaron las cosas así hasta que el Sr. Capn. Zamorano hizo una contrarevolución en Monterey, organizando una compa. de vecinos y otra de estrangeros. Últimamente los dos gefes contendientes hicieron un convenio para evitar la efusión de sangre, y formaron dos Comandas. Generales, una del Sur con Echeandía al frente, y otra del Norte que reconocía por gefe a Zamorano.[19]

---

[17]Rosaura Sánchez, 236. Sánchez declara que a Manuel Victoria se le pusieron en contra la mayoría de los líderes californianos porque lo consideraban un "gobernante déspota." Los liberales de California lo criticaban por no haber convocado a la Deputación, y, quizás más importante, lo percibían como amigo de los misioneros que estaban tratando de frenar la secularización de las misiones.

[18]Beebe y Senkewicz, 332. Los autores indican que Romualdo Pacheco era oficial militar que provenía de Guanajuato, México. Llegó a California en 1825 durante el tiempo que José María Echeandía fue nombrado gobernador. Pacheco sirvió como comandante interino de Santa Bárbara en los años 1827 y 1828. Su hijo, que también llevó el nombre de Romualdo, logró ejercer el puesto de gobernador interino de California en 1875.

[19]Beebe y Senkewicz, 342. Según los escritores Agustín Vicente Zamorano nació en San Agustín, Florida en 1798. Como miembro del ejército mexicano acompañó a José María Echeandía cuando éste fue nombrado gobernador de Alta California en 1825. Zamorano sirvió como secretario del gobernador durante cinco años y se volvió comandante de Monterey en 1831. Después que José de Figueroa asumió el puesto de gobernador, Zamorano le sirvió como secretario. En los años 1836 y 1837, Zamorano estuvo involucrado en la insurrección en contra del gobernador Juan B. Alvarado.

Finally, at the end of the same year of 1831, a rebellion took place against Commander General Victoria in San Diego and it was seconded in Los Angeles.[17]

Victoria, accompanied by Captain Romualdo Pacheco, went there. Victoria's forces abandoned him and went over to the insurrectionists. There was hand-to-hand combat between Victoria and José María Ávila in the proximity of Cahuenga. Francisco Alviso, my father-in-law, who was present there, told this to me. Another person, whose name I do not remember, was also present there. He killed Captain Pacheco.[18] Ávila thrust his spear into Victoria while the latter took out his gun. Ávila then speared him again, which threw him off his horse and knocked him to the ground. The fallen Victoria fired his gun and Ávila fell from his horse, dead. Alviso told me that he was six **varas** away from the combatants. Finally, Victoria was picked up, and as badly wounded as he was, I believe, he was taken to San Gabriel. The rebels had made ex-Commander General Echeandía the leader of their movement. When it became possible to safely move him [Victoria], they embarked him on the frigate *Pocahontas* bound for a port in México. I was told that he refused to give up his command, saying that he would only do so when dead. I believe this was true because Victoria was a man of great valor, a true soldier, something that was not the case with Echeandía. Things remained unchanged until Captain Zamorano led a counterrevolution in Monterey, organizing one company of countrymen and another of foreigners. In the end, the two rival leaders reached an agreement to avoid bloodshed. They established two military jurisdictions, one in the south with Echeandía as commander and another one in the north, which recognized [Agustín Vicente] Zamorano as its leader.[19]

---

[17]Sánchez, 236. Sánchez notes that Manuel Victoria was opposed by most Californio leaders who branded him a "despotic ruler." Californio liberals criticized him for failing to convene the Deputation and, more importantly, they perceived him as a friend of the missionaries who wanted to halt the secularization of the missions.

[18]Beebe and Senkewicz, 332. The authors point out that Romualdo Pacheco was a Mexican military officer from Guanajuato. He arrived in California in 1825, when José María Echeandía was appointed governor. Pacheco served as acting commander at Santa Bárbara in 1827 and1828. His son, also named Romualdo, became acting governor of California in 1875.

[19]Beebe and Senkewicz note that Agustín Vicente Zamorano was born in San Agustín, Florida, in 1798 (342). While in the Mexican army, he accompanied José María Echeandía after he was appointed governor of California in 1825. Zamorano served as the governor's secretary for five years and became commander of Monterey in 1831. After José de Figueroa assumed the governorship, Zamorano became his secretary. In 1836 and 1837, he became involved in the revolt against Governor Juan B. Alvarado.

Continuó esta división hasta la venida del Gen. Figueroa. En el intérvalo Echeandía continuó su obra de secularizar las misiones del Sur, pero en las del Norte continuó el mismo régimen anterior.

Figueroa vino al finalizar el año del 1832 y tomó posesión de los mandos militar y político, como Gefe Político y Comandte. Gen., y se ocupó primeramente en pacificar el territorio. Publicó un indulto general de todos los que habían hecho armas contra Victoria, llamando a sus puestos a los oficiales del ejército que se habían pronunciado, entre los cuales estaba el alfz. Vallejo. Durante las conmociones pasadas Victoria había hecho salir del país a José Ma. Padrés, ayudante Inspector de las tropas. Padrés tenía mucha influencia con la juventud de Cal., en la que había imbuído las ideas del republicanismo más exaltado.

Figueroa después de algún tiempo de mando manteniendo las relaciones más cordiales con la diputn. y con el pueblo, instruyó ayuntamtos., instruyó a la Diputn. en las prácticas parlamentarias, y se hizo sumamente popular. Planteó la secularizn. de las misiones.

En esto en 1834 fue nombrado Dn. José Ma. Híjar, gefe político de California, por haber renunciado ese cargo Figueroa. Híjar y José Ma. Padrés, como Director el uno, y Vice Director el otro, trajeron una colonia de como 300 personas para esta California bajo la protección del Gobo. nacional. A Figueroa le vinieron órdenes de facilitar a los directores de la colonia todos los recursos necesarios. Según tuve entendido el Sr. Híjar traía autorización para que se le entregasen los bienes de las misiones; esto causó mucho disgusto aquí.

Pero antes de que Figueroa hubiese entregado el mando, hallándose Híjar todavía en San Gabriel en camino del sur pa. Monterey, llegó un correo extraordinario en un viage muy violento y que o se había visto hasta entonces, con órdenes a Figueroa del Gobo. nacional de no entregar la gefatura política ni las misiones a Híjar. Ese correo era sobrino mío, llamado Rafael Amador, hijo de la Baja Cal., que vino sin descansar día ni noche desde México. A su regreso murió arrojando sangre por la boca de la estropeada que se había dado. Yo no le vi porqe. no subió de Monterey al norte.

La diputación de acuerdo con el Gen. Figueroa convino en reconocer a Híjar como Director de Colonizn. con 4000 $ de sueldo anual, pero se negó a reconocer el derecho que reclamaba Híjar de que se le entregasen las misiones, ni la gefatura política. Pero se le proporcionaron todos los recursos para la colonia que fue a Sta. Rosa y Sonoma.

This division continued until the arrival of General Figueroa. During the interval, Echeandía continued his work of secularizing the missions of the south. However, the missions of the north continued under the same previous regime.

Figueroa came [to California] at the end of 1832 and took possession of the political and military administrations by becoming Political Chief and Commander General. He first concentrated on pacifying the territory. He published a general amnesty for all who had taken arms against Victoria and called all army officers who had rebelled to return to their posts. Among them was the Second Lieutenant Vallejo. During the previous administration, Victoria had forced José María Padrés, assistant inspector of the troops, to leave the territory. Padrés had a lot of influence over the youth in California, and they had been imbued with the most exalted ideals of republicanism.

Figueroa, after some time in command and maintaining cordial relations with the Deputation and the people, instructed town governments and the Deputation on parliamentary practices and he became extremely popular. He started the secularization of the missions.

Around this time, in 1834, Don José María de Híjar was named Political Chief of California when Figueroa resigned his post. Híjar and José M. Padrés, one as Director and the other as Vice-Director, brought a colony of 300 persons to California under the sponsorship of the national government. Figueroa received orders to facilitate the directors with all the necessary resources. It was my understanding that Híjar brought with him the authorization to obtain all the assets of the missions. This brought much displeasure around here.

Before Figueroa transferred his command and while Híjar was still in San Gabriel on his way to Monterey, an express courier, at a very fast pace that had never been seen before, arrived with orders to Figueroa from the National Government that he was not to surrender either the political leadership or the missions to Híjar. This messenger was a nephew of mine, Rafael Amador, a native son of Baja California, who came from México without resting day or night. On his return, he died, bleeding from his mouth, due to injuries he caused himself. I did not see him because he did not go further north than Monterey.

The Deputation, in agreement with General Figueroa, recognized Híjar as Director of Colonization, with the annual salary of 4,000 pesos, but it refused to recognize the rights claimed by Híjar of having control of the missions transferred to him as well as assuming the political leadership of the territory. Nonetheless, they gave him all the resources for the colonies that were going to be established in Santa Rosa and Sonoma.

Estaba Figueroa ocupado en la formación de un nuevo pueblo en el valle de Sta. Rosa que debía llamarse "Santa Anna y Farías" cuando le llegaron nuevas de un plan de revolución en Los Angeles para derrocarle por partidarios de Híjar y Padrés. Abandonó el proyecto del nuevo pueblo, y marchó violentamte. pa. el Sur. Allá hizo arrestar a los cabecillas, y después a los que estaban en Sonoma, recogió todas las armas que tenían los colonos, (este últo. lo llevó a efecto el Alférez Mariano G. Vallejo), y concluyó por embarcar pa. México a Híjar, Padrés y todos los demás cabecillas.[20]

De los colonos, muchos se volvieron pa. México, y los que se quedaron pacíficos, se establecieron y hallaron ocupación. Supe que había pasado mucha corresponda. entre Figueroa e Híjar sobre esos asuntos, pero yo no estaba en posición de saber su contenido, pues estaba en mi rancho.

El título de mi rancho lo había escrito Solórzano, un secretario o escribiente de Figueroa en un cuarto de la misión de San José. Yo lo puse en mano del Sr. Figueroa con cubierta rogándole que pasara la vista por aquellos documentos. El Gobr. estaba jugando malilla con dos Padres, y creo que el otro era Eugenio Montenegro. Al hacer yo la súplica, me pidió que le dispensara hasta concluir de jugar aquella mano. Ya estábamos él y yo de acuerdo de eso desde antes. Él me había prometido cuando iba a hacer visita a Sonoma estenderme el título en la misma misión. Concluída la mano de malilla le dijo el Gobr. al P. González que diera informe en favor mío. El Padre respondió que no podía, y el Sr. Gobr. le dijo, "Padre González, una población que tenga 3000 almas le corresponden ocupar 9 leguas por circunferencia. De aquí a la casa del Sr. Amador hay 5 leguas, quiere esto decir que el terreno que él pide no pertenece a la misión. Así debe Ud. hacer el informe favorable a él." El Padre quiera que no quiera, dio el informe como se le ordenó, y entonces Figueroa me entregó los documentos pa. que fuese a Monterey a completar los trámites. Fui allá, me aprobó el título la diputa., luego lo firmó Figueroa. Esto fue en 1834.

---

[20]Rosaura Sánchez, 136. Sánchez cree que cuando Figueroa se rehusa a permitir que Híjar y Padrés se hicieran cargo de la secularización de las misiones, él estableció las condiciones para que los Californios eventualmente asumieran control de ellas. Los Californios sostenían la creencia que, como nativos del territorio, ellos, no los fuerenses, tenían que ser los que deberían sacar provecho de los ganados de las misiones y que también merecían ser concedidos los ranchos de las misiones o por lo menos tener el derecho de comprarlos. Los Californios también pensaban que ellos deberían ser los que tenían el derecho de arrendar el trabajo de los neófitas de las misiones.

Figueroa was busy establishing a new town in the Valley of Santa Rosa, which was going to be called Santa Anna y Farías, when he heard of a revolutionary plan, by followers of Híjar and Padrés in Los Angeles, to overthrow him. He abandoned the project for the new town and hurriedly marched towards the south. There, he ordered the arrest of the leadership and later he did the same to those who were already in Sonoma; then, he confiscated all the weapons from the colonists. (Second Lieutenant Mariano G. Vallejo carried out this last action.) Finally, he ended by sending Híjar, Padrés, and the rest of the leadership back to México.[20]

Many of the colonists returned to México and those who had not become involved in the rebellion settled down and found an occupation. I found out that much correspondence had taken place between Figueroa and Híjar on this matter, but I was in no position of knowing its content since I was at my ranch.

Solórzano, Figueroa's secretary or scribe, had written the title for my ranch in a room at Mission San José. Along with a cover, I put it in the hands of Sr. Figueroa and urged him to look over the documents. The governor was playing manille with two priests and I believe the other person was Eugenio Montenegro. After I made my plea, he asked me to forgive him [for not looking at them] until he had finished playing his hand. He and I had previously arranged this. He had promised me that when he visited Sonoma he would grant me the title in that same mission. After the manille game was over, the governor told Father González to give a report in my favor. The Father answered that he could not. The governor told him, "Father González, a place that has 3000 souls has the right to occupy nine leagues in circumference. From here to the house of Amador there are five leagues; this means that the property he is asking for does not belong to the mission. You have to make the report favorable to him." Whether the Father liked it or not, he had to give a report according to what was ordered and then Figueroa gave me the documents in order for me to go to Monterey to complete the transactions. I went there, and the Deputation approved the title; then, Figueroa signed it. This took place in 1834.

---

[20]Sánchez believes that Figueroa's refusal to let Híjar and Padrés take charge of the mission secularization created the political climate that would allow the native Californios to eventually take control of the mission lands (136). The Californios felt that it should be the native-born, not the outsiders, who should profit from the mission cattle and who should be granted or allowed to purchase the mission ranchos. They also insisted that they should be the ones to have the right to lease the labor of the missions' neophytes.

Los partidarios de Híjar y Padrés atacaron a Figueroa con mucha violencia cerca del Gobo. nacional, obligándole a defender sus actos, y hasta su honor y veracidad como lo hacía ya en un manifiesto, cuando le atacó en 1835 el mal que le privó de la vida. Falleció si no estoy trascordado, en Nove. de 1835, muy sentido por los Californios. Figueroa con su fina política lograba vencer todas las dificultades, nunca ha tenido Cal. un gefe tan generalmte. apreciado por sus habitantes. No puede quedar duda que tomó empeño en grangearse la buena voluntad de los Californios desvelándose por asegurar los adelantos del país y el bienestar general. Su cadáver, según se dijo en aquel tiempo, fue embalsamado, y conducido a Sta. Bárbara en cuya iglesia se le dio sepultura.

Antes de morir Figueroa se separó el mando político del militar, dejando el primero a cargo de José Castro, como vocal 1° de la diputación, y el militar a su compañero de armas Tente. Coronel Nicolás Gutiérrez,[21] a quien había hecho venir de San Gabriel en donde residía como Comandte. del partido del Sur del territorio.

Comenzaron a desempeñar sus respectivos cargos, a la muerte del General, Castro y Gutiérrez. Al poco tiempo reclamó el 2° a Castro que le entregase la gefatura política, porqe., decía él, que Cal. como territorio fronterizo con el estrangero, debía según disposiciones del Gobo. Supmo., estar al mando de una sola persona, y ésta había ser la autoridad militar. Después de alga. corresponda. cedió Castro y entregó el cargo.

Nada de nuevo ocurrió en ese tiempo. A principios de 1836 vino el Gefe Político y Comandte. Gen el Coronel Dn. Mariano Chico.[22]

[21]Beebe y Senkewicz, 320. Los escritores comentan que José Castro era hijo de José Tiburcio Castro, un soldado que había dado sus servicios en San Diego y San José. Aunque José Castro había sido miembro de la Deputación de California y había fungido como gobernador interino, el se involucró en la revuelta en contra del gobernador Nicolás Gutiérrez. José Castro también participó en la rebelión en contra del gobernador Manuel Micheltorena. Durante la invasión norteamericana de California, él tenía el cargo de comandante militar de las fuerzas de California.

[22]Beebe y Senkewicz, 321. Los autores informan que Mariano Chico sirvió en el congreso nacional mexicano antes de ser nombrado gobernador de Alta California en diciembre de 1835. Su estancia en la gubernatura fue de poca duración, ya que a los pocos meses él fue expulsado de California. Habiendo llegado a California en abril de 1836, él se vio forzado a abandonar California para julio de ese mismo año cuando los Californios se rebelaron. En la década de 1840, Chico asumió la gubernatura del estado de Guanajuato en México.

The supporters of Híjar and Padrés attacked Figueroa very viciously before the national government, forcing him to defend his actions, even his honor and veracity, as he did in a manifesto that he wrote around the time he fell to the illness that would deprive him of his life in 1835. He succumbed, if I am not forgetful, in November of 1835, and [his death] was deeply felt by the Californios. Figueroa, with his practical sense of politics, managed to overcome all difficulties. California had never had a leader who was widely appreciated by its inhabitants. There can not be any doubt that he made an effort to win the goodwill of the Californios, [often] going without sleep in order to secure the betterment of the country and the general well-being. His body, as it was said at that time, was embalmed and taken to Santa Bárbara in whose church he was buried.

Before dying, Figueroa separated the political and military command. He left the first [office] in the hands of José Castro, who served as First Vocal in the Deputation, and the military [command] to his comrade in arms, Lieutenant Colonel Nicolás Gutiérrez.[21] [Figueroa had] made [the latter] come from San Gabriel where he was serving as commander of the southern region of the territory.

Castro and Gutiérrez started carrying out their respective duties after the death of the general. In a short time, however, the second requested Castro to turn over the political leadership to him. He argued that California, as a territory bordering a foreign neighbor, had to be under the command of only one person according to National Government decree, and that this person had to be the military authority. After some correspondence, Castro gave in and relinquished his position.

Nothing new occurred during this time. In the beginning of 1836, a new political chief and general commander arrived, Colonel Mariano Chico.[22]

---

[21]According to Beebe and Senkewicz, José Castro was the son of José Tiburcio Castro, a soldier who had served at San Diego and San José (320). Although he was a member of the California Deputation and became acting governor, José took part in the revolt against Nicolás Gutiérrez. He also participated in the rebellion against Governor Manuel Micheltorena. During the U.S. invasion of California, José Castro served as the military commander of the California forces.

[22]Beebe and Senkewicz point out that Mariano Chico served in the Mexican Congress before being appointed Governor of Alta California in December 1835 (321). His governorship lasted only a few months. Arriving in California in April 1836, he was expelled by the Californios in July. In the 1840s, Chico served as governor of the Mexican State of Guanajuato.

Nunca le vi. Sé que tuvo desacuerdos con el ayunto. de Monterey, con la diputa., y con particulares, pero no estoy al tanto de los pormenores, por lo que no me atrevo a dar cuenta de ellos.[23] Muy poco tiempo estuvo Chico, y se marchó el mismo año pa. Méx. con ánimo de volver con una fuerza considerable de tropas pa. castigar a los Californios y hacerles respetar su autoridad. Dicen que Chico era tan quijote como un español, y casi era loco. Quedó otra vez mandando el Sr. Gutiérrez pero a los muy pocos días se puso en pugna con la diputn., insultó a sus miembros, y de la noche a la mañana se sublevaron los jóvenes de Monterey con Alvarado y José Castro a la cabeza. Situaron la plaza de Monterey, tomaron el castillo, bombardearon el Comandte. Gen. en su cuartel, disparándole un solo cañonazo. Él se rindió con sus oficiales y tropa, y en breves días los embarcaron para México.

Poco puedo yo decir sobre los sucesos de esta época del mando de Alvarado (Juan Bta.) como Gobr., y de Mariano Guadalupe Vallejo como Comandte.

Sé que tuvieron muchas dificultades con los habitantes del Sur, que Carlos Anto. Carrillo reclamaba el Gobo., que hubo marchar y contramarchar de tropas, pero finalmente fue reconocido Alvarado como Gobr. por el Gobierno de México. Vallejo siguió actualmte. de Comandte. Gen., aunque era un simple Tente. de la Compa. de San Francisco cuando los revolucionados lo elevaron a ese puesto.

Durante el mando de Alvarado, más bien cuando acababa de entregarlo a su sucesor, el Comodoro Jones de la escuadra Ama. en 1842, se apoderó de Monterey, alegando que México y su país estaban en guerra; pero a los dos días bajo su bandera, hizo de nuevo la mexicana con los honores correspondtes., y devolvió la plaza a las autoridades mexicanas.

En 1840 Alvarado hizo arrestar a gran no. de estrangeros, súbditos Británicos y ciudadanos, Ams. Después de una corta investigación, los envió a México pa. ser juzgados allí del delito que se les imputaba. De haber formado el proyecto de derrocar el gobo., matar a Alvarado, José Castro y otros, y poner el país bajo la dominación de los Estados Unidos, o por lo menos bajo su protección. Se dijo también que Graham y sus conspiradores

---

[23]Rosaura Sánchez, 237. Sánchez hace mención de que la juventud liberal de Monterey se iban a rebelar en contra de Chico, ya que éste era un ferviente centralista y seguidor del General Antonio López de Santa Anna. Cuando Chico y sus acompañantes llegaron a Monterey, los jóvenes liberales salieron a recibirlos, exhibiendo las insignias rojas del federalismo puestos en las solapas de sus vestimentas.

I never saw him. I do know that he had misunderstandings with the Monterey town council, with the Deputation, and also with private individuals.[23] I am not familiar with the particulars; for this reason I will not dare to give an account of them. Chico stayed a very short time and he left in the same year for México with the intention of returning with a considerable number of troops to punish the Californios and force them to respect his authority. It is said that Chico was as quixotic as a Spaniard and was almost crazy.

Sr. [Nicolás] Gutiérrez again took command, but in a few days he began to quarrel with the Deputation and insulted its members. Almost immediately, the youth of Monterey, with Alvarado and José Castro as its leaders, rebelled. They besieged the plaza of Monterey, captured the fortress, and bombarded the commander general at his headquarters. With only one cannon shot, he surrendered along with his officers and his troops, and in a few days they were embarked for México.

I can only say a little on the events during the era of Alvarado (Juan Bautista) as governor and of Mariano Vallejo as commander.

I know that they had a lot of difficulties with the inhabitants of the south, that Carlos Antonio Carrillo claimed the governorship, that there were marches and countermarches by troops of the opposing camps until Alvarado was finally recognized as governor by the Mexican Government. Vallejo remained as commander general although he had been just a mere lieutenant in the company of San Francisco before the revolutionaries promoted him to that position.

During the rule of Alvarado, it is better to say, just before he transferred his rule to his successor, Commodore [Thomas Catesby] Jones of the American Squadron, took possession of Monterey in 1842, alleging that México and his country were at war. Yet, in two days he lowered his flag and raised anew the Mexican flag, with the corresponding honors, and returned the plaza to the Mexican authorities.

In 1840, Alvarado arrested a great number of foreigners, British subjects and American citizens. After a short investigation, he sent them to México in order that they be tried there on charges that they had planned to overthrow the government, kill Alvarado, José Castro, and others, and put the territory under United States domination, or at least under its protection. It was also said that [Isaac] Graham and his fellow conspirators

---

[23]Sánchez notes that the young liberals of Monterey revolted against Chico, an ardent Centralist and supporter of General Antonio López de Santa Anna (237). When Chico and his party arrived in Monterey, they rode out to welcome them wearing red federalist insignias on their lapels.

proyectaban un saqueo general.[24] No sé lo que había de verdad en todo eso; lo que sí parece cierto[es] que los presos llegaron a Tepic, y nada se les pudo probar, por lo cual el Gobo. de México tuvo que pagar una gran cantidad, y que algunos de los presos volvieron a Cal. con dinero.[25]

También es cierto que durante la admon. de Alvarado estaban muy indispuestos los ánimos de los habitantes del Norte y del Sur, pues los Abajeños querían la capital en Los Angeles, y la aduana y tesorería en San Diego. Por otro lado había antipatía ya contra los Mexicanos del interior, porque éstos se habían opuesto a los proyectos de separar a Cal. del resto de la Repa.

Había graves desavenencias entre Vallejo y su sobrino Alvarado, quienes presentaban quejas continuas ante el gobo. de Mexo., el uno contra el otro. El despilfarro en Monterey era grande; y el país todo presenció cosas escandalosas, cuales fueron los robos y saqueos de las misiones.

La misma suerte que le cupo a la misión de San José, tuvieron todas las demás. Las órdenes del gobo. pa. que pagasen los gastos despilfarrados suyos se sucedían sin intermisión. El Gobo. hacía préstamos de ganados a sus partidarios y secuaces, que nunca se pretendió reclamarles, y creo en muy raros, rarísimos casos, se recobró alguna parte de esos préstamos. Sé que de los préstamos de San José que fueron muchos y muy crecidos, sólo dos individuos los pagaron. Juan Alvires González y Anto. Buelna. que habían recibido 200 vaquillas cada uno. Es un hecho que cuando entregó el mando Alvarado ya las misiones estaban escuálidas, casi todo su ganado había desaparecido.[26] La mayor parte de los admores. habían por su parte cometido robos escandalosos, llevándose a sus ranchos y casas hasta las ollas de las cocinas.

---

[24]Beebe y Senkewicz, 326. Según los autores, Isaac Graham llegó a California en 1833 y se estableció en Natividad en las afueras de Monterey, donde fundó una destilería. En 1836, Graham respaldó la revuelta de Juan Alvarado, y en 1844 y 1845 respaldó al gobernador Manuel Micheltorena.

[25]Rosaura Sánchez, 243. Según Sánchez los prisioneros fueron liberados cuando el gobierno mexicano recibió protestas de las embajadas de Inglaterra y Estados Unidos en la ciudad de México.

[26]Amador no fue el único Californio que culpaba al gobernador Juan B. Alvarado por el saqueo de las misiones. Rosaura Sánchez escribe que un miembro de la familia Pico, quien había servido como administrador de la misión San Luis Rey y que había sido despedido por el gobernador, declaró que durante su estancia en la misión las bodegas de la misión estaban repletas, y además la misión era dueña de miles de ovejas y ganado. Sin embargo, un año más tarde, cuando él estuvo de visita en la misión no encontró nada más que un poco de licor que se estaba fabricando en ella (157).

planned a widespread ransacking.[24] I do not know how much truth there was in all this; what appears to be true [is] the prisoners arrived in Tepic, and nothing was proven. The Mexican Government had to pay a great sum of money, and some of the prisoners returned to California with money.[25]

It is also true that during the Alvarado Administration there was considerable antipathy between the people of the north and those of the south since the **Abajeños** wanted to move the capital to Los Angeles and the Custom House and Treasury to San Diego. In addition, there was already much dislike for the Mexicans of the interior because they had opposed the plans to separate California from the rest of the Republic.

There were serious disagreements between Vallejo and his nephew Alvarado, both of whom repeatedly complained to the National Government about each other. The squandering that took place at Monterey was immense and the people of the entire territory witnessed scandalous things, such as the robbery and sacking of the missions.

The same fate suffered by [Mission] San José was experienced by the rest. Government orders that [the missions] pay for their financial squandering were issued continuously. The government forced [the missions] to loan cattle herds to its cronies and followers. There was never any attempt made to demand repayment from them; only on rare, very rare occasions, were parts of those loans recovered. I know that of the loans from [Mission] San José, which were many and very large, only two people paid them. They were Juan Alvires González and Antonio Buelna, who each received 200 young cows. It is fact that when Alvarado surrendered his office, the missions were already in a squalid condition and almost all the cattle had disappeared.[26] The majority of their administrators had committed scandalous robberies, taking to their ranches and houses even the pots from the kitchens.

---

[24]According to Beebe and Senkewicz (326), Isaac Graham came to California in 1833. He settled in Natividad, outside of Monterey, where he operated a distillery. In 1836, Graham supported a rebellion by Juan B. Alvarado; in 1844 and 1845, he backed Manuel Micheltorena.

[25]Sánchez notes that the prisoners were released because of protests from the British and U.S. embassies in Mexico City (243).

[26]Amador was not the only one to blame Governor Juan B. Alvarado for the despoliation of the missions. Rosaura Sánchez writes that one member of the Pico family, who was serving as administrator for Mission San Luis Rey but was dismissed by the governor, stated that when he was residing at the mission, its storehouses were full and it had thousands of sheep and cattle. Yet, one year later when he visited the mission, he found nothing but a small amount of liquor that was being manufactured (157).

El Visitador Gen. Hartnell que era todo un caballero y hombre honrado, hizo cuanto pudo para salvar las misiones de la rapiña, pero no logró nada, y renunció un destino que no le traía ni honra ni provecho y sí muchos sinsabores y penalidades.[27]

Esas ricas misiones que eran la admiración del mundo desaparecieron sus riquezas como por encanto. ¿Y qué han sacado en limpio los que las robaron? Ni ellos, ni sus descendientes disfrutaron mucho tiempo de sus mal-adquiridos bienes, casi todos ellos están en la pobreza, y algs. hasta en la indigencia.

Parece que el Gobo. de México, cansado de las desavenencias entre los gobernantes político y militar de Cal., y del mal estado en que se hallaba el país, y deseoso al mismo tiempo de afirmar su autoridad, pensó en nombrar un gefe de conocida inteligencia, integridad y buena intención, para esta parte tan importante de la República. Se fijó en un hombre que ciertamente poseía esas dotes, y éste era el Genl. de brigada Dn. Manuel Micheltorena, hombre de buen nacimto. y educación, de talento e instrucción, de maneras distinguidas, y que gozaba de prestigio en toda la repa. Al determinar mandarle aquí resolvió enviar con él una fuerza militar suficiente para apoyar su autoridad así como también pa. defender el territorio y que ya estaba amagado de invasión por parte de los aventureros o emigrantes que en grandes números se habían introducido al país y continuaban viniendo en contravención de las leyes de México sin que las autoridades pudiesen impedirlo.

Efectivamente, se propuso enviar un batallón de buena tropa pero, por desgracia, no le entregaron el batallón bien disciplinado que pensó el Gobo. poner a sus órdenes porque el Gen. Paredes en Guadalajara lo necisitaba para sus propias atenciones. De aquí resultó que con festinación formaron un batallón que se componía en su mayor parte de desalmados; de hombres sacados de las cárceles y del presidio de Chapala, con gran número de oficiales que hubieran adornado a las cadenas. No quiero decir con esto que todos

---

[27]Beebe y Senkewicz, 327. Los autores comentan que William Hartnell, nacido en 1798, era originario de Lancashire, Inglaterra. Hartnell arribó a California en 1822 como representante de una firma inglesa que comerciaba con las misiones. En abril 30, 1825, Hartnell se casó con María Teresa de la Guerra, hija de una prominente familia californiana. Hartnell recibió título sobre el rancho Alizal, lugar en donde ahora está situada la ciudad de Salinas. Después de la guerra contra México, Hartnell obtuvo un puesto con el ejército norteamericano como intérprete y traductor.

Visitor General [William Edward] Hartnell, who was a complete gentleman and an honest man, did whatever he could to save the mission from pil-
laging, but he did not accomplish much.[27] He resigned from a destiny that
would bring him neither honor nor benefit but a lot of grief and hardship.

The rich missions that were admired all over the world lost their wealth as
if by magic. And what have those who stole from them profited? Neither
they, nor their descendants enjoyed their ill-gotten gains for very long.
Almost all of them are living in poverty and some of them are indigent.

It appears that the Mexican government, tired of enmity between the military and political rulers of California and of the poor condition in which the
country found itself, and desirous at the same time of enforcing its authority, thought about naming a governor of well-known intelligence, integrity,
and good intentions for this part of the nation, which was so important to the
republic. A man was chosen who certainly possessed these talents, and this
was Brigadier General Don Manuel Micheltorena, a man of good birth and
moral education, of talent, and high schooling, of distinguished manners, and
one who enjoyed an excellent reputation throughout the Republic. When it
was decided to send him [to California], it was resolved to provide him with
a military force large enough to support his authority as well as to defend the
territory that was already being threatened by an invasion of adventurers or
immigrants, who in large numbers had entered the country in violation of the
laws of México, and without the authorities being able to prevent it.

Indeed, it was proposed to send a battalion of good troops, but unfortu-
nately they did not give him the well-disciplined battalion that the government had proposed to put under his command because General Paredes, in
Guadalajara, needed it for his own needs. As a result, they hastily formed a
battalion that was composed mostly of heartless people, of men taken out of
prisons and from the presidio of Chapala, and with a great number of officers
who should have decorated the [prison] chains. I do not want to say that all

---

[27]According to Beebe and Senkewicz, William Hartnell was born in Lancashire, England, in
1798 (327). Hartnell came to California in 1822 as a representative of an English firm that
traded with the missions. On April 30, 1825, he married María Teresa de la Guerra, daughter of a prominent Californio family. Hartnell received title to Rancho Alizal, located in present-day Salinas. After the Mexican War, Hartnell was employed by the U.S. military as an
interpreter and translator.

eran gentes de esa calaña, porque había oficiales muy respetables entre ellos; pero muchos eran tan malos y aún peores que los más malvados soldados que tenían a sus órdenes.

Llegó Micheltorena a San Diego con unos 500 hombres, que formaban el Batallón Permanente Fijo de Californias. El gobo. había dispuesto que la aduana de Mazatlán sufragase 8000$ mensuales para los gastos de esas tropas, recurso que le falló a Micheltorena desde el principio. Después de disciplinar algún tanto aquella horda, marchó el general pa. Los Angeles, debiendo advertirse que en la Aduana de San Diego no halló fondos ni recursos, y se vio precisado a suplicar a su antecesor Vallejo que le enviase semillas para mantener la tropa. Vallejo, creo, que le mandó lo que pudo recoger. Uno de los primeros actos de Michelta. fue nombrar a Vallejo, Comandante de la línea del Norte, desde Sta. Inés. Ya en Los Angeles reclamó a Alvarado el gobo. político.

Si mal informado no estoy Alvarado entregó el mando al 1er. vocal de la Junta Departamental Dn. Manuel Jimeno, y éste con una comitiva pasó a Los Angeles y transfirió el gobo. político a manos de Michelta.[28]

Ya venía marchando el nuevo Gobr. pa. Monterey, y se hallaba en las inmediaciones de San Fernando cuando le llegó un correo avisándole de la toma de Monterey por el Comodoro Jones. Regresó a Los Angeles y empezó a fortificarse allí pa. hacerle frente a las eventualidades. Aún se hallaba allí cuando vino la nueva de la devoln. de Monterey por el Comodoro, y que éste pasaba a San Pedro para tener una entrevista con él. Efectivamente el Comodoro Jones le visitó con su plana mayor en Los Angeles y fue recibido con los honores debidos a su rango. Hicieron un convenio satisfactorio en el que se reconocía por el Comodoro la autoridad de Méx. sobre Cal. Yo vi una copia de ese convenio, pero no recuerdo los términos.

---

[28]Beebe y Senkewicz, 328. Según los autores, Manuel Jimeno Casarín llegó a California en 1828 para asumir los puestos de subcomisario y contador de la aduana de Monterey. Más tarde, él obtuvo otros puestos gubernamentales. Sirvió como síndico y alcalde de Monterey y también llegó a ser miembro de la Deputación de California. Jimeno Casarín también ocupó el cargo de secretario para los gobernadores Juan B. Alvarado y Manuel Micheltorena. A principio de la década de 1830, Jimeno Casarín se casó con Angustias de la Guerra. Después de la muerte de Jimeno Casarín en 1853, ella se casó por segunda vez con el norteamericano, el doctor Edward Ord.

of them were people fitting this character because there were officers who were very respectable among them, but many of them were as bad or worse than the most wicked soldiers who were under their command.

Micheltorena arrived in San Diego with 500 men who made up the Permanent Fixed Battalion of the Californias. The government had mandated that the customs house of Mazatlán pay [the battalion] 8.000 pesos monthly to cover the expenses of the troops but this revenue failed Micheltorena from the very beginning. After disciplining the horde somewhat, the general marched to Los Angeles. It should be noted that he did not find any funds or resources in the Customs House of San Diego, and he was forced to implore his predecessor, Vallejo, to send him grain to feed his troops. I believe that Vallejo sent him whatever he could gather. One of the first acts that Micheltorena took was to name Vallejo as commander of the northern line, which began at Santa Inés. After reaching Los Angeles, he requested from Alvarado the transfer of the political government.

If I am not ill informed, Alvarado turned over his authority to the First Vocal of the Departmental Junta, Don Manuel Jimeno, and he [the latter], with a commission, went to Los Angeles and placed the political government in the hands of Micheltorena.[28]

The new governor marched to Monterey, and while he was in the vicinity of San Fernando, a messenger arrived informing him about the takeover of Monterey by Commodore [Thomas Catesby] Jones. He [Micheltorena] returned to Los Angeles and he started to fortify himself there to confront whatever contingencies may occur. He was still there when news arrived of the commodore's return of Monterey [to its Mexican authorities] and that he would go to San Pedro to meet with him. In effect, Commodore Jones with his officers visited him in Los Angeles and he was received with the required honors appropriate for his rank. A satisfactory agreement was reached in which the commodore recognized México's authority over California. I saw a copy of the agreement, but I do not remember the terms.

---

[28]According to Beebe and Senkewicz, Manuel Jimeno Casarín arrived in California in 1828 to take the positions of **Sub-comisario** and **Contador** at the Custom House of Monterey (328). He later held several government positions. He was a **Síndico** and **Alcalde** of Monterey as well as a member of the California Deputation. He also served as secretary for Governors Juan B. Alvarado and Manuel Micheltorena. In the early 1830s, Jimeno Casarín married Angustias de la Guerra. After his death in 1853, Angustias married her second husband, Dr. Edward Ord.

Vino, por fin, Micheltorena con una parte de su batallón a Monterey. Ya estamos en 1843.

Su primera medida fue ver cómo se establecían economías en los gastos civiles para poderle hacer frente a los militares. Hubo junta de autoridades civiles y militares en la Capital, y se resolvió suprimir las prefecturas y subprefecturas y algunos otros empleos.

Mas como no le venían los recursos de Mazatlán tuvo muchos apuros el General, y en varias ocasiones hizo frente a serias obligaciones públicas con fondos propios suyos, así se dijo entonces, y creo que fundadamente.

Yo me hallaba por aquel tiempo en la misión de San José, empleado por el P. González en la reparación de los edificios, inclusa la iglesia. De consiguiente no puedo hablar de aquellos sucesos sino por informes de otras personas, que me aseguraron que el mal comportamto. de algunos oficiales y de gran parte de la tropa del batallón tenía alarmada a toda la población de Monterey y de otros lugares.

Una de las medidas de Michelta. fue decretar la devolución de las huertas y edificios de las misiones a los ministros.

Pero a pesar de que los Californios no tenían queja fundada contra Michelta., había entre ellos el deseo de deshacerse de sus gobernantes de la otra banda, así como de los criminales del Batallón Fijo. Habían formado la resolución de que las rentas del Depto. se gastasen entre ellos mismos sin que vinieran a participar de ellas las gentes de Méx.[29]

Michelta. procuró el bien del país en cuanto se lo permitieron las circunstancias, castigó los excesos de la tropa, pero no podía deshacerse de la única fuerza con que contaba para el caso de algn. movto. por parte de los del país contra su autoridad.

---

[29]Como muchos otros Californios y algunos eruditos de hoy en día, Amador hace una separación entre los nativos de California y los pobladores que provenían del centro de México, a los cuales él les llamaba "mexicanos." Algunos historiadores usan esta división para argumentar que los californianos ya se veían como un pueblo que era diferente a los mexicanos. En lugar de pensar que los californios ya sentían un nacionalismo incipiente, existe mayor posibilidad de que lo que los californianos estaban expresando era un fuerte amor por su patria chica. En ese tiempo la nación mexicana estaba al borde de la desolución política y el regionalismo crecía desenfrenadamente a través de todo el país. California no era el único territorio que estaba experimentando movimientos separatistas. Aún hoy en día, el cariño por la tierra natal perdura, ya que los mexicanos todavía demuestran un fuerte apego a ella. Cualquiera que fuese el caso, lo que está claro es que este ramo de la historia chicana y mexicana requiere de mucho más estudio al igual que un diálogo más extenso.

At last, Micheltorena, with a part of his battalion, came to Monterey. We are now in 1843.

His first measure was to see how to implement cuts in the civil budget to increase [the one for] the military. There was a meeting of civilians and military officers at the Capital and it was agreed to eliminate the Prefectures, Subprefectures, and some other positions.

Yet, since the funds from Mazatlán were not reaching him, the general was under a lot of pressure, and several times he had to resolve some severe public debts by using his own funds. This is what was then said, and I believe that it is fundamentally true.

At that time I was at Mission San José, employed by Father González in repairing the buildings, including the church. As a consequence, I can only talk about the events through information given to me by other persons who assured me of the bad comportment of some officers and a great part of the battalion's troops. They had alarmed the entire population of Monterey as well as people from other places.

One of the measures that Micheltorena decreed was the return of the missions' orchards and buildings to the priests.

Although the Californios did not have a legitimate complaint against Micheltorena, there was a common desire among them to get rid of rulers that belonged to the opposing faction as well as the criminals of the Fixed Battalion. They reached a consensus that the department's revenues should be spent amongst themselves [Californios] without the people of México coming to share them.[29]

Micheltorena tried to concern himself with the well-being of the country and he would punish the excesses of the troops whenever circumstances permitted him, but he could not rid himself of the only force he could count on in case there was a movement against his authority by the natives of the country.

---

[29]Like many other Californios and some contemporary scholars, Amador makes a distinction between the native-born Californios and those settlers who came from Central Mexico, whom he calls "Mexicans." Some scholars use this distinction as a way to argue that the Californios were already seeing themselves as a distinct people who were different from Mexicans. I believe that rather than the Californios undergoing a process of protonationalism, what the Californios were expressing was a strong connection to their **patria chica**. At this point in its political evolution, Mexico was at the edge of political dissolution and regionalism was rampant throughout its territory. California was not the only territory that had separatist movements. Even today, Mexicans still have a special affection towards their **provincia**—their native homeland—and continue to exhibit a strong attachment to it. Whatever the case, this area of Chicano/Mexican history is still in its infancy and it requires much more study and dialogue.

Trató de conciliar los ánimos, pero nada valió. Estaban resueltos los Californios a gobernarse a sí mismos, y por medio de la revolución le facilitaron al Gen. y a su esposa la ocasión de salir de Cal. pa. volverse a México, como uno y otra deseaban.

Si no me engaña la memoria, en Dic. de 1844 varios jóvenes de Monterey con Francisco Rico y Manuel Castro a la cabeza se salieron una noche de la capital, se dirijieron al rancho en donde el Gobo. tenía su caballada, y apoderándose de toda ella se la llevaron a la cañada de San Miguel.[30] Muy pronto salió en persecusión de ellos una fuerza al mando del Comandte. Abella. Los Californios se trasladaron a La Natividad y de aquí a La Soledad.

Cuando tuvieron noticia por los espías que colocó Joaqn. de la Torre que marchaba sobre ellos el Gen. Michelta. con 300 hombres, reunieron todo el vecindario y se prepararon pa. el combate. Yo creo que estaba José Castro al frente de ellos, pues le habían hecho venir con los 25 hombres de la Compa. de Monterey que tenía consigo fundando por disposición del Genl Michelta. un establecto. en el río Mercedes (río que viene de la sierra y desemboca en el San Joaquín). Pero en vez de combatir hubo negociaciones en la laguna de Alvírez, un poco más adelante en la parte del Norte. De resultas de esas entrevistas, Michelta. se volvió con sus fuerzas a Monterey, y Castro con las suyas se estableció en San José. El Subprefecto Anto. Suñol que estaba presente en las negociaciones me comunicó que la fuerza de Michelta. era muy superior a la de los otros, pero él no quiso hacer uso de medidas violentas, y por otro lado los Californios tenían miedo de apurar el lance.

Quedó convenido que Michelta. pediría al Gobo. de Méx. autorización para embarcar la tropa del batallón, e interim quedasen las cosas in status quo. Michelta. se comprometió a no atacar a los otros hasta saber la resolución del Gobo. Supmo. Permanecieron así algunos dos o tres meses, los Californios acampados en San José, hasta que tuvieron aviso de que venía Michelta. contra ellos con unos 500 hombres. Entonces los Californios se apresuraron a marchar para el Sur, pues no tenían fuerzas con qué hacerle frente a su contrario. Marcharon para San Buenaventura y Michelta.

---

[30]Beebe y Senkewicz, 320–21. Los autores comentan que Manuel Castro nació en 1821 en el puerto de Monterey. Entre los años de 1842 y 1844 fue secretario del prefecto de Monterey. Para 1845, él asumió la prefectura de Monterey y respaldó al gobernador Pío Pico en su lucha en contra del comandante José Castro. Manuel Castro también respaldó la rebelión de José María Flores que tomó lugar a fines de 1846 en contra de las fuerzas norteamericanas en el sur de California.

He tried to appease the discontented, but it was all in vain. The Californios were determined to govern themselves, and by means of revolution, they gave the general and his wife the opportunity to leave California and return to México, as both desired.

If memory does not deceive me, in December 1844, several young men, with Francisco Rico and Manuel Castro as their leaders, left the Capital one night, and they went to the ranch where the government kept its herd of horses.[30] After taking possession of the entire herd, they took it to the San Miguel ravine. In a short time, a force headed by Commander Abella left in pursuit of them. The Californios moved to La Natividad and from there to La Soledad.

When they found out from spies placed by Joaquín de la Torre that General Micheltorena with 300 men was marching against them, they gathered the local residents and prepared for combat. I believe that José Castro was their commander since they had asked him to join them with twenty-five men of the Monterey company, who were assigned to him by order of General Micheltorena so that he could establish a settlement on the Mercedes River (a river that originates in the Sierras and flows into the San Joaquín). Instead of fighting, negotiations were held at the Alvírez Lagoon, a little ways up the northern part [of the territory]. As a result of this meeting, Micheltorena returned with his forces to Monterey and Castro [with his troops] established himself in San José. Subprefect Antonio Suñol, who was present during the negotiations, told me that the forces of Micheltorena were superior to the other but he did not wish to resort to violence and, on the other hand, the Californios were afraid of rushing into a confrontation.

It was agreed that Micheltorena would request permission from the Mexican government to embark his troops of the battalion, and in the interim, things would remain *in status quo*. Micheltorena promised that he would not attack the others until he received orders from the Supreme Government. For two or three months, the Californios remained camped in San José until they received notice that Micheltorena was coming for them with 500 men. Then, the Californios quickly began to march south since they did not have the force to confront their opponents. They marched to San Buenaventura; Micheltorena

---

[30]Manuel Castro was born in Monterey in 1821 (Beebe and Senkewicz, 320–21). He served as secretary to the Prefect of Monterey in 1842 and 1844. In 1845, he was made Prefect of Monterey and supported Governor Pío Pico in his struggle against Commander José Castro. He also backed José María Flores' rebellion against U.S. forces in the southern part of California in late 1846.

en persecusión. Al pasar éste por la laga. de Alvírez, viniendo yo de Monterey, pasé a saludarle. Estaba él debajo de un roble, me preguntó de dónde venía y qué objeto traía. Yo le contesté que andaba en mis asuntos propios. Entonces me preguntó si yo tenía conexión con los pronunciados, o si tenía que pasar por entre ellos, a lo que respondí negativamente, asegurándole que yo nada tenía que ver con la revolución, que yo era un vecino pacífico de San José que iba para mi rancho. Me dio la mano al despedirme y con mucha política me deseó buen viage. Yo tomé un camino estraviado para llegar a mi casa sin verme con los pronunciados, temeroso de que me fuesen a detener. Yo no quise saber nada de revolución, ni entonces, ni nunca en toda mi vida. Siempre me negué a tener participación en complots o enredos políticos. En una ocasión el Sr. Guadalupe Vallejo me filió mis dos hijos Valentín y Celso sin mi conocto., pero yo se los quité y los envié a mi rancho. Tuvimos algunas palabras sobre ellos, pero yo no le dejé mis hijos.

En San Buenaventura hubo un tiroteo entre las dos fuerzas contrarias, resultando de él la retirada de los Californios más pa. el Sur.

Por mi desgracia me habían seducido a dos de mis hijos llevándolos en la compa. de rifleros en el bando Californio.

Con Michelta. marcharon Sutter (Juan Augusto)[31] con una compa. de infantería de indígenas organizada por él en su presidio del Sacramento, y una compa. de estrangeros, mandada por un Americano, a la que iba agregado Isaac Graham como voluntario.

Siguió Michelta. con su tropa tras los Californios, y se volvieron a avistar en Cahuenga. Allí tuvieron también algunos tiroteos, hasta que los estrangeros abandonaron a Michelta. por convenios que tuvieron con los paisanos suyos que servían en el otro bando.

En esos encuentros creo que no hubo ni muertos ni heridos, únicamte. unas bestias fueron las víctimas. Finalmente, hubo conferencias entre

---

[31]Beebe y Senkewicz, 339. Los autores escriben que Juan A. Suttter, quien nació en 1803, era originario de Alemania. Según ellos, el gobernador Juan B. Alvarado le concedió una gran propiedad en el valle de Sacramento para tratar de frenar la influencia de Mariano Guadalupe Vallejo en esa región. Sutter llegó a dominar la región como si fuera su propio feudo. En 1845, Sutter salió en respaldo del gobernador Manuel Micheltorerna cuando una gran parte de los californianos se rebelaban en contra de su gobierno. Sutter no resistió la invasión norteamericana en California. Después de que California fue integrada a la unión americana, Sutter fue miembro de la convención constitucional del estado. Eventualmente, él perdió la mayor parte de sus propiedades a anglosajones que las ocupaban ilegalmente.

went in pursuit of them. As he passed by the Alvírez Lagoon, and I was coming from Monterey, I stopped to greet him. He was under an oak tree and he asked me where I was coming from and what was the nature of my business. I answered that I was taking care of some personal matters. He then asked me if I was connected to the rebels or if I had run into them, to which I answered negatively, assuring him that I had nothing to do with the revolution, that I was a peaceful civilian from San José and was heading [back] to my ranch. He gave me his hand as I took my leave, and with much politeness he wished me a good trip. I took a circuitous road to get to my house in order not to run into the rebels, fearful that they might detain me. I did not want to know anything about revolution, not then, nor ever in my entire life. I always refused to participate in any plots or any political entanglements. On one occasion, Sr. [Mariano] Guadalupe Vallejo conscripted my two sons Valentín and Celso without my knowledge; I, however, took them away from him and sent them to my ranch. [He and I] exchanged a few words about them but I did not leave him my sons.

In San Buenaventura, there was a skirmish between the two opposing forces, resulting in the withdrawal of the Californios further to the south.

To my misfortune, two of my sons were seduced into joining the Californio company of riflemen.

With Micheltorena marched Sutter (Juan Augusto) with an Indian infantry company that he organized at the presidio of Sacramento.[31] [Also accompanying Micheltorena] were a company of foreigners led by an American, to which Isaac Graham added himself as a volunteer.

Micheltorena with his troops followed the Californios, and they again encountered each other at Cahuenga. There, they fired several shots at each other until the foreigners abandoned Micheltorena as a result of an agreement that they had reached with their countrymen that were serving the other faction.

I do not believe there were any deaths or wounded in those encounters; some animals were the only casualties. Finally, there were conferences between

---

[31]According to Beebe and Senkewicz, Juan Sutter was born in Germany in 1803 (339). They also note that Sutter received a huge land grant in the Sacramento Valley from Gov. Juan B. Alvarado to check the influence of Mariano Vallejo. Sutter ran the Sacramento region as if it were his own private fiefdom. In 1845, he supported Governor Manuel Micheltorena. He also did not oppose the U.S. invasion of California. After California entered the American union, he became a member of its constitutional convention. He eventually lost most of his land to Anglo-American squatters.

Michlta. por un lado, y Castro y Alvarado por otro, y quedó convenido Michelta. en embarcarse con sus oficiales y Batallón Fijo pa. México, quedando él reconocido como gefe Supmo. hasta su salida del país. Entregó el mando político a Pío Pico, como 1er. vocal de la Asamblea Departal., y la Comanda. Genl. de las Armas al Tente. Coronel José Castro.

Pasó Michelta. con su tropa a Los Angeles, de allí a San Pedro donde se embarcaron para Monterey. Aquí recogió el resto de su fuerza, y a su esposa, y salió de Cal. pa. uno de los puertos Mexicanos del Pacífico, Mazatlán, creo.

Hasta el últo. momento se le hicieron los honores de su rango. La artilla. que había llevado Michelta. en la campaña fue entregada al Comisionado del Comandte. Gen. Castro.

Los anteriores pormenores los adquirí de otras personas que fueron testigos oculares. Yo me hallaba arrinconado en mi rancho.

Ya tenemos a los Californios gobernando su suelo natal otra vez. Estamos en 1845.

Pío Pico, Gobr. interino.

José Castro, Comandte. Gen.[32]

El Gobr. fijó por su propia voluntad la capital en Los Angeles, y trató de trasladar a aquella sección del país la aduana y la tesorería. Viendo la gran oposición por parte de los arribeños y habiendo José Abrego, el tesorero, hechó renuncia de su cargo, nombró Pico a Dn. Ignacio del Valle pa. reemplazarle, pero antes de que éste hubiese tomado posesión, el Comandte. Genl. Castro prohibió a Abrego en tono amenazador que hiciese la entrega, y ésta no se efectuó.

Pico dividió el país en Prefecturas, nombrando segunda a la de Monterey pa. el Norte, y puso a su frente a su sobrino Manuel Castro. Después comenzó a expedir la serie de proclamas altisonantes que le dieron bastante celebridad. Pico puso todos los empleos en manos de sus parientes y secuaces, y entre éstos se dividían las rentas que le tocaban al ramo civil, teniendo por su parte la admon. de las misiones, las que acabaron de reducir a la miseria.

---

[32]Beebe y Senkewicz, 333. Los escritores dicen que Pío Pico nació en San Gabriel en 1801. Pico fue miembro de la Deputación de California en 1828 y asumió el puesto de gobernador interino en 1832. Después que Manuel Micheltorena fue desplazado de la gubenatura, Pico fue nombrado gobernador para la parte sur del estado.

Micheltorena on one side and Castro and Alvarado on the other and it was agreed that Micheltorena, his officers, and the battalion would embark for México. Until he left the country, he would be recognized as the supreme leader. [When he departed,] he transferred the political leadership over to Pío Pico as the First Vocal of the Departmental Assembly and the General Commandancy of Arms to Lieutenant Colonel José Castro.

Micheltorena, with his troops, went to Los Angeles and from there to San Pedro, where they embarked for Monterey. While there, he picked up the rest of his forces and his wife, and he left California for one of the Mexican ports on the Pacific, Mazatlán, I believe.

Up until the last moment, deference was paid him according to his rank. The artillery that Micheltorena had taken during his campaign was turned over to the commissioner of Commander General Castro.

The previous details I acquired from other persons who were eyewitnesses. I was living in the isolation of my ranch.

We have the Californios governing the land of their birth once again. We are now in 1845.

Pío Pico is Interim Governor and

José Castro is Commander General.[32]

The governor, on his own, chose Los Angeles as the capital and he tried to move the Customs House and the Treasury to that part of the country. After seeing the great opposition on the part of the **Arribeños** and having José Abrego resign his position as treasurer, Pico named Don Ignacio del Valle to replace him. But, before he [del Valle] could take office, Commander General Castro prohibited Abrego, in a threatening manner, from making the transfer [of his office], and it did not take place.

Pico divided the country into prefectures, designating Monterey as the second [prefecture] to administer the north and putting his nephew Manuel Castro in charge of it. Then, he started to issue a series of high-sounding proclamations that gave him a lot of notoriety. Pico placed all the jobs in the hands of his family and his followers, who amongst themselves divided the revenues that belonged to the civil branch [of government]; they also took control of the administration of the missions, which they reduced to the level of misery.

---

[32]Pío Pico was born in San Gabriel in 1801 (Beebe and Senkewicz, 333). He served in the California Deputation in 1828 and became acting governor in 1832. After the removal of Manuel Micheltorena he became governor for the southern part of California.

Finalmte., estaban las misiones adeudadas; los acreedores reclamaban el pago de sus créditos, y al fin, la asamblea de acuerdo con el Gobr. nombró una Comisión para que tomase el parecer de los prelados sobre el mejor modo de cubrir esos créditos pasivos. Al fin quedó autorizado el Gobr. para vender los bienes o arrendarlos.

Pío Pico y Castro lograron satisfacer al Gobo. Supmo. de que los Californios le eran leales, y que en lo sucesivo se mantendría la paz y el Gobo. sería acatado. En vista de todo esto, el Gobo. Supmo. aceptó la situación y nombró propietarios en sus cargos a los dos gefes superiores del Depto. Por este tiempo vino de comisionado del Gobo. Supmo. Dn. José Ma. Híjar, el mismo que fue Director de Colonizn. en 1834, pero no sé cual fue el objeto de su comisión. Oí decir que murió en Los Angeles.

Las relaciones entre Castro y Pico no eran nada cordiales. El primero desconocía en mucha parte la autoridad del 2°. Los recelos entre uno y otro así como entre sus partidarios, eran muy grandes. Los odios entre los habitantes del norte y del Sur eran día a día mayores, y amenazaban un rompimto. que traería la ruina del país. Contra los Mexicanos del resto de la Repa. existía también un odio que venía haciéndose más y más intenso. Así es que los Mexicanos apenas podían contar por segurar sus vidas y propiedades. Se les ultrajaba y hasta se les robaba con impunidad.

Ya en este tiempo llegaba una numerosa inmigración de los Estados Unidos a través de las llanuras. Esto era todo en violación de las leyes de México que prohibían la introdn. de estrangeros al país sin pasaportes. En las regiones del Sacramento, a inmediaciones del fuerte Sutter se había reunido una gran cantidad de emigrados, que ninguno traía documentos legales.

Castro corrió allá con Mariano G. Vallejo, y haciendo alarde de autoridad y de fuerza, permitió la permanencia de aquellos estrangeros bajo de la condn. de que pasados los rigores del invierno habían de retirarse del país, o legalizar su residencia. Nombró a Juan A. Sutter, comandante del distrito, y ya él ejercía las funciones de Juez de Paz.

Muy a fines de 1845 o principios de 1846 se presentó el Capn. Juan C. Frémont, del ejército de los Estados Unidos, en Monterey, con una pequeña escolta, se dijo que para pedir autorizn. del Gobo. pa. esplorar la Cala. Frémont había indebidamente entrado al país con una fuerza militar.

In the end, the missions were so indebted that their creditors demanded repayment of their loans. Finally, the Assembly, with the agreement of the governor, appointed a commission to examine the views of the priests on the best ways to repay the outstanding loans. The governor was authorized to sell [the missions'] assets or rent them.

Pío Pico and Castro managed to convince the Supreme Government that the Californios were loyal to it and that in the future peace would be maintained and it would be obeyed. In view of this, the Supreme Government accepted the situation and formally named both of them as the two superior leaders of the department. Around this time, Don José María Híjar, the same one who had served as Director of Colonization in 1834, arrived [in California] as commissioner of the Supreme Government but I do not know the objectives of his commission. I heard that he died in Los Angeles.

Relations between Castro and Pico were not cordial at all. The first one largely refused to recognize the authority of the second one. Jealousy between the two and among their supporters was very great. Hatred between the inhabitants of the north and the south grew day by day and it threatened to create a split that would have brought ruin to the country. Hatred towards the Mexicans of the rest of the republic also became more and more intense. Hence, the Mexicans could barely feel that their lives and their properties were safe. They were mistreated and robbed with impunity.

By that time there was a large immigration from the United States across the [Great] plains. This was a violation of Mexican laws that prohibited the entry of foreigners to the country without passports. In the region of Sacramento, near Fort Sutter, there was a large concentration of emigrants, and none had legal documents.

Castro, with Mariano Vallejo, rushed there, and boasting of his authority and power, allowed the foreigners to stay under the condition that once the harshness of winter had dissipated they would have to leave the country or legalize their residency. He named Juan A. Sutter district commander, and he already was performing the duty of justice of the peace.

Close to the end of 1845 or at the beginning of 1846, Captain Juan C. Frémont, a member of the U.S. Army, presented himself in Monterey with a very small escort. It was said that he wanted permission from the government to explore California. Frémont illegally entered the country with a military force.

El Gobo. le contestó que no habría inconvente. en concederle ese permiso a él con alg. sirvientes, pero no con una fuerza armada. Creo que se le exigió que hiciese salir a su fuerza del territorio inmediatamte. Frémont salió molesto de Monterey, se reunió con su fuerza que se decía ser de unos 70 hombres, entre blancos e indios Walla-Walla, y a pocos días se supo en Monterey que estaba acampado en el cerro del Gavilán, y que ondeaba sobre su campamento la bandera Americana. Esto naturalmente produjo grande conmoción, por considerarse un acto de cuasi-invasión del país, o un desconocto. de la supremacía de México.

El Comandte. Gen. Castro, el Prefecto Manuel Castro, Alvarado, Franco. Rico y muchos otros hombres prominentes se apresuraron a organizar una fuerza respetable pa. ir a castigar la insolencia de Frémont. Primeramente mandaron esploradores para descubrir la manera cómo estaba el gefe invasor, quiénes informaron que estaba fortificado con trincheras ta. en una parte difícil de atacar. Los Castros y la fuerza llegaron a San Juan, y dejaron correr el tiempo.

Supo Frémont de la fuerza formidable que se le venía encima, (más de 300 hombres) levantó su campo y se retiró como en dirección pa. el Oregón. Se supo más tarde que Frémont obtuvo ese aviso de boca de Capistrano López, uno de los esploradores que habían sido enviados pa. averiguar cómo estaba situado. Se dijo también que el mismo López confesó haber recibido de Frémont 6 onzas mexicanas ($96) de gratifn.

Frémont siguió su marcha; no sé si llegó al Oregón o no. Más tarde del mismo año de 1846 se presentó en el Sacramento, y se le llamó a ponerse al frente del movimto. de independencia de Cal. que habían inaugurado varios estrangeros.

Una fuerza de aventureros cayó sobre Sonoma y se apoderó de la plaza sin resistencia. Tomaron prisioneros al Coronel Mariano G. Vallejo, al Capn. Salvador Vallejo, al Tente. Coronel Víctor Pradón, y al cuñado de los Vallejos, Amo. de nacimto., Jacob P. Leese. Esa fuerza llevaba una bandera en que estaba pintado un oso (mirado en California como enemigo mortal. Esa bandera del oso inspiró muchos temores sobre los planes de los que la ondeaban) con una estrella y unas fajas rojas, según me esplicaron. Yo nunca la vi.

Después supieron que venían contra ellos una fuerza de tropa, la que mandaba el Capn. Joaqn. de la Torre. Le atacaron, hubo muertos y heridos

The governor responded that there were no objections to granting permission to him and some of his servants but not to an armed force; I believe that it was demanded that he withdraw his force from the territory immediately. An annoyed Frémont left Monterey and gathered his force, which was said to be made up of some seventy men, including white men and Walla Walla Indians. In a few days, the people of Monterey learned that he was camped at Mount Gavilán and that an American flag was flying over the camp. This naturally caused a great commotion since this act was considered a quasi-invasion of the country or the non-recognition of México's supremacy [over the territory].

Commander General Castro, Prefect Manuel Castro, Alvarado, Francisco Rico, and many other prominent men set out to quickly organize a respectable force to go and punish Frémont's insolence. First, scouts were sent to reconnoiter the condition of the invader and they reported that he had fortified himself with trenches at a location that would be difficult to attack. The Castros and their force reached San Juan and allowed time to pass.

Frémont became aware of the formidable force that was coming against him (more than 300 men), picked up his camp and retreated in the direction of Oregon. It was discovered later that Frémont had been warned by Capistrano López, one of the scouts who had been sent to investigate his [group's military preparedness]. It was said that the very same López confessed to having received from Frémont six Mexican ounces (ninety-six pesos) in recompense.

Frémont continued his march and I do not know if he reached Oregon or not. Later in the same year of 1846, he presented himself in Sacramento, and he was called to lead the independence movement of California that had been initiated by various foreigners.

One force of the adventurers arrived in Sonoma and took possession of the plaza without encountering any resistance. They took as prisoners Colonel Mariano G. Vallejo, Captain Salvador Vallejo, Lieutenant Colonel Víctor Pradón, and the brother-in-law of the Vallejos, the American by birth, Jacob P. Leese. This force had a flag with a bear painted on it (since the bear was seen in California as a mortal enemy, the bear flag inspired much fear about the plans of those who flew it) with a star and some red stripes, as it was explained to me. I never saw it.

After they found out that troops were coming against them, headed by Joaquín de la Torre, they attacked them. There were deaths and wounded on

de la parte de la Torre, entre los muertos el Alfz. Cantúa. Torre logró apoderarse de una lancha en el Sauzalito, y en ella se escapó con su gente pa. San Pablo. Antes del encuentro con la Torre ya los estrangeros le habían quitado al Tente. Franco. Arce toda la caballada que venía custodiando.

Los estrangeros encontraron por San Rafael a los jóvenes gemelos Haro y al anciano José de los Reyes Berreyessa, y les dieron muerte. Los Haros habían ido allí a llevar órdenes al Capn. de la Torre, y Berreyessa en busca de unos hijos suyos, temerosos de que éstos hubiesen tomado parte en los sucesos ocurridos en que una partida al mando de un tal Padilla había asesinado a unos Americanos, con crueldades inauditas. Segn. me dijeron unos, fueron muertos los tres por suponérseles espías, y otros que fue por venganza, por el asesinato de aquellos estrangeros. Sea lo que fuere aquellas escenas de una y otra parte fueron demasiado tristes para relatarse con calma aún después del largo tiempo transcurrido. Lo que sí no se puede negar es que esos actos no hicieron honor ni a unos ni a otros de los autores, porque con ellos se violaron las leyes divinas y humanas, y se pisotearon los principios de la civilizn.

Siguieron las cosas en ese estado alarmante hasta que en Julio de 1846 el Comodoro Amo. Sloat tomó posesión de Monterey y de toda la Califa. a nombre de su gobo., y en virtud del estado de guerra en que se hallaban Méx. y los Estados Unidos. La toma de Mont. fue seguida inmediatamte. por la del puerto de Yerbabuena por el Capn. Montgomery, quien enarboló su bandera en la plaza. Sucedió en seguida en el mando de la escuadra Ama. el Comodoro Stockton, quien se tituló Gobr. militar de Cal.

Cuando estos sucesos se venían sucediendo el Comandte. Gen. Castro corrió pa. el Sur con su fuerza, y Pío Pico que recelaba de sus intenciones se salió al encuentro con otra fuerza armada; pero no hubo hecho de armas porqe. Manuel Castro tranquilizó a Pico, haciéndole saber la verdadera situación en el Norte, y la necesidad de trabajar de consuno las dos autoridades superiores y todos en defensa del país.

Se abrazaron ambos gefes, pero a pesar de las palabras melosas de uno y otro, no hubo cordialidad, ni espíritu patriótico, ni inteligencia, ni pericia militar, ni nada. Esas malas cualidades de los gefes descorazonaban a los subalternos, a la tropa y al pueblo, faltaron los recursos, que sólo con la unión

de la Torre's side; among the dead was Second Lieutenant Cantúa. De la Torre managed to take possession of a launch in Sausalito, and he escaped in it, with his soldiers, to San Pablo. Before the encounter with de la Torre, the foreigners had already taken from Lieutenant Francisco Arce the entire horse herd that he had been guarding.

The foreigners found the Haro twin brothers and the old man José de los Reyes Berreyessa around San Rafael, and they killed them. The Haro brothers had gone there to deliver orders to Captain de la Torre. Berreyessa had gone in search of some of his sons, fearful that they had gotten involved in the events in which a party at the command of someone by the name of Padilla had killed some Americans, with unspeakable cruelty. As I was told by some, the three were killed because they were suspected of being spies, and by others that they were killed to avenge the assassination of the foreigners. Regardless of the causes, the actions by one side or the other are too sad to narrate with calmness even after so much time has transpired. What cannot be denied is that those actions did not bring much honor to one or the other responsible groups because with these [actions] they violated divine and human laws and they trampled the principles of civilization.

This situation continued in its alarming state until July 1846 when the American Commodore [John Drake] Sloat took possession of Monterey and the rest of California in the name of his government and because México and the United States were in a state of war. The occupation of Monterey was followed immediately by the taking of the port of Yerba Buena by Captain [John Berrien] Montgomery, who planted his flag at the plaza. Commodore [Robert Field] Stockton, who had just assumed command of the American Squadron, declared himself military governor of California.

As these events were taking place, Commander General Castro fled to the south with his troops, and Pío Pico, who distrusted his intentions, went out to confront him with another armed force. A clash did not take place because Manuel Castro calmed Pico down, convincing him of the real situation up north and of the necessity of having the two superior authorities and everyone else working together in defense of the nation.

Both leaders embraced each other, but in spite of each other's sweet words, there was no cordiality, patriotic spirit, intelligence, or military expertise— nothing at all. These bad qualities of the leaders disheartened their subordinates, the troops, and the people. With a shortage of funds, only unity

y el patriotismo se hubieran tal vez allegado muchos pa. defender la patria como hombres de honor, o morir en la pelea. Pero nada. En cuanto supieron que venía Frémont con una fuerza considerable, Castro mandó desbandar su fuerza. Pico hizo otro tanto, y cada uno de ellos se fugó de su deber bajo pretestos ridículos de ir en busca de ausilios que sabían muy bien no iban a conseguir (México no los tenía pa. si, por las mismas causas que he detallado arriba.). El uno se huyó por la vía de Sonora y el otro por la de la Baja Califa.[33] Se dio por muy válido en toda la California que Pico se llevó $22,000 en efectivo que produjo la venta de algs. bienes de misiones, y que nunca dio cuenta de esos fondos. Sobre este punto, sería bueno preguntarle.[34]

Quedó todo el país en pacífica posesión de la Unión Americana, hasta que en 1847, por motivos que no conozco, hubo una sublevación en el Sur que puso a su cabeza al Capn. Dn. José Ma. Flores.[35] Sobre la marcha vinieron para el Norte Franco. Rico, Manuel Castro, José Anto. Chávez y otros con la mira de dar un golpe de mano, y apoderarse de algunos prisioneros, y de la caballada que tenía la fuerza apostada por Frémont en San Juan Bautista.

En el camino Chávez con algunos hombres cayó sobre el rancho de Los Vergeles de Dn. Joaqn. Gómez, en donde sabían que estaba pasando la noche el Consul Amo. en Monterey Dn. Tomas O. Larkin. Hallaron a Larkin dormido y le hicieron prisionero. Después de esto, que hasta cierto punto desbarató el plan de los Californios de dar un golpe de mano antes que los Americanos supieran de su presencia en el Norte, tuvieron los Californios y Americanos un encuentro o dos en La Natividad, con muertos y heridos de una y otra parte. Los Americanos se quedaron dueños del campo, y los otros se fueron pa. el Sur, (segn. dijeron, por no tener ya municiones) llevándose al prisionero Larkin. En ese combate murieron los Capitanes Ams. Burroughs y Foster y otros, por parte de los Mexicanos varios, quedando entre los malheridos el José Anto. Chávez, y Juan Igno. Cantúa.

---

[33]Amador no fue el único que consideró a Pío Pico y a José Castro como cobardes. Rosaura Sánchez dice que en los testimonios de Mariano Guadalupe Vallejo, Estevan de la Torre, y Narciso Botello, fueron juzgados como individuos que no tuvieron la valentía para defender su patria de la invasión norteamericana.

[34]Amador le tenía tanto desprecio a Pico que le pidió a Thomas Savage que si él tuviera la oportunidad de entrevistarlo para el proyecto histórico de Bancroft que le preguntara qué había hecho con el dinero que se había llevado.

[35]Beebe y Senkewicz, 324. Los escritores indican que José María Flores llegó a California en 1842 como secretario del gobernador Manuel Micheltoena. Después de dirigir la resistencia en contra de la invasión norteamericana de California, Flores regresó a México en 1847. Flores se integró al ejército mexicano y eventualmente logró alcanzar el rango de general.

and patriotism could possibly have brought many people together as men of honor to defend the motherland or die in the battlefield. But nothing happened. As soon as it was found out that Frémont, with sizeable force, was coming, Castro gave orders to disband his troops. Pico did the same. Each one of them abandoned their duties under the ridiculous pretext that they were going to go get help when they knew very well that they were not going to get it. (México did not have it for itself for the same reasons that I have stated above.) One fled by way of Sonora and the other through Baja California.[33] It was well-known throughout California that Pico took 22,000 pesos in cash that came out of the sale of some mission assets and he never gave an account of those funds. It would be good to ask him about this point.[34]

The entire country came into the peaceful possession of the American Union until 1847, when for reasons that I don't know, there was a rebellion in the south that was led by Captain José María Flores.[35] Francisco Rico, Manuel Castro, José Antonio Chávez, and others marched north with the goal of giving a surprise attack, taking some prisoners as well as the horse herd that Frémont's forces were keeping in San Juan Bautista.

On the way, Chávez, with some of his men, came to the Los Vergeles Ranch of Don Joaquín Gómez, where they knew that the American Consul in Monterey was spending the night. They found [Thomas Oliver] Larkin asleep and they took him prisoner. This action, to a certain extent, ruined the Californios' plan to deliver a severe blow to the Americans before their presence was discovered in the north. There were one or two encounters between the Californios and the Americans in La Natividad, with deaths and wounded on both sides. The Americans won the battle and the others left for the south (according to them, they did so because they ran out of ammunition), taking with them the prisoner Larkin. In this battle, the American Captains Burroughs and Foster died as well as others, and on the side of the Mexicans, [there were] various [casualties]; among the badly wounded were José Antonio Chávez and Juan Ignacio Cantúa.

---

[33]Amador was not the only person to consider Pío Pico and José Castro cowardly. Rosaura Sánchez notes that the **testimonios** of Mariano Guadalupe Vallejo, Estevan de la Torre, and Narciso Botello portray them as individuals who lacked the courage to fight the U.S. invasion of their homeland.

[34]Amador has so much contempt for Pico that he hoped that if Savage ever got a chance to take his narrative for the Bancroft history project that he should ask him what happened to the money.

[35]José María Flores came to California in 1842 as the secretary of Governor Manuel Micheltorena (Beebe and Senkewicz, 324). After leading the resistance to the U.S. invasion of southern California, Flores returned to México in 1847. He remained in the Mexican army and eventually attained the rank of general.

Ya en la parte del norte no hubo más acciones de guerra, en el Sur sí. Los Californios recobraron Los Angeles y San Diego para volverlos a perder. Hubo varios combates entre los más notables el de Sn. Pascual y el de San Gabriel, pero los Americanos al mando de Stockton y Kearney se apoderaron de Los Angeles. Los Californios que habían estado a las órdenes de Flores se vieron abandonados por su gefe, quien también se huyó pa. México. Frémont, que venía con un batallón a unirse con Stockton, recibió proposiciones de rendición. Frémont concedió condiciones honorosas a todos y garantías para los Californios, y así terminó esa campaña que fue el últo. esfuerzo en favor de nuestra unión con México.

Concluída la guerra de los Estados Unidos con México en el tratado que celebraron sus plenipotenciarios quedó esta California cedida a los Estados Unidos, mediante unos cuantos millones de pesos que éstos le pagaron.

Pero durante el tiempo de las campañas las tropas Americanas se apoderaban de las caballadas, sillas, frenos, armas y cuanto más fuese útil pa. la guerra, de los ranchos, quedando algunos desprovistos hasta de las bestias más precisas pa. su servicio, y de armas para defenderse de los indios. A mí me quitaron de una vez de mi rancho de San Ramón, 60 bestias, pero no me quitaron ni armas ni ninga. otra cosa. Mandé a donde Frémont a reclamar mis caballos o su valor, y me mandó a decir con el enviado que me los pagaría con una onza de plomo que llevaba cada rifle de su tropa.[36]

En otra ocasión, pocos días después, vino Sutter a mi rancho y se llevó otras 20 bestias que había yo comprado con dinero para los trabajos de mi finca.

Después de esa, vino una partida de 50 Americanos, entraron a mi casa, registraron el banco de armas en que tenía yo 20 y tantas entre rifles y fusiles, un cajón de cartuchos. Revisaron todas las armas, y las pusieron en su lugar otra vez sin quitarme ni una siquiera. Me preguntaron si tenía carne seca, les bajé dos tercios, y les puse leña pa. cocinarla. No aceptaron ésta. Se comieron cruda la carne que estaba muy buena; se llevaron un poco cada uno. En seguida me preguntó el Capn. cuánto era el valor de la carne, y yo le contesté que nada, que la daba de obsequio.

---

[36]Margaret Mollins y Virginia E. Thickens, eds, *Ramblings in California: The Adventures of Henry Cerruti* (Berkeley: Friends of the Bancroft Library, 1954), 129. En su autobiografía, Cerruti recuerda una entrevista que él condujo con la viuda de Feliciano Soberanes en cual ella declara que los soldados de Frémont eran solamente un poco mejor que aquellos que el general Manuel Micheltorena había traído con él a su llegada a California. Ella declaró que la pequeña banda de Frémont "se portaron mal y se robaron todo lo que pudieron agarrar con sus manos."

In the northern part [of the territory] there would no longer be any more military conflicts, but there were some in the south. The Californios retook Los Angeles and San Diego only to lose them again. There were various battles; among the most notable were the ones at San Pascual and San Gabriel. Yet the Americans under the command of [Robert Field] Stockton and [Stephen] Kearney took possession of Los Angeles. The Californios who had fought along with Flores were abandoned by their leader, who also fled to México. Frémont, who was coming with a battalion to reinforce Stockton, received offers of surrender. Frémont granted honorable concessions to everyone and guarantees for the Californios and this is how the campaign ended, which was the last attempt in our efforts to retain our union with México.

The United States' war with México concluded with a treaty that their plenipotentiaries signed and California was ceded to the United States, by means of several million pesos that [the United States] paid it [México].

During the military campaigns, the American troops confiscated from the ranches the horse herds, saddles, bridles, weapons, and whatever equipment was useful for war, leaving some of them lacking even the livestock that was vital for their maintenance or the weapons to defend themselves against Indians. One time, they took sixty animals from my San Ramón Ranch, but they did not take my weapons or anything else. I sent Frémont a claim for my horses or their proper monetary compensation and he sent word through the messenger that he would pay it with an ounce of lead from each gun of his troops.[36]

On another occasion, a few days later, Sutter came to my ranch and took twenty horses that I had bought with money from the work of my ranch. Later, a party of fifty Americans came and entered my house and examined the armory that I had, where I kept about twenty guns and rifles and a box of ammunition. They checked all the weapons and they put them back in their place without them again taking a single one. They asked me if I had dried meat; I brought them two **tercios** and I lit a fire to cook it. They did not accept the cooked meat. They ate the meat raw; it was very good. Each one took a little of it. Afterwards, the captain asked me the cost of the meat, and I answered that it was nothing, that I gave it to them as a gift.

---

[36]Margaret Mollins and Virginia E. Thickens, eds. *Ramblings in California: The Adventures of Henry Cerruti* (Berkeley: Friends of the Bancroft Library, 1954), 129. In his autobiography, Cerruti recounts an interview that he conducted with the widow of Feliciano Soberanes in which she states that Frémont's soldiers were only a little better than those that Governor Micheltorena had brought with him at his arrival in California. She said that Frémont's small band "behaved badly and stole everything they could lay their hands upon."

Tenía yo en el corral ocho o 10 bestias encerradas, agenas y mías, entre ellas había dos mulas y un caballo tordillo que eran de mi propiedad. Un sargento me abocó el rifle pa. quitarme las mulas y el caballo (este era bonito y me había costado $80, el único que tenía), pero el Capn. se lo impedió. Ordenó a un soldado que me sacara los 3 animales, entonces cogieron los otros caballos del corral y se los llevaron. Esos caballos no eran míos. Lo que es cierto es que yo no perdí esa vez nada, ni el valor de una aguja.

Esa partida fue para el Monte del Diablo, y allí sacaron de los ranchos cuanto encontraron de algún valor. En los caminos, a los que encontraban montados, les quitaban los caballos y las monturas.

En el pueblo de San José me acusaban mis paisanos de ser adicto a los Americanos, porqe. éstos no me quitaban mis bestias, ni armas ta.

Estas cosas sucedían cuando Francisco Sánchez se levantó con unos 100 hombres en Sta. Clara; hubo sus escaramuzas, pero por la mediación de Santiago Alex. Forbes, Vice Consul inglés, los Californios se rindieron y entregaron los prisioneros que habían hecho, bajo la garantía de no sucederles nada.[37]

Yo fui un día a San José y Charles Weber me dijo que metiera mi caballo en su casa pa. que nadie me lo tocara. A esto el Comandte. de las tropas ams. que estaban allí (como 500 hombres) haciendo ejercicio, le dijo a Weber que no era necesario, que quedara mi caballo afuera amarrado a un poste, con mis espuelas a la cabeza del fuste.

Entró a la casa de Weber y estendió un documento en que decía que nadie me estobarse el paso ni me molestase en nada, presentando ese salvo conducto. Así fue que nunca se me molestó por las partidas que andaban por los caminos, y por esto mis paisanos decían que yo estaba americanado. El secreto de todo esto es que las autoridades Americanas sabían bien que yo era hombre pacífico que no me metía en conspiraciones ni trácalas. Todos me miraban con respeto, desde el gefe al soldado.

---

[37]Beebe y Senkewicz, 336. Los escritores escriben que Francisco Sánchez era hijo del famoso combatiente de indios José Antonio Sánchez. Francisco fue soldado en la compañía de San Francisco desde 1824. Para 1846, él era el comandante interino en ese presidio, y en enero de 1847, él comandó las fuerzas mexicanas en Santa Clara durante una escaramuza con los norteamericanos. Después de la ocupación estadounidense de California, Francisco fue electo a la mesa de supervisores de San Francisco.

In the corral, I had eight to ten animals. Some of them were mine, but some belonged to others; among them were two mules and a dapple-gray horse that were my property. A sergeant pointed his rifle at me to take away the two mules and the horse, which was beautiful and cost me eighty pesos (it was the only one that I had), but the captain stopped him. He ordered a soldier to separate the three horses for me and then took out the rest of the horses from the corral and left with them. Those horses did not belong to me. The truth is that I did not lose anything that time, not even the value of a needle.

The party headed for Mount Diablo and there they stole from the ranches whatever of value they could find. On the roads, they took the horses and saddles from those they found riding.

In San José, my countrymen accused me of sympathizing with the Americans because they [Americans] did not take away either my animals or my weapons.

These things were taking place when Francisco Sánchez, with 100 men, rebelled in Santa Clara.[37] There were several skirmishes but through the mediation of Santiago Alex Forbes, the British Vice-consul, the Californios surrendered. They released the prisoners that they had taken and were given the guarantee that nothing would happen to them.

I went one day to San José and Charles Weber told me to put my horse inside his house so that no one would take it. The commander of the American troops (about 500 men) that were drilling there, told Weber that it was not necessary, that my horse could stay outside tied to a post, with my spurs on the head of the saddle.

He went inside Weber's house and issued me a document that stated that no one should impede my movement or bother me in any way when I presented this letter of safe-conduct. This is why the parties that roamed the roads never bothered me, and for this reason my countrymen said that I was Americanized. The secret of all this is that the American authorities knew very well that I was a man of peace who did not get involved in conspiracies or schemes. Everyone looked at me with respect, from the commander to soldier.

---

[37]Beebe and Senkewicz (336) note that Francisco Sánchez was the son of the famous Indian fighter José Antonio Sánchez. Francisco was a soldier at the San Francisco company starting in 1824. In 1846, he was acting commander there and led the Mexican forces at Santa Clara during the skirmish with the Anglo-Americans in January 1847. After the U.S. occupation of California, Francisco was elected to the San Francisco Board of Supervisors.

Lo único que siento es que nunca se me han pagado las 60 bestias que me quitaron primero. El Capn. Weber ofreció pagármelas a cuatro y cinco pesos cada una, pero yo le respondí que prefería perder el valor de todas a someterme a eso, porque esas bestias me habían costado desde 50$ hasta 100$ cada una. Porque es de advertir que yo había tenido de mucho tiempo atrás la costumbre de que cuando alguno pasaba por mi casa montado en un caballo que me llamaba la atención por sus buenas cualidades (era ramo que yo entendía porque había andado a caballo, desde que empecé a pararme desde niño) proponía al dueño comprárselo si me lo quería vender. Hacíamos nuestro trato y yo le pagaba el precio estipulado, además de darle otro caballo ordinario pa. que siguiese su viage. Pero el caballo que me había llenado el ojo no salía de allí, sino que iba pa. mi corral. Así me había yo hecho de esa caballada escogida y valiosa, por la que me ofrecía Weber 4 y 5$, como acostumbraban pagarles a los borrachitos, y a los ladroncitos que vendían caballos agenos.[38]

Ya quedó California bajo la bandera de las estrellas.

En 1848 se descubrió el oro en el molino de Sutter en el Sacramento. Como 8 días después salimos de mi rancho un francés llamado Sansevain y yo para aquella localidad. Llegamos a Sutters Fort como a las 8 de la noche y encontramos a Sutter bastante ebrio; sin embargo, nos recibió bien y nos dio bastante cena y licor de buena calidad. Después de cenar seguimos nuestro viage hasta el molino que había como 25 leguas. Creo que fue esto por Mayo o Junio. Llegamos allá casi al amanecer, y entre las piedras dormimos un ratito. En la mañana fuimos a almorzar a casa de unos estrangeros, a quienes les pedimos el almuerzo y que nos lo sirvieron. Después del refrigerío pasamos el río Americano, en donde trabajaba el molino de aserrar. Tomamos nuestras bandejas y nos pusimos a sacar oro, en cada bandejada sacábamos de seis reales a un peso de oro. Después fuimos río abajo del Sacramento, en donde había un campamento de "Mormones." Allí sacaban de cada dos paladas una onza de oro, cuando menos 10$. Entonces yo le dije a Sansevain, "esto es como el que viene a robar, vámonos, y volveremos."

---

[38] Aparte de Amador, Antonio Berreyessa, hermano de José de los Reyes Berreyessa, quien fue asesinado junto a los hermamos Haro por norteamericanos, relató que Weber también le robó caballos a él y a otros Californios. Rosaura Sánchez menciona que en el testimonio de Berreyessa, él reporta la pérdida de 35 a 40 caballos durante una incursión de Weber a su rancho al igual que a otros (295).

My only resentment is that I have never been paid for the first sixty animals that were taken from me. Captain Weber offered to pay for them at four or five pesos each, but I told him that I would rather lose the entire value rather than to accept it [this ridiculous amount] because these animals had cost me from fifty to 100 pesos each. It should be noted that for a long time I had had the habit that whenever someone passed by my house riding a horse that got my attention for its good qualities, I would offer to buy it from him if he was willing to sell it. (This was an area that I knew well since I have been riding horses from the time I started walking as a boy.) We would make the deal and I would pay the agreed upon price and, in addition, I would give him an ordinary horse so that he could continue his journey. The horse that caught my eyes did not leave anywhere but to my corral. This is how I managed to have such a carefully selected and valuable herd of horses, for which Weber offered four to five pesos, as was the custom to pay the **borrachitos** and the **ladroncitos** that sold stolen horses.[38]

California was now under the flag of the stars.

In 1848, gold was discovered at Sutter's mill on the Sacramento [River]. Eight days later, I and a Frenchman called Sansevain left my ranch for that location. We reached Sutter's Fort around eight o'clock at night and we found Sutter extremely drunk; he, nevertheless, received us very well and gave us a large dinner and good quality liquor. After dinner, we continued our journey to the mill that was about twenty-five leagues away. I believe this was around May or June. We got there almost at dawn and we slept a short while in between the rocks. In the morning, we went to have breakfast at the house of some foreigners; we asked them for breakfast and they served us. After the light repast, we went to the American River where there was an operating lumber mill. We got our pans and started taking out gold and, in each panning, we would remove from six **reales** to one peso worth of gold. Then, we went downstream on the Sacramento, where there was a Mormon camp. There, from every two shovelfuls, an ounce of gold was taken, that is, at least ten pesos [worth]. I then told Sansevain: "This is like coming to steal, let's go [home] and we shall return."

---

[38]In addition to Amador, Antonio Berreyessa, the brother of José de los Reyes Berreyessa, who was killed by Americans along with the two Haro brothers, stated that Weber also stole horses from him and other Californios. Rosaura Sánchez writes that in his **testimonio**, Antonio reported the loss of 35 to 40 horses during a Weber raid on his ranch and others (295).

Efectivamente nos volvimos a Sutter's Fort [sic], y en la tarde nos despedimos de él, y vinimos a amanecer al estrecho de Carquinez. Ocho días después estábamos de vuelta, pasamos el río de San Joaqn. en balsas con los víveres y animales que llevábamos. Había harina de trigo, pinole de trigo y de maíz, carne seca, frijol, garbanzo, lenteja, y 16 reses en pie. Esto era por mi cuenta. Conmigo iban además 10 indios de mi servicio ganándose 1$ diario. Me acompañaban Sansevain y Antonio Suñol que también llevaban sus pacotillas y 10 indios entre los dos. Llegamos al campamento de los Mormones. A Sansevain y Suñol no les gustó la localidad por escabrosa, y seguimos al molino de Sutter. Allí supimos del placer seco.

Ellos se fueron allá y yo me quedé en el río con una canoa de como 4 varas, que la compré allí en 10$. Volteando peñascos de los que el río arrojaba fuera en sus crecientes, barríamos la arena con escobas de ramas y la echábamos en la canoa, con el agua al pescuezo, y en la tarde pesaba el oro que habíamos sacado una libra más o menos. Esto era cosa diaria. Todo el oro que saqué allí lo vendí a 18$ onza por plata acuñada. Era oro muy fino y muy limpio revuelto con platina.

Me escribieron Suñol y Sansevain que fuera a donde estaban ellos a descubrir. Me fui para allá al 3er. día con mis víveres, indios y ganado. Esploté aquella tierra. Me puse a trabajar en compa. con ellos, mis indios ganando un peso diario. Sacábamos oro diariamte. de siete a nueve libras en compa. hasta que llegó Rosignon con una partida de aguardiente y vinos.

Se vendía el vino a 10$ botella, el aguarte. a 15$, una frazada ordinaria a 20$, las piezas de indiana a 30$. Mis víveres y reses los vendí a los precios siguientes: las reses a 150$ cada una; pinole de trigo y maíz revuelto me lo arrebataban de las manos a 10$ el almud, o sea 120$ fanega; carne seca 5$ arroba, no era muy apetecida; frijol, garbanzo, lenteja, 10$ almud, sin repugnancia ninguna.

Vendí todo. A los 14 días me contaban los asociados que andaban ladrones por allí, y dispusieron mis tres compañeros venirse. Hicimos la cuenta de lo que nos tocaba a cada uno, me tocaron $13,500. Los entregué a Suñol para que los entregase a mi esposa si no naufragaban en la lancha.

In effect, we went back to Sutter's Fort, and in the evening, we said farewell to him [Sutter], and by dawn we were at the Carquinez Strait. Eight days later, we were on our way back [to the gold fields]; we crossed the San Joaquín River on rafts with our supplies and the animals we were taking. We had wheat flour, **pinole** of wheat and corn, dried meat, beans, garbanzo beans, lentils, and sixteen head of live cattle. This was only my list. I had with me ten Indians in my service who were earning one peso daily. Accompanying me were Sansevain and Antonio Suñol who also were carrying their own goods and together had ten Indians [in their service]. We arrived at the Mormons' camp. Sansevain and Suñol did not like the place because of its ruggedness and we continued to Sutter's mill. There, we discovered dry panning.

They [Amador's companions] went there and I stayed on the river with a canoe that was four **varas** long; I bought it there for ten pesos. In water up to our necks, we would turn the large boulders that had been pushed to the sides by the river's currents, and we would sweep the sand with brush brooms and we would put it in the canoe. In the evening, I would weigh the gold we had taken out, a pound more or less. This was a daily occurrence. All the gold that I took from there I sold for eighteen pesos an ounce in silver coins. The gold was of very fine quality, very clean, and mixed with platinum.

Suñol and Sansevain wrote me and invited me to go where they were searching [for gold]. On the third day, I went there with my supplies, Indians, and cattle. I worked that terrain. I started working in partnership with them; my Indians earned one peso daily. We would take out gold daily, from seven to nine pounds in partnership until Rosignon arrived with a supply of **aguardiente** and wines.

Wine would sell for ten pesos a bottle, **aguardiente** for fifteen pesos, an ordinary common blanket for twenty pesos, and Indiana cloth [printed calico] for thirty pesos a piece. I sold my supplies and cattle at the following prices: cattle at 150 pesos per head; mixed wheat and corn **pinole** would be grabbed from my hands at ten pesos the **almud** or 120 pesos the **fanega**, dried meat at five pesos an **arroba**, it was not very appetizing; the beans, garbanzo, and lentils at ten pesos the **almud** with no complaints by anyone.

I sold everything. By the fourteenth day, my associates told me that robbers were roaming around and my three partners decided to leave. We made an accounting of each one's share; my part amounted to 13,500 pesos. I gave the money to Suñol so that he could give it to my wife, if he did not become shipwrecked on the boat.

Otro dineros llegaron a San Francisco; con él se embarcó Rossignon pa. Lima pa. emplearlo, el mío como el de ellos, sin mi permiso. Yo me quedé en los placeres con mi hijo Valentín que ya se había reunido conmigo. Trabajamos unos dos meses; mis indios me abandonaron. Quedamos mi hijo y yo, y otros trabajando cada uno por su cuenta, en el campo de Amador, en el Condado de mi nombre, donde todos los días sacaba como 22 onzas. Cuando salí del placer pa. mi casa me traje 12,000$ en oro limpio. Llegué a mi casa, y pasé al pueblo a buscar mi otro dinero. Me encontré con que lo habían despachado pa. Lima. Al tiempo me pagaron $1001, hasta ahora me deben el resto. Se llevó el diablo a Rossignon y nadie me ha pagado.

Volví como 3 meses después al mismo placer con 300 reses (novillos y vacas) a medias con José Suñol (hijo de Antonio). Las vendí a 100$, a 80$ y a 70$ cada una. Cuando acabé de vender entregué el producido a José Suñol, tanto lo mío como lo de él. Era un joven muy honrado. Me fui al campo de Amador otra vez, trabajé allí 2 meses en compañía de uno de la Baja Cal, repartiéndonos cada tarde nuestra parte. Reunimos 10,000$ cada uno y nos vinimos para mi rancho. Me vine porque mi muger me mandó decir que se hallaba enferma. Ya no volví más a los placeres.

Other monies reached San Francisco with Rosignon; however, he sailed to Lima [Peru] to invest my money, as well as theirs, without my permission. I stayed working in the placers with my son Valentín who had just joined me. We worked for some two months; my Indians abandoned me. My son, myself, and others remained working, each one on his own at Amador's Camp, in the county that bears my name. Each day I would take out some twenty-two ounces. When I left the placers for my house, I brought 12,000 pesos in pure gold. I arrived at my house and then went to town to get my other money. I found that it had been dispatched to Lima. In time, I was paid 1,101 pesos; to this very day they still owe me the rest. The devil has taken Rossignon, and no one has paid me.

Three months later, I went back to the same placer with 300 head of cattle (heifers and cows) in partnership with Jose Suñol (son of Antonio). I sold them at 100, 80, and 70 pesos each. When I finished selling, I gave the earnings to José Suñol, mine as well as his; he was a very honest young man. I went to Amador's Camp once again. For two months I worked in partnership with someone from Baja California; each evening we would split our shares. We each accumulated 10,000 pesos and we came to my ranch. I came because my wife wrote me that she was sick. I did not go back to the placers again.

CAPÍTULO 4

OTRAS REMEMBRANZAS DE DON JOSÉ MARÍA AMADOR

Anoche se me vino a la memoria una ocurrencia que sucedió en el pueblo de San José con el Gobr. Solá.

Estaba de comisionado el Sargto. Luis Peralta. Yo estaba de guardia, pues formaba parte del destacamto.

Llegó de visita procedente de Monterey el Gobr. Solá. El Sargto. Peralta tocó la caja para llamar a toda la gente que viniesen a saludar al Gobr. que los quería ver. Vino toda la gente y Solá les dijo que se alegraba mucho de ver un vecindario tan honrado. Los más viejos pobladores, sea por ignorancia o por reverencia a la persona del Gobr., muchos de ellos se le acercaban y le besaban la mano como si fuera un Padre ministro o sacerdote. Después del saludo general se presentó un anciano llamado José Ramón Bojorques. Éste dijo al Gobr. que su esposa se hallaba embarazada y tenía muchos deseos de conocer a Su Señoría. Adviértase que la señora pasaba de 100 años de edad, el marido tenía de 80 a 90. El Gobr. ordenó a Peralta que nombrara 4 hombres que le acompañasen a la casa de Bojorques. A esto Peralta se reía mucho, pero se tapaba la boca con el pañuelo, y me hacía señas para que yo no me diese por entendido. Fui nombrado entre los 4. El Gobr. no se apercibía de nada. Atravesamos las 500 varas que mediaban a la casa de Bojorques; el viejo iba con nosotros. Entró el Gob. a la casa, y dijo, "¡Alabado sea Dios!" "Por siempre sea," contestó la viejita.

"Pase Ud, Señor Gobr." (La viejita era natural de Guadalajara y bachillera. No se levantó porque sus años no se lo permitían, estaba impedida.) Solá se le acercó, le dio la mano, y la saludó. Entonces ella se escusó de no poderse levantar, diciéndole que estaba impedida, que se sirviera sentarse en uno de los huesos de ballena, porque no tenía sillas mejores. Se sentó Solá junto a ella, y le dijo al viejo, "Señor Bojorques, es Ud. un tunante, grande, grandísimo,

CHAPTER 4

JOSÉ MARÍA AMADOR'S OTHER REMEMBRANCES

Last night I remembered an occurrence that took place in the town of San José with Governor Solá.

Serving as commissioner was Sergeant Luis Peralta. I was performing guard duty since I was part of the detachment.

Governor Solá came from Monterey on a visit. Sergeant Peralta sounded the drums to call all the people to come and greet the governor, who wished to see them. All the people came, and Solá told them that he was very happy to see such an honest town. The oldest dwellers, many of them, either from ignorance or reverence towards the person of the Governor, approached him and they kissed his hand as if he were a Father Minister or a priest. After the general greeting, an old man called José Ramón Bojorques presented himself and told the governor that his wife was pregnant and had a great desire to meet His Excellency. It should be noted that the woman was over 100 years old and the husband was between eighty and ninety years. The governor ordered Peralta to choose four men to accompany him to Bojorques' house. Peralta was laughing a lot at hearing this but he had covered his mouth with his handkerchief and made gestures to me to pretend I did not know what was happening. I was chosen to be one of the four. The governor did not have an inkling of what was going on. We walked five hundred **varas,** which was the distance to the Bojorquez house. The old man accompanied us. The governor entered the house and said, "Praise be to God." "Forever," responded the little old lady.

"Please come in, **Señor Gobernador.**" (The old lady was a native of Guadalajara and was very talkative. She did not get up because her years prevented her; she was disabled.) Solá approached her, gave her his hand, and greeted her. She then excused herself for not being able to get up because she was disabled and asked that he sit himself on one of the whale bones because she did not have better chairs. Solá sat next to her and told the old man: "Mr. Bojorquez, you are sly, a great,

muy gran bicho. ¿no me ha dicho Ud. que la muger está embarazada?" La vieja rompió a reír. El Sargto. Peralta y nosotros nos reíamos a más no poder. La Señora le dijo, "Señor Gobr., no conoce Ud a Ramón, es hombre que no se le puede creer ni cuando habla el Evangelio." El viejo Bojorques no se cortó por eso, sino dijo, "Señor Gobr., yo no le he engañado a Su Señoría, mi muger está embarazada." Solá le reprendió entre loco-serio porque no le había esplicado la clase de embarazo de que su muger adolecía, desde antes de emprender la marcha pa. su casa. Así terminó la visita muy alegre el Gobr. y todos los demás, después le mandó un regalo a la viejita.

* * *

Dije antes que estuve varios años de cabo de la escolta y mayordomo de la misión de San José, que ya había antes de ir estado en la de San Franco. Solano y más tarde [estuve de] mayordomo y administrador de la de San José. De manera que he tenido como 15 años de esperiencia en misiones. Puedo dar informes no sólo de esas dos sino también de la de Sta. Clara en donde dirigí los trabajos alguna que otra vez.

El régimen ordinario de la misión de San José era el siguiente. Se levantaban los indios a las 6 ó las 7 según la estación, almorzaban, pasaban a la iglesia a rezar en su propio idioma por conducto del intérprete. De allí iban a la plaza para hacer la distribn. de los trabajos. Hacía yo las distribuciones pa. abrir valladas, otros al telar, otros a los carpintería; los albañiles a sus obras, y en fin, cada partida a su destino. Yo me iba a ver los trabajos del campo, la agriculta., los vallados ta., que trabajaban por tequio o tarea. A la hora de concluído su tequio se retiraban para descansar.

La misión tenía una casa destinada pa. hacer la comida de la comunidad, en dónde la tomaban los indios a la madrugada pa. almorzar, al medio-día para comer, y a la tarde pa. cenar.

El almuerzo consistía de atole de pinole, de cebada o trigo. La comida y la cena eran lo mismo. Cada sábado se mataban en la misión 100 a 120 reses para abastecer la gente de ración de carne. Los mismos indios las mataban y cuarteaban bajo la dirección del mayordomo, quien repartía las raciones.

very great urchin! Did you not tell me that this woman was pregnant?" The old lady broke out laughing. Sergeant Peralta and the rest of us laughed until we could no longer do so. The woman said, "**Señor Gobernador,** you do not know Ramón, he is a man that no one would believe, even when he says the gospel." Old Bojorquez did not hold back but instead said, "**Señor Gobernador,** I did not deceive Your Excellency, my woman is pregnant." Solá reproached him for being a prankster because he did not explain what kind of impediment his wife was suffering before coming over to his house. This is how the very happy visit of the governor and everyone else ended; afterwards, he sent the little old lady a gift.

* * *

I stated earlier that I had been at Mission San Francisco de Solano before going to Mission San José, and while there, I served for several years as corporal of the guard and as well as the foreman. Later, I became foreman and administrator of Mission San José. In this manner, since I came to have about fifteen years experience in the missions, I can provide information about these two missions as well as the one in Santa Clara, where I occasionally directed several work projects.

The daily routine of Mission San José was the following. The Indians would get up around six or seven o'clock [in the morning] depending on the time of the year. Then they would have breakfast and go to church to pray in their own language; [the prayers] were conducted through an interpreter. From there, they would go to the plaza where they would receive their work assignments. I assigned some of them to build fences, others to the looms, and others went to the carpentry shops. The masons went to their work. In the end, all persons were sent to do their corresponding chores. I would go to inspect the work on the property, the planted fields, and the **vallados**; [this last work] was done by the **tequio** or chore. Whenever they completed their **tequio**, [the workers] would retire to rest.

The mission had designated a house to prepare the food for the community, where the Indians would go to take their breakfast at dawn, their lunch at noontime, and their dinner in the evening.

Breakfast consisted of **atole de pinole** of barley or wheat. Lunch and dinner were the same. Each Saturday, 100 to 120 head of cattle were slaughtered at the mission to provide the people with their meat rations. The Indians themselves would kill them and quarter them under the direction of the foreman, who would distribute the rations.

El vestuario se les daba cada 6 meses, a cada hombre camisa, pantalón, frazada o sarape. A las mugeres, naguas, camisa y frazada. A los niños de uno y otro sexo se les daba también de los mismos artículos.

Las raciones de semilla se repartían cada sábado por la tarde. Además de esa ración iban los indios todos los días a tomar la ración de la pozolera. En Sn. José no conocían el hambre los indios, también estaban bien vestidos.

Los vaqueros recibían sombrero, camisa, pantalón, chaqueta, zapatos y botas.

Los indios trabajaban desde las 8 hasta las 11. Después de la 1 o 1½ hasta 4 o 5 de la tarde. Los que trabajaban por tequio se retiraban cuando lo hubieron concluído. Los que trabajaban de gañanes necesariamte. lo hacían hasta ponerse el sol por cubrir las semillas que estaban tiradas en la tierra. Los del telar, albañiles y carpinteros trabajaban hasta ponerse el sol. En el telar trabajaban por tequio; cada telar tejía 5 frazadas diarias. El que hacía sarapes 1½, de modo es que cada semana entregaban 30 frazadas de cada telar y 9 serapes. Había 5 telares empleados en hacer frazadas que rendían 150 cada semana.

El trato que se daba a los indios era riguroso. No se les perdonaban faltas sino raras veces, o por mucha consideración. Una falta muy leve era castigada con 15 azotes, más grave con 25. El que faltaba al trabajo de dos semanas arriba por andar fuera sin licencia, o por holgazanería, u otra causa no justificada, llevaba 50 azotes. Otras faltas graves, como querellas en las rancherías, golpes, o flechazos, 100 azotes y un par de grillos en la guardia por una o dos semanas en las horas de descanso, sin perjuicio de trabajar en el telar cargando lana o haciendo otras tareas durante las horas de labor del día.

La única instrucción que se les daba a los indios, además de enseñarles a trabajar era la de enseñarles a rezar. En los últimos tiempos, como de 1827 en adelante, se puso un preceptor llamado Antonio Noreña (Mexicano) para enseñarles a leer y escribir.

Muchos de los inditos aprendieron a leer, escribir, y contar un poco. A cierto número se les enseñaba a cantar música de iglesia y a tocar algn. instrumento para que sirviese en la orquesta del templo.

Clothing was given every six months. Each man received a shirt, a pair of pants, and either a blanket or serape. The women would get a skirt, a shirt, and a blanket. Depending on their gender, the children would get the same articles.

Grain rations were distributed every Saturday evening. In addition to this ration, the Indians went every day to eat their **pozole** ration. At Mission San José, the Indians did not know hunger and they were well clothed.

The cowboys received a hat, a shirt, and a pair of pants, jacket, shoes, and boots.

The Indians would work from eight to eleven in the morning, then from one or one thirty until four or five o'clock in the evening. Those who worked on the **tequio** basis would leave as soon as it was completed. Those who worked as **gañanes** necessarily would work until sunset so that they could cover the seeds that had been strewn on the soil. Those from the looms, masons, and carpenters would work until sundown. At the looms, they worked by the **tequio**; each worker would weave five blankets daily. The ones who made the serapes would finish one and a half daily; in this way each week they would deliver thirty blankets and nine serapes from each loom. There were five looms assigned to make blankets and they would produce 150 every week.

The treatment of the Indians was rigorous. Only on rare occasions or after much thought would their transgressions be forgiven. A minor fault was punished with fifteen lashes and a more serious one with twenty-five lashes. Someone who missed work for more than two weeks because he was out of the mission without permission, or because of laziness, or an unjustified cause, would receive fifty lashes. Other serious offenses, such as complaints from the **rancherías** and fist or arrow fights, would be punished with 100 lashes and a pair of shackles at the guardhouse for one to two weeks during hours of rest. [The punishment was carried out] without a disruption of their duties at the looms, carrying the wool, or performing other tasks during the work hours of the day.

In addition to teaching them how to work, the only instruction that was given to the Indians was to teach them to pray. In past times, beginning in 1827, a teacher named Antonio Noreña (a Mexican) was assigned to teach them to read and write.

Many of the Indian children learned to read, write, and to count a little. A group of them was taught to sing church music and to play an instrument in order to play in the Church's orchestra.

Antes de la secularizn. el P. Durán emancipó 4 indios, los únicos que se emanciparon en la misión antes de secularizarse ésta. A esos se les dieron sus tierras, 15 vacas, 5 caballos, y una yunta de bueyes.

* * *

Durante la dominación española, el emancebamiento era mal mirado y castigado con severidad. Todo individuo que se le pillase llevando semejante vida era sentenciado irremisiblemte. a 10 años de presidio con grillos, y enviado, si vivía en San José, a Monterey a sufrir allí su condena. A la muger la tusaban como un caballo, le ponían un muñeco al pecho y la hacían pararse todos los domingos a la hora de misa en la puerta de la iglesia, por espacio de un mes, para que sirviese del ejemplar.

Réstame ocuparme de la vida ordinaria de las diversas clases de nuestras gentes en las épocas de la dominación espa. y mexicana en este país.

* * *

Empezaré detallando la vida diariamte. de los Padres ministros de las misiones.

Desde la fundn. de las misiones se pusieron dos ministros en cada una. Por regla general uno de ellos, que presumo sería el más esperto para el caso, se ocupaba de las temporalidades, y el otro se dedicaba casi esclusivamte. a lo espiritual. Sin perjuicio de que el primero también cumpliese con sus deberes de misionero en bautizar, enterrar, enseñar ta.

Los Padres por lo general tenían una cartilla de agricultura por la que se dirijían para el culto. de las tierras. Para la siembra de trigo nunca usaron los padres la piedra del cardenillo pa. preparar la semilla, sino la batían en agua de lejía, y luego la tiraban a la tierra. Esta era la regla en tiempo de España, y siguió siéndolo después que el país se separó de aquella nación.

Hasta el año de 1828 no tuvieron los P. P. mayordomos, sino de los mismos neófitos sacaban los más hábiles para encargarles de los trabajos agrícolas. Ahora, de los almacenes cuidaban los mismos Padres, atendiendo ellos hasta al corte de la ropa de los indígenas, y a la repartición de alimentos. En aquellos años tenían los P. P. ministros muchísimo más trabajo que después del año 1828. Muy pocas misiones tenían sirvientes de razón, y si acaso lo tenían, era el llavero. Alguna que otra vez ocupaban al cabo, o algún soldado antiguo

Before secularization, Father Durán emancipated four Indians, the only ones who were freed before secularization. These Indians obtained lands, fifteen head of cattle, five horses, and a pair of yoke oxen.

* * *

During the Spanish domination, living out of wedlock was disapproved of and was severely punished. Any individual who was caught living such a lifestyle was irremissibly sentenced to ten years at the presidio with shackles, and if he lived in San José, sent to Monterey to carry out his sentence. The woman would have her hair cut like a horse, they would put a doll on her chest, and they would make her stand every Sunday during mass by the door of the church for an entire month so that she would serve as an example to others.

* * *

I will now occupy myself with the lifestyles of the various classes of our people during the periods of the Spanish and Mexican domination of this territory.

I will start by detailing the daily lives of the mission priests.

From the founding of the missions, two priests were placed in each one. As a general rule, one of them, I assume the one with the most experience in these matters, would dedicate himself to the temporal [affairs] and the other almost exclusively would devote himself to spiritual [matters]. The former would also carry out his duties as a missionary such as baptizing, [performing] burials, and also teaching.

In general, the priests relied on an agricultural primer to instruct them on the cultivation of fields. In the planting of wheat, the priests never used the **cardenillo** stone to prepare the seed but they instead would stir them in **agua de lejía**, then they would strew them on the soil. This was the custom since the time of Spain and continued being so after the territory separated itself from that nation.

Until 1828, the priests did not have foremen, since they would choose the ablest from the neophytes and give them supervision over the agricultural tasks. However, the priests would take responsibility for the warehouses; they would even take care of cutting the material for the Indians' clothes and the distribution of the food supplies. In those years, the priests had much more work than after 1828. Very few missions had **gente de razón** servants and if they had one, he would be the **llavero**. Other times, they would hire a corporal or a retired soldier

que entendía de trabajos de campo; pero esto no agradaba a los Comdts. de los presidios, porque. decían que después que el militar se había congraciado con el Padre, y acostumbrándose a las grangerías y comodidades de la misión, se le relajaba la disciplina, y ya se disgustaba con sus obligaciones militares. Esa cosa como que cuando un cabo se hacía favorito de algn. Padre, le motejaban eso, y lo quitaban de la misión. Nunca hubo buena inteligencia, sino aparentemente, entre los Comandtes. y lo Padres. Después que ya las misiones empezaron a progresar y a producir más de lo que necesitaban pa. las atenciones de sus neófitos y otros indígenas ya los habilitados de los presidios, por orden Supma., obtenían sus semillas de las misiones, y ya gradualmte. cesaron de venir muchas de ellas en la memoria de San Blas.

Sobre estas entregas de semillas ocurrían bastante a menudo choques entre los habilitados y los Padres, quejándose éstos de que aquéllos eran muchas veces demasiado exigentes, pero siempre suministraban lo que se les pedía.

Las misiones tenían también telares de frazadas y sarapes y de otros géneros de lana para vestir sus indios y pa. las tropas. Hacían zapatos y botas, sillas de montar, frenos, espuelas, jabón y alga. que otra cosa, incluso arados y otros instrumentos primitivos pa. el uso de las misiones.

Desde los primeros años el Gobo. puso maestros de albañelería, carpintería, herrería, de tejer ta., pa. la enseñanza de los indios; a quienes pagaba el Gobo., y luego se resarcía con lo que cada misión contribuía por la enseñanza de sus neófitos. Sin embargo, el encargado de la jabonería era siempre un hombre de razón pagado por la misión; y se hacía jabón de varias clases, y todo muy bueno.

En el ramo de géneros de lana era todo trabajo ordinario para las necesidades de la época. Al principio del país el gobo. no permitía que nadie usara de cosas lujosas. Cada ramo de manufactura tenía su gefe o encargado. Al principio eran indios, más tarde fueron poniendo gente de razón. Lo mismo sucedía en las trojas.

El Padre misionero se levantaba todos los días a las 6 a.m., mandar a su primer page y sacristán tocar a misa. Después de decir su misa el Padre tomaba un pocillo de chocolate y una rebanada de pan tostado. Después llamaban a los indios (éstos estaban ya desayunados desde antes) a rezar en la iglesia, pues ellos no asistían a misa sino en los domingos y días de fiesta.

who had farming experience. Yet, this did not please the commanders of the presidios because they claimed that after the military person ingratiated himself with the priest and became accustomed to the advantages and comforts of the missions, he would become lax in discipline and would become unhappy with his military obligations. Whenever a corporal became a priest's favorite, they would censure him, and they would remove him from the mission. Apparently, good relations never existed between the commanders and the priests. After the missions began to progress and produce more than they needed to satisfy the needs of the neophytes and other Indians, the residents of the presidios, by order of the Supreme Government, obtained their grain from the missions. Hence, gradually [the grain] stopped coming from San Blas as was done traditionally.

As a result of these grain deliveries, there quite frequently occurred many confrontations between the presidios and the priests; although the latter complained many times that the former were very demanding, they always supplied what was asked of them.

The missions also had looms for making blankets and serapes and other wool fabrics to clothe the Indians and troops. They made shoes and boots, riding saddles, bridles, spurs, soap, and a few other things, including plows and other primitive tools for the use of the missions.

From the early years, the government sent instructors in masonry, carpentry, blacksmithing, and also textile production to teach the Indians. The government would pay them [instructors] and then it would indemnify itself with what each mission contributed for the teaching of its neophytes. Nonetheless, the person in charge of soap production was always a **gente de razón** individual who was paid by the mission; various types of soap were produced, and all of it was of good quality.

In the area of wool fabrics everything consisted of ordinary work to satisfy the basic needs of the period. At the birth of the [Mexican nation], the government did not permit anyone to wear luxury items. Each manufacturing sector had an administrator or someone in charge. At the beginning, [the administrators] were mostly neophytes but, later on, **gentes de razón** were put in charge. The same was happening in the granaries.

The mission priest would get up every day at six o'clock in the morning and he would order his page and sacristan to ring the bells for mass. After celebrating mass, the priest would drink a cup of chocolate and eat a slice of toasted bread. After this, the Indians (who had already had their breakfast) were called to the church for prayers only, since they only attended mass on Sundays and on feast days.

Concluído el rezo salía el ministro (cuando no tenía mayordomo) a hacer la distribn. de la gente, para lo cual llevaba en la mano el padrón de la indiada. Hacía sus distribuciones, y se retiraba a su celda. Los indios que habían faltado de presentarse a la puerta de la iglesia se apuntaban. No se buscaba nunca al indio, pero cuando se presentaba, se le "socorría" (esta era la palabra que se usaba, decía el Padre "dénle el socorro espiritual") según la falta. Si era de un día con unos 6 azotes, si dos días a una semana de 15 a 25 azotes. El Padre Durán acostumbraba en esos casos preguntárle al mismo delincuente qué viento hacía. El indio contestaba Sur; "pues que llueva," decía el Padre, y le aplicaban al pobre diablo el "socorro espiritual," y el Padre muerto de risa de las súplicas y contorsiones del paciente. Alga. vez se compadecía y mandaba parar antes de completarse el no. de azotes que había recetado. Todos los días había azotados de 10 para abajo. El que faltaba a la iglesia o al trabajo (a no ser que hubiese tenido licencia, o que probase haber estado enfermo, o haber ido por leña para su casa, si era casado) llevaba azotes irremisiblemte. Lo mismo sucedía en los jayuntes. Todos los días se pasaba lista por el padrón, y el que faltase la pagaba en la misma puerta con su ración de azotes, y se levantaba alegre y contento pa. ir a su trabajo, porqe. es un hecho que los indígenas se reían de esos cortos castigos. Yo nunca vi en las misiones de Sta. Clara, San José y Sn. Francisco de Asís, San Francisco Solano, ni San Rafael que los P.P. diesen los castigos crueles de que he oído hablar sobre Santa Cruz, San Antonio y otras.

En las que nombro arriba los castigos equivalían a represiones sin visas de crueldad.

Vi yo una cosa célebre en la misión de Santa Clara (estando de ministro Fray José Viader).[1] Le faltaron tres indios en el jayunte, y había un hoyo a corta dista. del jayunte. Allí estaban enterrados los 3 indios que habían faltado, cubiertos con sacate. Ellos se habían metido allí por consejo de un soldado llamado Leandro Galindo, quien después incendió el sacate. Los indios saltaron fuera

---

[1]Geiger, 263. Geiger menciona que el padre José Viader era oriundo de España y fue asignado a la misión de Santa Clara en 1796. Él participó en varias expediciones al Valle Central. Viader, al igual que el padre Durán, estuvo presente en el funeral del padre Andrés Quintana. Aunque el padre hizo repetidas súplicas para permitirle regresar al centro de México, Viader permaneció en la misión de Santa Clara hasta que ésta fue transferida a los franciscanos del colegio de Zacatecas.

After prayers, the priest (when he did not have a foreman) would go out and make work assignments for which he had in his hands a list of the Indians. After distributing the workforce, he would retire to his cell. The names of the Indians who had not presented themselves at the doors of the church were written down. They were never sought out, but when they finally presented themselves, they were given a "**Socorría**" (This was the word that was used—the priest would say: "Give him spiritual assistance."), according to the [severity of] the offense. They would receive six lashes if it was one day and if it were two days and up to a week, [they would get] from fifteen to twenty-five lashes. Father Durán was in the habit in those situations of asking the delinquent which wind was blowing and if the Indian answered [the] south [wind], he would say, "let it rain," and the poor devil would receive "spiritual assistance." The Father would die of laughter listening to the pleadings or seeing the contortions of the patient. Sometimes, he would take pity and order that the punishment be stopped before the completion of the lashes that had been prescribed. Every day, there were ten [individuals] or fewer who were punished. The one who did not go to church or to work (unless he had permission or could prove that he was sick or if married, he had gone to get firewood) would get an unpardonable flogging. The same would take place at the **jayunte**. Daily attendance was taken from a list and the persons who were absent would take their ration of lashes at the door and then they would happily get up and with joy go to work because it was true that the Indians would laugh at such a light punishment. I never saw in the Missions of Santa Clara, San José, San Francisco de Asís, San Francisco de Solano, or San Rafael that the Fathers would give such cruel punishments as I have heard were given at Santa Cruz, San Antonio, and others.

In the ones that I have mentioned above, the punishments equaled the offense without the intention of cruelty.

I saw a notable event at Mission Santa Clara (Fray José Viader was serving as Minister).[1] He was missing three Indians in the **jayunte** and there was a hole at a very short distance from the **jayunte**. The missing three Indians were buried there, covered with grass. They had hidden themselves there because they followed the advice of a soldier by the name of Leandro Galindo who, then, set the grass on fire. The Indians jumped out

---

[1] José Viader was born in Spain (Geiger, 263). Geiger notes that Viader was assigned to Mission Santa Clara in 1796. He participated in several expeditions in the Central Valley. Viader, along with Father Durán, was also present at the funeral of Father Andrés Quintana. Despite repeated appeals to be allowed to return to central México, Viader remained at Mission Santa Clara until it was turned over to the Franciscans from the College of Zacatecas.

algo chamuscados, y el P. Viader se río de la ocurrencia. Vinieron los indios, le besaron al padre la mano, él riéndose los dejó ir sin castigo.

Por costumbre el Padre ya no tomaba alimento hasta las 12 del día, sin perjuicio de que a las 11 había bebido su copita de aguardte. de España acompañado de unos panecitos dulces y un pedacito de queso, "pa. hacer boca."

El Padre por lo general tenía dos cocineros, un panadero, y cinco pages pa. su servicio personal y de iglesia, además un sacristán.

Su comida era: una sopa de fideos, de arroz o de pan, una olla de borrego o de res con su jamón, bastante verdura y demás. Este era plato de fuerza que no faltaba ningún día. Algunas veces comían frijoles, o lentejas, o garbanzos separados, pero casi siempre esas menestras entraban en la olla. Concluía la comida el Padre con frutas frescas, o secas segn. apetecía, conservas y queso. Durante la comida se lavaba ésta con sendos vasos de buen vino.

En la misión de San José se hacía vino bueno y aguardiente. El padre Narciso Durán me enseñó a mí a hacer el vino y el aguardte. de uva porqe. era hombre inteligte. en esos ramos. El aguardte. estaba como agua cristalina, y se le daba color con sirope hecho con azúcar quemada. Quedaba de un amarillo claro, y era de doble saca, de consigte. muy fuerte.

Entre la comida de las 12 y la cena era raro que el P. ministro comiese nada. La cena era a las 7 u 8 (hablo de la misión de San José, y era, puede decirse, costumbre de los P.P. de todas las misiones). Un pichoncito asado o cosa parecida y su pocillo de chocolate. Esto era diario, a no ser que hubiera huéspedes, ya de oficiales, algunas veces sargentos, comerciantes u otros particulares decentes. Entonces, no sólo eran alojados en el departamento de huéspedes que todas las misiones tenían establecido, sino que los Padres los convidaban a su mesa, y en esos casos se ponían platos estraordinarios. A ningún huésped se le cobraba nada por la asistencia de él, ni de sus criados, ni bestias. Al contrario, se les facilitaba a los transeúntes no sólo esa asistencia, sino bestias frescas y bastimentos para seguir su viage todo libre de costo. Lo mismo se hizo práctica general en todos los ranchos de particulares con los transeúntes que se presentaban. La hospitalidad en el país no tenía límites.

A más de los trabajos arriba citados, atendían los P.P. a sus deberes espirituales, esforzándose constantemte. en aumentar el no. de cristianos, en mantener a éstos en la fé dándoles la instrucción religiosa conveniente, muy a menudo en sus propias lenguas pa. que comprendiesen mejor los principios y dogmas de la religión.

and were somewhat scorched; the Father laughed at the occurrence. Afterwards, the Indians came and kissed the Father's hand. Still laughing, the
Father let them go without punishment.

As a matter of habit, the Father would not take any more food until twelve
noon, yet he would faithfully drink a small glass of **aguardiente** from Spain
at eleven; it was accompanied by some sweet breads and a small piece of
cheese to "make hunger."

Generally, the Father had two cooks, a baker, and five pages for his personal service and that of the church. He also had a sacristan. His meals consisted of noodles, rice, or bread soup; a dish of lamb or beef with its ham;
and plenty of vegetables and other items. This was the main dish of the day
and it was never skipped. Sometimes they ate beans, lentils, or garbanzo
beans separately but almost always these stews could be found in the pot.
The priest would finish his meal with either fresh or dried fruit, according to
his desire, and fruit preserves, and cheese. He would wash his meal down
with generous glasses of good wine.

At Mission San José, good wine and **aguardiente** were produced. Father Narciso Durán taught me to make wine and aguardiente of grapes because he was a
man of vast expertise in those areas. The **aguardiente** was like crystalline water
and it was given its color with syrup made from burnt sugar; it turned to a color
of clear yellow and it was of double **saca** and consequently, it was very strong.

Between noontime and dinner, it was rare that the Father Minister would
eat anything. Dinner was between seven and eight (I am speaking about Mission San José and it could be said that this was the custom for the rest of the
missions). [It consisted of] a small roasted pigeon or a similar food and a cup
of chocolate. This was a daily routine unless there were guests [such as] officers or sometimes sergeants, merchants, or other decent folks. If this was the
case, not only were they placed in the guest chambers that all the missions had
established but the priests would also invite them to their tables, and in those
cases, they were given some extraordinary dishes. No guest was charged for
the assistance given to him, his servants, or his horses. On the contrary, the
travelers were not only given this assistance but they would also receive fresh
horses and supplies to continue their trip; they received all this at no cost to
them. This also became a general practice in all the private ranches with the
travelers that visited them. Hospitality in this country knew no boundaries.

In addition to the work cited above, the priests also attended to their spiritual obligations and constantly tried to increase the number of converts to Chris-
tianity. [The priests would make] sure that they kept the faith by frequently giving them the necessary religious instruction in their own languages so that they
could better understand the principles and dogmas of the [Catholic] religion.

A todas horas, día y noche, estaban prontos para ir a desempeñar su ministerio ya pa. bautizar, catequizar, o ausiliar a los enfermos y moribundos; debiendo advertirse que también hacían las veces de médicos y suministraban medicinas tantos a los neófitos y catecúmenos de la misión, cuanto a los gentiles que venían a pedir el ausilio. Los mismos gentiles eran a menudo socorridos con alimentos, y de este modo muchos se prestaban a reducirse a la vida de misión.

En los primeros tiempos los P.P. acostumbraban alejarse de sus misiones sin escolta militar, yéndose a rancherías distantes, en donde corrían graves riesgos de perder la vida. Después del asesinato del P. Quintana en Sta. Cruz, adoptó el Gobr., medidas severas para prohibir a los misioneros el que corriesen esos riesgos. Así es que las escoltas tenían órdenes estrictas bajo la responsabilidad del cabo o de los soldados respectivos, de no dejar nunca la persona del Padre sin irle escoltando, fuese eso de la voluntad de éste o no. Hubo el caso de un soldado llamado Salvador Espinosa que estando de escolta en una misión, se vio obligado a emplear la fuerza para impedir que el P. ministro se marchase adelante, por tener mejores bestias, sin que le acompañase Espinosa. Éste fue puesto en el cepo, y por queja del fraile se le hizo comparecer ante el Gobr. (creo que fue Solá), y cuando éste se enteró de las circunstancias, aprobó lo hecho por el soldado, alabándole la manera como había cumplido con las órdenes del Gobo. porque es de advertir que en aquellos tiempos, "cuando todavía se amarraban los perros con longanizas," o en otra palabra cuando las gentes de Cal. no habían abierto los ojos, el poner la mano en ademán de amenaza o violencia sobre un Padre ministro era un delito gravísimo que se castigaba con la mayor severidad, y al mismo tiempo hacía perder al delincuente su posición en la sociedad.

Entre otras cosas se le escomulgaba por el hecho, y quedaba el individuo en el ostracismo.

Las escoltas de las misiones tenían por obligación, además del servicio puramte. militar de la guardia y la conservación de sus armas y municiones, protejer las personas de los ministros ya en la misión misma, o ya cuando salían del cuadro de ella pa. ir a las rancherías. El cabo de la escolta era el encargado de justa. criminal, y en aquellos casos de delitos graves que ya salían de la jurisdición del P. ministro, él mandaba administrar el castigo de azotes y cepo. En casos más graves formaba las primeras diligencias de investigación, y después mandaba al reo al presidio para ser allí juzgado. El cabo tenía a su cargo la defensa de la misión, en caso de ataque repentino de enemigos internos o esternos, podía ejercer facultades estraordinarias hasta el punto de privar de la vida. Sin embargo, esto era sólo en el caso de que no hubiese tiempo para ponerlo en conocto. del Comandte. del Presidio.

At all hours, whether day or night, they were ready to go and carry out their ministry, that is, baptizing, teaching catechism, or aiding the sick or the dying. It should be noted that sometimes they [would assume the duty of] doctors and would administer medicines to the neophytes and the **catecú-menos** of the missions as well as the gentiles that came to seek assistance. The same gentiles were frequently assisted with food, and in this manner, many of them came to accept mission life.

In the early days, the priests were in the habit of leaving their missions without military escort, going to the distant **rancherías**, where they ran the great risk of losing their lives. After the killing of Father Quintana in Santa Cruz, the government adopted severe measures to prohibit the missionaries from taking these risks. Hence, the escort had strict orders that required that either the corporal or the respective soldiers never leave the priest alone, whether he wished it or not. There was the case of a soldier by the name of Salvador Espinosa who, while serving as an escort for a mission, was compelled to use force against the Father Minister to keep him from going ahead without him because he had better horses. He was put in the stocks and because of the friar's complaint was forced to appear before the governor (I believe it was Solá). When the governor learned the circumstances, he approved of the soldier's actions, and praised him for the manner by which he complied with the government's order. It must be said that in those days it was still possible to "tie dogs with sausages"; in other words, it was before the people of California had opened their eyes. Putting a hand on or threatening a priest with violence was a very grave crime that was punished severely, and caused the violator to lose his position in society. Among other things, he was excommunicated for the crime and ostracized.

In addition to performing their military duties as guards and maintaining their weapons and ammunition, the mission escorts had the obligation of protecting the lives of the ministers whether in the mission itself or when they left its boundaries to go to the **rancherías**. The corporal of the guard was in charge of administering criminal justice and in the case of serious crimes that were committed outside the jurisdiction of the Father Minister, he would issue orders for punishment by either flogging or the stocks. In the more severe cases, he began the initial investigations and then he would send the prisoner to the presidio so that he would be judged there. The corporal was in charge of the defense of the mission and in case of an unexpected attack by internal or external enemies, he could exercise extraordinary authority even to the point of taking [someone's] life. Nonetheless, this was possible only if there was no time to notify the commander of the presidio.

En los primeros años, hubo ocasiones de ponerse escoltas dobles, algunas veces mandadas por Sargentos. En esos años el cabo de escolta era nombrado por el Gobr. mismo, y sólo él podía quitarle. Esto no impedía que en un caso urgente le suspendiese el Comandte. de la tropa del presidio a cuya jurisdn. pertenecía la misión. La escolta tenía siempre de día un soldado vigilante, y de noche centinela con campana pa. dar los cuartos de la noche, esto es, prima, segunda, tercera, y alba. El centinela era relevado por el cabo, quien por supuesto tenía que levantarse pa. cada relevo. En caso de falta de un soldado, tenía el cabo que hacer su cuarto de centinela, que era en prima o en alba. Las raciones de carne y semillas de la escolta las suministraba la misión, la que después pasaba la cuenta o la habilitación.

Los cabos y soldados casados tenían sus familias consigo en la misión, y habían una cuadra de casas dedicadas a la tropa. Los soldados solteros eran atendidos por las mugeres de los casados sin remuneración ninguna, sólo entregaban la ración en la casa donde comía. Era costumbre que los P.P. gratificasen a la tropa y a las familias, ya con frutas, vino u otras cosas. Esto era en ocasiones estraords. de fiestas ta.

Si como sucedió conmigo, que el cabo era al mismo tiempo mayordomo de la misión, entonces tomaba su sueldo de ella, sin contar otras gajes. El socorro que yo tenía como mayordomo era de unos 10$ mensuales en lo que pedía pa. mis atenciones. La escolta común de una misión ya organizada era de 1 cabo y 5 soldados.

La hora general de levantarse las gentes fue siempre la de 6 a 7, según la estación del año. Esto era pa. gentes de posibilidades o pobres. Las gentes que no eran militares no tenían más ocupación que la agricultura. Desde temprano, después del desayuno que ya espliqué en otro lugar, tomaban sus yuntas y se iban a trabajar, o atendían a las necesidades de sus siembras y terrenos, y a la asistencia de sus animales de servicio. La costumbre del país era que los hombres atendieran a los trabajos del campo, a lazar reses; en fin, todo trabajo fuera de casa. Las mugeres atendían al servicio doméstico y a la crianza de sus hijos, cuidado de sus maridos, padres, hermanos ta.

Las mugeres Californias se hicieron siempre notables desde que yo he tenido conocimiento (téngase presente que en 1790 tenía yo 8 o 9 años de edad) por su buen comportamto., su amor filial, y por sus maridos, hijos y hermanos.

In the beginning, there were occasions when double escorts were needed; sometimes they were supervised by sergeants. During these years, the governor himself named the corporal of the escorts and only he could remove him. This did not impede the commander of the presidios in whose jurisdiction the mission was located from suspending him in urgent cases. The [mission] escort always had a soldier during the day serving as a sentry and, at night, a sentinel with a bell would give the quarters of the night: first, second, third, and dawn. The corporal, who obviously had to wake up for every changing of the guard, relieved the sentinel. In case a soldier failed to report for duty, the corporal had to take over his quarter, which was first or dawn. The meat or grain rations of the escort were provided by the mission, which then submitted the bill to the presidio's paymaster.

The corporals and married soldiers had their families living with them in the mission and a block of houses was assigned for the troops. The women of the married ones tended to the single soldiers; they did not receive any remuneration. [The single soldiers] gave their rations to the houses where they ate. It was the custom that the Fathers reward the troops and their families with fruit, wines, or other things. This was also done on extraordinary occasions, including fiestas.

When the corporal was also the foreman of the mission, as in my case, then he would receive wages from it [the mission] as well as other wages. The assistance that I received as a foreman was around ten pesos monthly, which I requested for my needs. The average escort for each established mission consisted of a corporal and five soldiers.

The people's usual hour for waking up always was from six to seven, depending on the season of the year. This was the same for both the people of means as well as for the poor. The people who were not in the military did not have any other occupation but agriculture. Very early, after breakfast, which I have explained elsewhere, they would take their yoke oxen to plow the soil, or they would tend to the needs of their cultivated fields and other properties, or they would care for their service animals. It was the custom of the country that the men work on the land and rope cattle, or perform all the work outside the home, in other words. Women would do all the domestic work, raise the children, and take care of their husbands, parents, and also their siblings.

The women of California have been known since I have had consciousness (keep in mind that in 1790 I was around eight or nine years old) for their good conduct and their filial love for their husbands, children, and siblings.

Eran virtuosas, e industriosas, constantemte. entregadas a los deberes de su familia, los cuales nunca descuidaban.

Los hombres hasta por los años de 1830 eran de buenas costumbres, con raras escepciones, sin prejuicio de que hubieren casos de prostitución, borrachera, afición al juego y abandono de las familias. Esos casos existieron pero eran escasos. El respeto por los padres, y la autoridad de estos era indispustada. No cesaba ni aún después que los hijos eran casados, y a su vez padres o madres. De 1830 en adeltante, empezó a relajarse la sociedad debido al mayor roce con gentes de fuera (que no toda era buena) la mayor facilidad de adquirir recursos, y las convulsiones políticas acabaron de introducir las malas costumbres, haciéndolas bastante comunes entre nuestros hombres. El juego, la prostitución, la vagancia, y embriaguez se hicieron muy comunes, y con esos vicios pronto se hizo bastante común el robo pa. sostenerlos.

Los trabajos de campo de los ranchos, ya agrícolas, ya de rodeo y herradero duraban hasta eso de las once am. a cuya hora se retiraban a comer, y descansar hasta las 2 de la tarde. Las familias pobres hacían ellas mismas sus trabajos domésticos de limpieza, cocina, lavado, coser y demás. En las que tenían posibles., muchos de esos servicios los hacían indígenas de uno y otro sexo. Después de las 2 volvían todos, ricos y pobres, a los trabajos hasta el oscurecer. Los ricos tenían, por su puesto, operarios que les ausiliasen.

En los días de mi padre recuerdo que él pagaba a sus operarios de razón que se ocupaban en barbechar, limpiar o regar las milpas, u otros trabajos de campo, 6 reales diarios y la comida. Los 6 reales se pagaban en plata al que lo exigía, o en efectos. Yo mismo, en años posteriores, los pagaba a 15$ mensuales y su mantención.

Esta no incluía nada de bebida, ni café, ni té. La ración del operario era lo que cada uno podía comer. Se le daba semanario, y consistía de carne de res, manteca, maíz, frijol, lenteja o garbanzo. De otras cosas como calabazas, cebollas, chiles, ta ta, lo sembraban ellos mismos en el rancho en el pedazo de terreno que se les prestaba para eso, y que escogían ellos mismos. Ese sueldo de 15$ mensuales, que se pagaban en efectos o en dinero (a voluntad del trabajador), estaba asignado a los operarios de la gente de razón. A los indios, de los que tenían los rancheros muchos empleados, se les daban 2 vestidos, desde zapatos hasta el sombrero anualmte., ración semanaria como en las misiones.

They were virtuous, industrious, and always devoted to their family obligations, which they never neglected.

Until 1830, the men, with rare exceptions, had good habits. There was no prostitution, drunkenness, addiction to gambling, or family abandonment. These cases did exist but they were rare. Respect for parents and authority went unquestioned and it did not end even when children got married, even after they themselves became mothers and fathers. From 1830 on, society became more lenient due to the greater contact with outsiders (this was not all good) and a greater ease in acquiring resources; the political uprisings led to an even greater introduction of bad habits, making them very common among our men. Gambling, prostitution, vagrancy, and drunkenness became very common and to sustain these vices robbery quickly became a common occurrence.

The work in the ranches, whether agricultural, livestock round-ups, or blacksmithing, would last until eleven in the morning at which hour they would retire to eat and rest until two in the afternoon. The poor families themselves would do their own domestic work such as cleaning, cooking, washing, sewing, among other things. In families of financial means, Indians of either sex performed many of these services. After two PM, everyone, wealthy or poor, would return to work until it grew dark. The wealthy, obviously, had workers who assisted them.

During my father's time, I remember that he would pay **gente de razón** workers that he employed to plow, weed-out, irrigate **milpas**, and to perform other types of field work, six **reales** daily and gave them their meals. The six **reales** were paid in silver to those who requested it or in supplies. I, myself, in the later years paid fifteen pesos monthly and gave them their sustenance.

This did not include alcoholic beverages, coffee, or tea. The ration of the workers was whatever they could eat. It was given weekly and it consisted of beef, lard, corn, beans, lentils, or garbanzo beans. They planted other things, like squash, onions, and chilies, at the ranch on a piece of land that was lent to them for this purpose; they chose [the plot] themselves. The wage of fifteen pesos monthly was assigned to the **gente de razón** and it was paid in goods or money (it was the workers' choice). The Indians, of whom the ranchers had many employees, received annually two changes of clothes, from shoes to hats, as well as their weekly rations, just like in the missions.

Mis operarios de razón eran por lo general hijos del país. Alguna qe. otra vez tuve mexicanos, casi siempre tenía yo de éstos en la fabricación de sillas. Nunca tuve entre ellos presidarios, como otros rancheros, y no sé cómo les pagaban. En mis matanzas de ganado pagaba a todo el que mataba 6 reales res, beneficiada toda: manteca, sebo limpio, picada la carne, y los huesos pelados para freírse y sacarles la manteca del tuétano. Todos estaban conformes con eso, pues mataban de 4 a 6 reses cada uno. Esos eran operarios estraords. Indios y blancos, todos ganaban lo mismo, y además se les daba la carne que necesitaban pa. sus familias. Este era mi régimen 60 reses cada 3er. día hasta completar el no. de 1000 reses que era lo corriente anual. Yo pagaba en efectivo, y el que prefería efectos, los tomaba de mi almacén.

Otros rancheros tenían sus arreglos, pagando con reses en pie. Los matadores preferían trabajar para mí que para los otros.

La cueramenta que ellos adquirían fuera venía a parar a mi poder, y la pagaba yo a 2$ cada cuero, en efectivo o efectos, y los vendedores gustosamte. las estacaban pa. secarse. Nunca me fallaron cueros pa. llenar mis compromisos.

En los ranchos después de concluídas las tareas del día y de cenar, se iban todos a dormir, o hacían alga. diversión ya jugando a los naipes, o tocando vihuelas, cantando y bailando caseramente. En los juegos de baraja apostaban (en mi rancho) cueros, dinero, cigarros, y algunos viciosos hasta la camisa. El dinero y cueros de algún modo siempre venían a parar a mi poder por aguardte. u otros efectos. Esto sucedía poco más o menos lo mismo en todos los ranchos en que había comercio (que no eran muchos, tal vez no pasaban de dos o tres). Pero el juego existía en todos lados, y más tarde se generalizó el vicio de la bebida, y el de la prostitución. En los primeros años de Cal. la sífilis era ya conocida, pero en los años posteriores se hizo tan común que la mayor parte de los hombres, y muchas mugeres estaban contaminados. Esto era más, en las indiadas, pero no faltaba en los hombres de razón. En verdad, conocí hombres de respetable posición que tenían el mal desarrollado en su sistema, y que murieron de él.

Los oficiales y soldados de las Campas. presidiales, en las horas que no estaban ocupados en el servicio militar, se empleaban en procurar leña y otras cosas pa. sus familias. Algunos eran zapateros, y otros sastres ta., y trabajan pa. procurarse recursos con que mantener a sus familias. Mucha falta les hacía ese recurso, puesto que de muchos años atrás no se les pagaba el prest.

My **gente de razón** workers generally were native sons of the country. Once in a while I had Mexicans; almost always I hired these [workers] in the manufacturing of chairs. I never had prisoners as workers as did other ranchers and so I do not know how much they were paid. For the killing of cattle I would pay all who killed them six **reales** per head and they would benefit from everything such as lard, clean tallow, minced meat, and bare bones that were fried in order to extract the lard from the marrow. Everyone was satisfied with this arrangement, since they would each kill from four to six head. They were extraordinary workers, both Indians and whites, all of them earned the same wage and, in addition, they would get the meat that they needed for their families. This was my routine: killing sixty head of cattle every third day until completing one thousand head, which was the annual goal. I paid cash, and those who preferred goods could receive them from my storehouse.

Other ranchers had their own arrangements; they would pay with live cattle. The slaughterers preferred working for me rather than for the others.

The hides that they acquired elsewhere would reach my hands and I would pay two pesos each for the hides, either in cash or in goods; they would gladly put them in stakes so that they could get dried. I never ran short of hides to fill my obligations.

After finishing the daily chores and dinner, the people of the ranches went to sleep or they entertained themselves by playing cards or by playing the **vihuela**, singing, and dancing at home. In the games of cards (at my ranch), [people] would bet hides, money, cigarettes, and some [gambling] addicts would even [bet] their shirts. Money or hides, in one way or another, always ended with me in exchange for **aguardiente** or some other goods. This more or less would take place in every ranch that had commerce (there were not very many, perhaps no more than two or three), but gambling existed everywhere, and later the vices of alcoholic consumption and prostitution also became fairly common. In the early years of California, syphilis was already known but in the later years it became so common that most of the men and many women were infected. This was more common among Indians but it was not rare among the **gente de razón**. In truth, I knew many respectable men who had the illness in their bodies, and they died from it.

The officers and soldiers of the presidial companies would devote themselves to gathering firewood and other things for their families whenever they were not performing their military service. Since some of them were shoemakers or tailors, they would perform these types of work to earn income to support their families. They were in need of this resource, since for many years back they had not been paid their **prest**.

Si mal no recuerdo desde 1815 o 1816, si acaso vino algún situado después de esos años, no pasaría de uno o dos.

Cuando yo servía en la Compa. de Sn. Franco. el prest. del soldado era de $17.50 mensuales. De aquí salía la ración, vestuario y demás. A mi me dieron la ración que montaría a unos 10$ mensuales. Ropa, zapatos, ta muy raras veces me los dieron. Así es que podré decir que el Gobo., primeramte. el Espl. y después el Mexo. me debieron como unos 6$ mensuales, que en 10 años 5 meses son $750, los que nunca me pagaron. Cuando estuve 8 años en la artilla. no recibí más que mi ración y vestuario y munición.

Serví, pues, 18 años 5 meses. Sin contar las colillas que me pagaban después pa. ir en persecusión de indios y otros servicios, y nunca me puso el gobo. un peso en la mano. El único prest. que recibí del gobo. (español o mexicano) fueron los 14 agugeros de flecha que tengo en mi cuerpo, y que los puedo mostrar al que dude mi palabra. Tal era la recompensa del pobre infeliz soldado que trabajaba, sufría la fatiga de guardias, trasnochadas, marchas y contramarchas a todas horas y en todas las estaciones, conducciones de correos, cuidado de caballadas. Y no hablemos de la humildad, sumisión ta. que debía manifestar a sus superiores. En fin, estar hecho un esclavo. Al retirárseme no se me dio mi pensión, ni tierras, ni nada.

Se necesitaban haber servido 18 años consecutivos en el mismo cuerpo pa. poder pasar a inválidos. Yo serví 18 años 5 meses, pero no consecutivos. Sin embargo, al inválido tampoco le pagaban su pensión.

Mi padre que sirvió 47 años y se retiró de alférez vivo y efectivo en 1797 ó 1798 a 1800 (no recuerdo) con medio sueldo, o sean 200$ anuales, quedó muchos años sin recibir su retiro. Y no me es posible decir cuánto le debían, y que jamás se ha cobrado. Yo lo mantuve con mis arbitrios, y al fin tuve que vender mi casa para poder continuar socorriéndole, y comprar otra en que alojarle. Estuvo ciego como 15 años antes de morir, su muerte ocurrió 8 mayo 1825.

Cuando tenía de 15 a 16 años de edad esto es, por los años 1796 o 1797, vestían las mugeres de este modo. Nagua blanca de abrigo con un bordado de 4 dedos de ancho, sobre la nagua otra de sorga azul, verde, o negra. La media negra o colorada de seda; zapato bajo de hebilla de metal o plata con taconcito regular. El rebozo de hilo o seda; collar de perlas, o más bien, imitación de ellas.

They had not received it, if I remember correctly, since 1815 or 1816. If they did receive a salary after these years, I do not believe it was more than one or two.

When I was serving in the company of San Francisco, the **prest.** was 17.50 pesos monthly; from it came the food rations, clothing, and other things. I received a ration that consisted of some ten pesos monthly; only on very rare occasions did I receive clothing or shoes. Hence, I can say that first the Spanish government and then the Mexican government owed me some six pesos monthly that in ten years and five months would total 750 pesos that they never paid to me. When I served in the artillery for eight years, I only received food rations, clothing, and ammunition.

I then served eighteen years and five months. Without taking into consideration the scraps that they paid me for going in pursuit of Indians and performing other services, the government never put a single peso in my hands. The only **prest.** that I received from the government (Spanish or Mexican) were the fourteen arrow holes that I have in my body and that I can show to anyone who doubts my word. Such was the recompense of the poor wretched soldier who had to work and who suffered the fatigue of performing guard duty and all-night vigils, who conducted marches and countermarches at all hours and all year round, and who served as mail carrier and caretaker of the horse herds. Let us not mention the humility and submission that he had to show to his superiors. In the end, he had become a slave. When I retired, I did not get a pension, land, or anything. It was required to have served eighteen years consecutively in the same company to become a retired soldier. I served eighteen years and five months but not consecutively. Regardless, not even a retired soldier would receive his pension.

My father, who served forty-seven years and retired as an active second lieutenant with all the rights and responsibilities, either in 1797, 1798, or 1800 (I do not remember), was supposed to receive half a salary, that is 200 pesos yearly; for many years he did not receive his pension. It is not possible for me to know how much they owed him and it has never been paid. I supported him with my own means and finally I had to sell my house so that I could continue helping him, and I bought another one to lodge him. He was blind for the last fifteen years before he died. He died on May 8, 1825.

When I was fifteen or sixteen years old, this was around 1796 or 1797, the women would dress in the following manner: a white underskirt with embroidery four fingers wide; over the underskirt, another skirt of blue, green, or black coarse cloth. The stockings were black or red made of silk; the shoes were low and had regular size heels and either metal or silver buckles. The **rebozos** were either cotton or silk; the necklaces were made of pearls, or to be more precise, imitation pearls.

El anterior era el vestido corriente de una señora de algunas posibilidades, para recibir o hacer visitas, o para ir a las diversiones. Ahora para cuando estaba ocupada en los trabajos de su casa, se puso nagua blanca de crea o pontivil, sobre esa nagua de sarga barata de agn. color.

La muger pobre vestía por el mismo estilo que la de recursos, pero la calidad de sus géneros era inferior. Esto es, en lugar de sorga, bayeta o franela muy basta. En los años de 1816–8, usaban gerga hecha en las misiones, y la consideraban como la mejor muselina.

Ricas y pobres se vieron precisadas a usar la gerga; de medias la que tenía posibles. compraba lana, y mandaba hacer las medias a los mexicanos o a los indígenas. Las mugeres pobres usaban las medias "naturales."

Mi primera esposa fue de las que les tocó la suerte de ponerse las dichas "muselinas de las misiones," o sea la gerga.

Yo llegué a usar "pana fina tejida a brincos," o sean calzones hechos de cuero de venado, y cuando estaban bien hechos con galor de plata blanca valían 12$. Esto fue desde 1816 hasta 1819, poco más o menos.

Desde que yo abrí los ojos hasta 1819 usaban los hombres, militares y paisanos, calzón corto de paño, o pana, media de lana o de hilo, charretera en el calzón con hebilla de metal o plata. El pantalón tenía tapabalazo, unas veces fue ancho, otras angosto. Chaqueta corta, el militar la usaba con vuelta colorada, con collarín y francas coloradas. El chaleco de paño grana también, corbatín negro bien ajustado para no colgar la cabeza. El soldado, además cuando estaba de servicio llevaba su cuera, hecha de 7 pieles de gamuza, en 3 piezas, como un chaleco. Se abrochaba con correas del mismo cuero de bajo de los brazos. La cuera llegaba hasta cerca de la rodilla y servía de protección contra las flechas de los indios. Llevaba adarga ovalada, de cuero de res pasmado de dos haces, con maniguera por dentro pa. el brazo. Esta adarga servía pa. proteger la cara y el cuerpo.

Bota de forma de una media en la entrada del pie, encima iba el zapato. La bota llegaba hasta cerca de la rodilla con atadera de seda o de hilo, según la posibilidad del individuo.

This description was the common dress that women of some means wore to receive guests or make visits, or to go out to entertain themselves. When she was doing her house chores, she would wear a white underskirt of linen or **pontivil,** and a skirt made of cheap serge of some color over it.

Poor women would dress in the same style as those with means but the quality of their items was inferior, that is, instead of serge, they would wear a coarse wool fabric or very coarse flannel. In the years 1816 and 1818, they wore a coarse cloth that was made in the missions, and they considered it the best muslin.

Both rich and poor women were forced to use this coarse cloth. In regards to stockings, the women of means would buy wool and send it to the Mexicans or Indians to make it into stockings. The poor women would wear "natural" stockings.

My first wife was one of those whose fate was to wear the said "mission muslin," that is, the coarse cloth.

I came to wear the "fine corduroy knitted while skipping" or, that is, pantaloons made from deerskin, and when they were well made with a lace of white silver; they cost twelve pesos. This was from 1816 until 1819, more or less.

From the day of my birth to 1819, the men, whether military men or civilians, would wear woolen or corduroy short pants, stockings that were made from wool or cotton, and leg belts with metal or silver buckles. The pants had a flap, sometimes wide, other times narrow. The short jackets that were used by the military men had a red inner lining as well as a small red collar and fringe. The vest was made of scarlet wool; also worn was a small tie so well adjusted that it did not hang out from the head. In addition, when the soldier was in service, he would wear his leather jacket, made from seven hides of chamois leather in three pieces, like a vest. It was fastened under the arms with laces made from the same hide. The jacket would go down almost to the knees and it served as protection against Indian arrows. [The soldiers carried] an oval-shaped **adarga** made from cattle hides, hardened on both sides, and had the handle inside for the arm. This shield served to protect the head and body.

The boots were in the shape of a stocking down to the foot. The shoes went over them. The boot reached almost all the way to the knee, and it had either a silk or cotton cord, depending on the means of the individual.

El zapato del berruchi abotinado hasta más arriba del tobillo, con abrochadera al lado de afuera.

El sombrero bajo de copa, a la ancha de lana, con su barbiquejo.

El oficial usaba el mismo trage que el soldado con la diferencia de que sus materiales eran más finos; llevaban por supuesto sus insignias distintivas, y el sombrero de tres picos para gala, para servicio ordinario usaban el mismo que el soldado.

De armas ofensivas, el oficial llevaba espada de 4 o 5 cuartas flamencas, con vaina de acero, que servía de bastón. En campaña llevaba, además, puñal, lanza, pistolas, y carabina. Las mismas armas portaban los soldados.

En mis primeros años no había escuelas en Cal. Así es que ningún niño tuvo las ventajas de un instituto en donde aprender siquiera a leer y escribir. Yo y mis hermanos la poca instrucción que adquirimos nos fue dada por nuestro padre y madre en nuestra propia casa. Así como nosotros, hubo otros que disfrutaron de la ventaja de que sus padres conociesen esos ramos, y estuviesen dispuestos a enseñárselos. Mi señora madre y algunas otras señoras que sabían leer y escribir gratuitamente enseñaban a algunas niñas y niños cuyos padres no podían hacerlo, y venían a suplicar que se les hiciese ese beneficio. Así hubo ocasión de tener mi madre hasta 25 niños de ambos sexos, y aún hombres también.

A los prims. les enseñaba a leer, escribir y rezar. A los 2os. (vi 3 soldados, José Tiburcio Castro, padre del qe. fue Comandte. Gen. José Castro, Manuel Briones, y Cornelio Rosales) los enseñó a leer y escribir en San Franco., y después que aprendieron ascendieron a cabos de plaza (porqe. ya no eran legos) en las compañías, porqe. hay que advertir que habían muchos cabos legos que estaban habilitados de cabos, pero no podían pasar lista porqe. no sabían leer.

Dn. José Joaqn. Arrillaga vino de Gobr., y se puso una escuela sostenida por el gobo., de la que se hizo cargo el cabo retirado Miguel Archuleta. En seguida se puso otra en San Francisco, que se puso a cargo de un mexicano llamado Mariano Guerrero. En el pueblo de San José se puso una escuela con un mexicano a su frente llamado Villavicencio; era el Sacristán de la Capilla. Lo relevó Mariano Duarte. Este Duarte era descendte. de india de la misión de San Antonio. Se le acusó de haber desflorado a seis niñas de la escuela; las mismas niñas lo acusaron. Fue llevado preso a San Francisco,

The **berruchi** shoes covered above the ankles and they had buckles on the outer sides.

The wool hats had small crowns and brims, and guard ribbons.

The officer wore the same uniform as the soldier with the difference that his materials were of finer quality. Obviously, they displayed their distinctive insignias and wore the three-corner hat for full dress but, for ordinary use, they wore the same [hat] as the soldier.

In regards to offensive weapons, the officer carried a sword of four or five **cuartas flamengas**, with a steel scabbard, which served as a [walking] cane. In addition, during campaigns, he also carried a dagger, a spear, pistols, and a carbine. The soldiers carried the same weapons.

During my early years there were no schools in California. Hence, no child had the benefit of an institution where he could at least learn to read and write. Our father and mother gave my siblings and me whatever little instruction we had in our own home. Like us, there were others who had the advantage of having parents who knew these subjects and were willing to teach them. My dear mother and some other women who knew reading and writing taught, without charge, some of the boys and girls whose parents did not know, and who came and begged them to perform this benefit. There was a time when my mother had twenty-five children of both sexes as students; some of them were men.

She taught the former reading, writing, and prayers and, to the latter (I saw three soldiers—José Castro, father of the one who became Commander General José Castro, Manuel Briones, and Cornelio Rosales), she taught them reading and writing in San Francisco. After [the soldiers learned these skills], they were promoted to corporals of the plaza (because they were no longer illiterate) in the various companies. It must be noted that there were many illiterate corporals who had the rank of active corporals but could not take roll because they did not know how to read.

When Don José Joaquín Arrillaga became governor, a school was established and funded by the government; Miguel Archuleta, a retired corporal, took charge of it. Soon, another one was established in San Francisco and a Mexican by the name of Mariano Guerrero was put in charge of it. In the town of San José, a school was built and a Mexican by the name of Villavicencio, the sacristan of the church, was chosen to head it. Mariano Duarte succeeded him. This Duarte was a descendant of an Indian woman from Mission San Antonio. He was accused of having deflowered six girls from the school; the same girls made the accusation. He was taken prisoner to San Francisco

encausado y sentenciado a obras públicas. Estuvo rompiendo piedras y barriendo la plaza pública ta. Cuando cumplió su condena, lo pusieron en libertad y murió pronto después. La misma pena le impusieron a Cornelio Rosales por haber violado a una entenada; murió preso, engrillado en el cuerpo de guardia de San Franco., después de más de un año de prisión trabajando en su oficio de sastre.

Los indígenas tenían supersticiones, y algunas de ellas las creían los que no eran indios. Por ejemplo, creían que el tecolote tenía la facultad de manearse los caballos en las noches oscuras, de manera que se quedaban las bestias paradas sin poder andar.

Los indios entendían algo de juegos de manos y brujerías. Estando yo de mayordomo en la misión de San José, había un indio llamado Firmo de la misión de Sta. Clara, que solía ir a la de San José a dar bailes y diabluras a nuestros indios. Cuando él venía nuestros [indios] faltaban al trabajo. El Padre González me encargó que averiguara la causa de esas ausencias. Yo me disfracé y fui al bosque en donde bailaban. Llegué y me introduje entre los indios quienes me conocieron, pero no dijeron nada al hechicero. Este se echó a la boca a la pita y la tragó. Dijo que pronto se saldría una vívora del dedo gordo del pie. Como lo dijo salió. Dos veces se hizo la exhibición y a mi me pareció cosa verdadera porqe. la vi con mis mismos ojos. Concluido el hecho, lo tomé prisionero y lo llevé amarrado a la misión. Se le puso una barra de grillos y se le aplicó un novenario de a 25 azotes para que no volviera a hacer esas diabluras, y que los demás indios escarmentasen.

En Cal. he conocido yo buenos caballos desde mi niñez. Los Californios siempre han sido buenos ginetes y buenos vaqueros, pero no como los mexicanos. Sin embargo, para los rodeos, lazar toros, caballos, y aún osos, los Californios se han distinguido. Nunca se han hecho notables como toreros, ni tampoco han manifestado mayormente gran afición al trabajo. Hablo de los hombres, las mugeres sí han sido siempre muy trabajadoras y de buen gusto.

Los bailes que se bailaban en Cal. cuando yo era joven, eran: jarabe, pontórico, navamba, el cuando, el queso, y otros varios sones que no me acuerdo. Concluía el baile siempre con la jota, o con cuadrillas.

La casa no tenía más piso que el natural. Los dueños de la casa compraban dos tablas, y les ponían 3 burros y las clavaban para ver bailar sones a las mugeres y a algs. hombres que sabían bailar muy bien. Había un tecolero

and, after being prosecuted, he was sentenced to perform public works. He broke rocks and swept the public plaza. After completing his sentence, he was set free and died soon after. The same sentence was given to Cornelio Rosales for having raped a stepdaughter. He died while a prisoner, shackled, in the guards' company of San Francisco after more than a year in prison. While there he worked in his trade as tailor.

The Indians had superstitions, and some of them were believed by those who were not Indian. For example, they believed that owls had the capacity to fetter horses during dark nights in such a way that they became immobile and unable to walk.

The Indians knew a little of games of magic and witchcraft. When I was serving as a foreman at Mission San José, there was an Indian named Firmo of Mission Santa Clara, who tended to go to San José to teach dance and commit devilries on our Indians. When he would come around they would miss work. Father González gave me the responsibility of finding out the cause of their absenteeism. I disguised myself and went to the woods where they were dancing. I arrived and joined the Indians, some of whom recognized me but they did not say anything to the sorcerer. He put a piece of century plant into his mouth and ate it. He said that very soon a snake would come out from the toe of his foot. Just as he said, it came out. The exhibition was performed twice and to me it appeared very real since I saw it with my own eyes. After the event was finished, I took him prisoner, and took him to the mission tied up. He was put in shackles and a novena of twenty-five lashes was applied to him so that he would no longer make these devilries and so that the rest of the Indians would learn a lesson.

In California, I have known good horses since my childhood. The Californios have always been good horsemen and good cowboys, but not like the Mexicans. Yet, the Californios distinguished themselves at rodeos for lassoing bulls, horses, and even bears. They have never been recognized for being bullfighters, nor have they generally demonstrated a great affinity for work. I am speaking of the men; the women have always been very hard working and take pleasure in it.

The dances that were danced in California when I was young were **jarabe**, **pontorico**, **navamba**, **el cuando**, **el queso**, and other **sones** of which I do not remember. The dance would always finish with **la jota** or with **cuadrillas**.

The houses had no floors but the natural ones. The owners of the houses would buy two wooden boards and they would put them on three stands and they would nail [the boards] to them to see the women dance **sones**; they also saw some men who knew how to dance very well. There was a **tecolero**

o bastonero que iba zapateando y echando mudanzas pa. ir a sacar a las señoras. Las sacaba una a una, y algunas veces ponían un hombre y una muger a bailar juntos en las tablas, a ver cuál hacía más mudanzas. Después que cada señora había bailado se volvía a su puesto, y el tecolero sacaba otra. Cuando alga. sobresalía por su habilidad entonces la cubrían de sombreros, y le arrojaban sombreros y pesos duros a los pies, luego cada cual tenía que rescatar su sombrero por 4 reales o 1$ que se le entregaba a la bailadora. Ese baile se llamaba el son, se bailaba al son de harpa, guitarra o violín. Algunas veces, aunqe. muy raras, se cantaban los sones.

El jarabe lo bailaban con compañeros hombres y mugeres, dos, tres, o 4 parejas; haciendo redobles o mudanzas con los pies, a ver cuál hacía más. Junto a la vihuela se sentaban a cantar versos análogos al baile, los que se llamaban cantadores.

La jota, salían 6 parejas que hacían revoluciones, cedazos, mudanzas, y cambios pa. todas partes. Los cantadores estaban en su punto, cantando versos, y algunas veces tomaban parte los mismos bailadores. Cada uno de estos sacaba su compa[ñera]. Entre los muchos cantos que se cantaban, citaré algunos.

> Yo tenía una rata
> con 30 ratones
> Unos sin cabezas
> Y otros cabezones;
> Unos sin colitas
> Y otros muy colones

El estribillo decía:

> Cuando yo era chico
> Bebía chocolate,
> Ahora que soy pobre
> Agua de metate.

Otro:

> Yo me enamoré
> De una melindrosa,
> de nada bonita,

or a **bastonero,** who while tapping his feet and making movements, would take out women to dance. He would take them out one by one and sometimes he would put a man and a woman to dance together on the wooden boards to see which one would make the most movements. After each woman had danced, she would be returned to her place and the **tecolero** would take another one out. When one of the women excelled in her ability, she would be covered with hats, and [people] would toss her hats and peso coins at her feet. Then, everyone had to go and rescue his hat for four **reales** or a peso, which was given to the female dancer. This dance was called a **son** and it was danced with the accompaniment of the harp, guitar, or violin. Sometimes, although very rarely, one could sing the **sones.**

The **jarabe** was danced by men and women as partners—two, three, or four couples. They would make **redobles** or **mudanzas** with their feet to see who would make the most. Persons who were called **cantadores** would sit next to the **vihuela** to sing verses analogous to the dances.

In the **jota,** six couples would make revolutions, **cedazos, mudanzas,** and **cambios** in all directions. The **cantadores** would reach their climax singing verses and sometimes they would be joined by the dancers. Each one of the male dancers would seek out his female partner. I will quote some of the many songs that were sung:

> I had a rat
> With thirty mice
> Some without heads
> And others with very big heads;
> Some without little tails
> And others with very big tails.

The refrain would say:

> When I was a child
> I drank chocolate
> Now that I am poor
> I drink **metate** water

Another verse:

> I fell in love
> with a fuzzy woman
> none too pretty

de nada graciosa.
Tenía un ojo tuerto
Y el otro apagado

Otro:

Vamos arriba, muchachos.
Amarresen bien las botas
Vámonos a Monterey
A comer puras bellotas

Seguía la jota otra vez bailando y cantando.

Seguido, Seguido
Hasta qe. en tus brazos
me quedé dormido.
Si la piedra es dura
tú eres un diamante.
Pues no ha podido
mi amor ablandarte.
Si te hago un cariño
me haces un desprecio
Y luego me dices
Que yo soy el necio,
como si el quererte
fuera necedad,
Pero anda, ingratota,
Que algún día entre sueños
Tú te acordarás que yo fui tu dueño.

Concluían con:

el Ay! Ay! Ay! y más Ay! Parece que llueve y es agua que cae, muchachas
bonitas y dinero no hay.

En los fandangos se cantaban décimas, no me acuerdo de ninguna de ellas.

none too gracious
She was blind in one eye
And the other one was shut

Still another verse:

Awaken, my fellows
Tighten your boots real well
Let's go to Monterey
To eat nothing but acorns

The **jota** would continue again with dancing and singing.

I will follow you, I will follow you
Until in your arms,
I will fall asleep
If the stone is hard,
you are a diamond
Since my love
has not been able to soften you
If I try to caress you,
You snub me
Later you tell me
That I am the stubborn one,
As if loving you
were a necessity,
But, go on, you great ingrate
That one day in your dreams
You will remember that I was your Master

The song would conclude with "Ay! Ay! Ay! Ay! And more Ays!" and then:

It appears that it is raining
And water is falling
So many beautiful girls and there is no money

At **fandangos,** the **décimas** were sung but I do not remember even one of
them.

Se ha dicho que era costumbre que hombres se metieran a caballo en la sala del baile. Esto es verdad hasta cierto punto. Se vio, algs. veces hombres ebrios hacerlo, pero muchas ocasiones salían escarmentados con golpes o heridas.[2]

En mis primeros años había muy poca distinción social. Los oficiales y sus familias, los sargentos, cabos, y soldados y los suyos, así como los pobladores y los suyos, alternaban juntos en las reuniones. Sólo se exigía que fuese gente honrada. Luego gradualmente, según fueron desarrollándose los recursos, aumentando la riquesa, creciendo la población con gentes de fuera, se fueron separando las clases. Con todo aún después de 1840, cuando ya estaban bien separadas las clases, era bastante común ver a un soldado presentarse a la puerta de un baile de alto tono y pedir permiso para bailar un jarabe o un son, y aún se vió a alguna señora de posición salir a bailar con él. Esto al fin cesó. Ya la sociedad de Monterey, San Francisco, y demás poblaciones, no bailaba sino en los bailes de salón que se acostumbran en los países civilizados. Últimamente ya pa. antes de la anexión de Cal. a los Estados Unidos, hasta la clase casi ínfima del pueblo bailaba los mismos bailes que la alta sociedad— valses, contradanzas, cuadrillas ta— habiendo quedado el son, jarabe, y demás bailes de antes relegados al olvido excepto en algunos ranchos. Hoy apenas se ve de eso.

Los niños chicos de ambos sexos jugaban varios juegos como gallina ciega en las noches de luna; daban carreras en las lomas montados en caballos de palo, [jugaban] a rayuela, o maruca en que se hacían apuestas de botones, o reales. Muchas veces se quitaban los botones de la ropa pa. jugarlos. Las niñas también jugaban a las muñecas.

Hablando de la maruca y rayuela, algunos señores copetudos los he visto yo públicamente, y sin pudor, dar el mal ejemplo a la juventud, apostando dinero sobre el tangano o maruca. Se ponían las piezas una sobre otra. El que iba tumbando, iba sacando la parte que le tocaba, y si de un tiro echaba abajo el tangano y quedaba el peso que se tiraba sobre el dinero, todo este era del tirador. Se volvía a empezar otra partida.

---

[2] Es interesante observar que Amador menciona este punto que contradice los comentarios del historiador H. H. Bancroft. Bancroft afirmó que era muy común que los hombres entraran a las pistas de baile montados en sus caballos y era entonces cuando se bajaban de ellos para bailar con sus parejas. Al finalizar el baile, escribó Bancroft, "Los hombres se remontaban en sus caballos y se hiban cabalgando" (*California Pastoral*, 409).

It has been said that it was the custom that the men would ride their horses inside the dance halls. This is true up to a certain point. There were some cases where drunken men would do it but on many occasions they came out punished by being beaten up or wounded.[2]

During the early years there were very few social distinctions. The officers and their families, the sergeants, corporals, and the soldiers and their families as well as civilians and their families would mix together during the social gatherings. The only condition was that they had to be honest people. As people acquired resources and thereby increased their wealth, and with a greater population due to the arrival of people from elsewhere, gradually the classes began to separate themselves. Even after 1840, when the classes were well separated, it was fairly common to see a soldier present himself at the door of an upper class dance and ask permission to dance a **jarabe** or a **son** and it would be possible to see a woman of society dance with him. This finally came to an end. By then, the upper class of Monterey, San Francisco, and the rest of the towns would only dance the dances that were common in the dance halls of civilized nations. A little before California was annexed by the United States, even the less refined class of the people would dance the same dances as the high society—waltzes, **contradanzas**, and also **cuadrillas**—relegating the **son**, **jarabes**, and other [traditional] dances to oblivion, except in some ranches. Today, only rarely do people dance them.

Children of both sexes played various games such as the **gallina ciega** during moonlit nights. The children would race each other on the hills, riding wooden horses. They would play **rayuela** or **maruca** where bets were made of buttons or **reales**. Many times, they would remove buttons from their clothes to bet them. The girls also would play with dolls.

Going back to **maruca** and **rayuela**, I have seen some full grown men publicly and without shame setting a bad example for youth, betting on **tangano** and **maruca**. The pieces would be put one on top of the other. As the player knocked [the pieces] down, he would take possession of the piece that belonged to him, and if in a single shot he managed to bring down the **tangano**, and only the **peso** that was on top of the money remained, all of it belonged to the shooter. A new round would then begin.

---

[2]It is interesting that Amador makes this point, which contradicts H. H. Bancroft. The latter claimed that it was fairly common for the men to ride their horses to the dance areas and only then would they get off their horses to dance with their partners. At the end of the dance, Bancroft noted that they would mount their horses and ride away (*California Pastoral*, 409).

Esto lo he visto yo, con mis mismos ojos, hacer a los S.S. Alvarado, Jesús Vallejo, Anto. Suñol y otros en el corredor de la misión de San José.

En los primeros tiempos cuando yo era joven había la costumbre de acostarse todo el mundo de las 8 a las 9 p.m. inmediatamte. después de cenar, y encerrados, cada joven, varón o muger soltero, dormía en su cuarto bajo llave. Muy temprano se levantaban el padre y la madre, y les abrían las puertas; el padre a los varones, y la madre a las hembras. Si había alga. diversión ésta duraba hasta las 10 o las 11, y entonces se retiraban las familias a sus casas. Según fueron pasando los años las diversiones se fueron haciendo más largas en la noche, notándose ya esto desde 1817 o por esas inmediaciones. Y al fin llegaron a durar toda la noche los bailes.

En 1840 recuerdo un baile en casa de Salvio Pacheco en San José que no sólo duró toda la noche (fue en el casamto. de un hijo mío) sino que a las 9 a.m. del día sigte. se bailaba todavía. Volvió a comenzarse como a las 8 de la noche y siguió hasta el amanecer.

Creo que fue en 1843 que se casó Antonio Amador, mi 3er hijo, en el Agua Caliente y la gente bailó 3 días con sus noches. [Hubo] gasto de vino, aguardte. y comestibles de todas clases, sin límites. Jacinto Rodríguez de Mont., que vive aún, se halló presente.

Rancho de San Andrés, Julio 16 1877
Por orden de mi Señor Padre José Ma. Amador, que está imposibilitado
María Antonia Amador de Rodríguez

The following men I saw, with my very own eyes, playing this game in the corridors of San José: Misters Alvarado, Jesús Vallejo, Antonio Suñol, and others.

In the early days when I was young, it was the custom that a person would go to bed between eight and nine o'clock at night, immediately after dinner. Every youth, whether single male or female, slept in his/her room under lock and key. The father and mother would get up very early to open the doors; the father would do so for the males and the mother for the females. If there was entertainment, it would last until ten or eleven and then the families would retire to their homes. As the years passed, the entertainment events would last much longer into the night; this could already be seen around 1817. Finally, dances came to last all night.

I remember a dance that took place at the house of Salvio Pacheco in San José in 1840 and it not only lasted the entire night (it took place during the wedding of one of my sons) but people were still dancing until nine o'clock in the morning of the following day. The dance started again at eight o'clock that night and continued until dawn.

I believe that it was in 1843 when Antonio Amador, my third son, got married in Agua Caliente [Warm Springs] and people danced for three days and their corresponding nights. Money was spent on wine, **aguardiente,** and food of all kinds without limits. Jacinto Rodríguez of Monterey, who is still alive, was present.

San Andrés Ranch, July 16, 1877
By order of my honorable father José María Amador, who is disabled.
María Antonia Amador de Rodríguez

GLOSSARY

Words defined here are in boldface in the text.

Abajeños   Before the U.S. annexation of California, the people of the southern part of the territory identified themselves as **Abajeños**.

Adarga   A soldier's shield made from cowhide

Agua de lejía   Lye

Aguardiente   Liquor distilled from herbs, flowers, or fruit

Alcalde   A town mayor. However, Thomas Savage uses the same term to refer to the indigenous authorities chosen by the priests as heads of the mission Indians.

Alférez   A second lieutenant or an ensign

Alforja   A saddlebag made from rawhide and used for carrying food or supplies

Almud   A measure of grain and dry fruit, in some places half a **fanega**.

Almuerzo   A main breakfast

Antepasados   A person's ancestors

Arribeños   When California was still a part of the Mexican Republic, the people of the northern part of the territory called themselves **Arribeños.**

Arroba   A Spanish weight measure of 25 pounds.

Asaderas   Small, flat cheese made by beating the curd of the richest milk

Atole   Gruel made by boiling ground corn or wheat

Atole de Pinole   Gruel made by boiling ground corn

Azumbre   A container for liquids equivalent to about two liters

Baño   A type of cloth

Bastonero   Marshall or manager of a ball, steward of a feast

Berruchi   According to H. H. Bancroft, a **berruchi** was a peculiar form of men's shoes that were used by Californios in old times. Possibly the term was also applied to the materials that the shoes were made from.

Borrachitos   Habitual drunkards

Buñuelos   A tortilla-like bread that is fried in cooking oil or lard

Cabrones   Men who consent to the adultery of their wives

Cambios   A dance movement

Cantadores   Singers

Cardenillo   Verdigris

Catecúmeno   A newly arrived individual who is being instructed in the doctrine and mysteries of the Catholic faith with the objective of receiving baptism

Cedazos   A dance movement

Chamisal   A thicket of chamiso, a densely growing shrub

Chinela de coletilla   A locally made shoe, probably a sandal

Compadres   Godfather and Godmother. The word by which the godfather and godmother address the father and mother of their godson or goddaughter and by which the father and mother address them

Compañeros   While the word means "companion" in English, Lorenzo Asisara used it to refer to a man's testicles.

Contador   Accountant

Contradanza   Square dancing or country dancing

Cortes   Parliament

Coyote	A person who has three-fourths Indian blood and one-fourth European
Criollo	An individual who was supposedly of pure Spanish blood born in the New World
Cuadrillas	Dance performed by four couples
Cuarta	A measurement the width of an open hand
Cuartas Flamengas	Length sizes for Spanish swords
Cuartos	A type of measurement. One **cuarto** probably equaled the length of a man's hand.
Curandera	A traditional female folk healer
Décima	A Spanish stanza consisting of ten verses of eight syllables
Desayuno	A light breakfast
Ermita	Probably a type of military drill
Fandango	A lively Spanish dance, festive entertainment
Fanega	A measurement equaling 55½ liters or 1½ bushels
Gañan	A day worker
Gallina Ciega	Blind man's bluff or hood man's blind
Gente de Razón	The word means " people possessing reason." While in New Spain the term generally described someone of pure Spanish blood, in California it was given to anyone who was not indigenous.
Gerga or **jerga**	A coarse cloth
Gobernador	Governor
Jarabe	On the American continent, a popular dance consisting of hand clapping and tapping
Jarazo	A cistus or rock rose labdanum tree
Jayunte	According to H. H. Bancroft, **Jayunte** is the vulgarization of **Ayunte.** Ayunte was the act of assembling

	indigenous grown-up boys or men. It also referred to their quarters in the mission.
Jerga or **gerga**	A coarse cloth
Jota	A Spanish folk dance
Ladroncitos	Petty thieves
Llavero	Keeper of the keys
Licenciado	A title given to lawyers
Manta	Course white cotton cloth
Maruca	Hob, a game among boys, using bone or stone
Mestizo	An individual of mixed indigenous/Spanish background
Metate	A curbed stone, in the shape of an inclined plane, resting on three feet, used for grinding maize for tortillas or cacao for chocolate
Migas	Crumbs of bread or tortillas fried in a pan, with lard, salt, and pepper
Milpas	Farm fields
Morisco	A person of Mulato and Spanish ancestry. A person who is lighter than a **Pardo**.
Mudanza	A certain number of motions in a dance
Mulatto	An individual of mixed African/Spanish background
Panocha	Ungranulated brown sugar
Paño	A woolen cloth
Pardo	A person of Indigenous/African/European extraction.
Patria Chica	A person's native homeland
Pelado	In Mexico, a poorly educated rascal who lacks manners
Pesos	Money used in California when under Mexican and Spanish rule. Symbol is the same as for dollars.

Peón	Usually it refers to a field worker but in this case it is a game of hidden objects
Pinole	Parched corn, ground and mixed with sugar
Pita de Inmortal	A plant with thorns and yellowish flowers, probably a type of maguey plant.
Pontivil	A type of fabric
Pontorico	A traditional dance
Pozole	Boiled barley and beans
Presidio	A frontier military garrison. In addition to the military structure, it also included the civilian settlement that was built around it.
Prest.	The daily wage of a soldier. Probably abbreviation for either préstamo or prestación.
Pretina	A waistband
Provincia	Province
Rancherías	The name that the Spaniards used for the traditional settlements of indigenous peoples in New Spain
Ranchero	A horseman
Rayuela	Hopscotch
Reales	Spanish coins weighing an ounce of silver each
Rebozo	A Mexican shawl
Redobles	Redoublings
Saca	The alcohol content in **aguardiente**
Saya Saya	Chinese Silk
Señor/ Sr.	Mister
Síndico	A member of the town council
Socorría	The word orignates from **socorrer,** which means "to aid" or "to help."

Soldaditos	Little soldiers. Lorenzo Asisara used the this term in a denigrating way to suggest that these individuals were ill-fit to be soldiers.
Soldado de Cuera	Presidio soldier who used a multi-layered leather coat for protection when campaigning against Indians.
Sones	In Mexico and Central America, a generic name for a variety of popular dances that reflect the cultural mixture of these regions.
Sub-comisario	Sub-commisioner
Tangano	The Anglo-American game of ducks and drakes.
Tapojo	Probably a flower of some sort, possibly cactus flowers
Tecolero	The master of ceremonies during a dance. H. H. Bancroft notes that he would often invite women to dance.
Temascal	A sweat lodge used by the indigenous peoples of California
Tequio	A labor system of Meso-America that required that individuals perform work for the community. In California, mission priests assigned specific chores to individuals under this system.
Tercerola	A medium-sized barrel
Tercios	Half a load
Troje	A brick container for storing fruit or grains. H. H. Bancoft, however, claims that **trojes** were also granaries.
Tulareños	The indigenous people who resided in what is now Tulare County
Untos	Cattle fat used for making soap and lard
Valcarra	A type of man's sideburns
Vallados	A fence that consisted of a mound and a trench adjacent to it. Workers would dig the trench and deposit the soil on one side to make a mound. On the

mound, **magueys**, cactus, **piñuelas**, blackberry vines or other thorny plants would be grown.

Vara   A distance measurement equalling .836 meters

Vecinos   Civilian residents of the towns

Vihuela   A type of Spanish guitar

Zanjón   Ravine

BIBLIOGRAPHY

Archives

San José Historical Museum, Pueblo Archives, San Jose, California
The Bancroft Library, University of California: Berkeley, California
Amador County Historical Archives, Jackson, California

Primary and Secondary Sources
Diaries, Autobiographies, Books, and Dissertations

Almaguer, Tomás. *Racial Fault Lines: The Historical Origins of White Supremacy in California.* Berkeley: University of California Press, 1994.

Arbuckle, Clyde. *History of San Jose.* San Jose: Memorabilia of San Jose, 1986.

Archibald, Robert. *The Economic Aspects of the California Missions.* Washington, DC: Academy of American Franciscan History, 1978.

Argüello, Luis Antonio. *The Diary of Captain Luis Argüello, October 17–November 17, 1821: The Last Spanish Expedition in California.* Berkeley: Friends of The Bancroft Library, University of California, 1992.

Bancroft, Hubert Howe. *History of Californa.* 7 vols. Santa Barbara, CA: Wallace Hebberd, 1963.

Bancroft, Hubert Howe. *California Pastoral.* San Francisco: The History Company, 1888.

Bannon, John Francis. *The Spanish Borderlands Frontier, 1513–1821.* New York: Holt, Rinehart and Winston, 1970.

Barrera, Mario. *Race and Class in the Southwest: A Theory of Racial Inequality.* South Bend, IN: University of Notre Dame Press, 1979.

Barrios de Chungara, Domitila. *Let Me Speak.* Translated by Victoria Ortiz. New York: Monthly Review Press, 1978.

Beebe, Rose Marie, and Robert M. Senkewicz. *The History of Alta California: A Memoir of Mexican California by Antonio María Osio*. Madison: The University of Wisconsin Press, 1996.

Beilharz, Edwin. *San Jose: California's First City*. Tulsa: Continental Heritage Press, 1980.

Botello, Arthur R. *Don Pio Pico's Historical Narrative*. Glendale: The Arthur Clark Co, 1973.

Bouvier, Virginia M. *Women in the Conquest of California: Code of Silence, 1542–1840*. Tucson: University of Arizona Press, 2001.

Browning, Peter, ed. *The Discovery of San Francisco Bay: The Portolá Expedition of 1769–1770*. Lafayette, CA: Great West Books, 1992.

Bryant, Edwin. *What I Saw in California; Being the Journal of a Tour in the Years 1846–1847*. New York: D. Appleton and Company, 1848.

Castañeda, Antonia I. "Presidarias y Pobladoras: Spanish/Mexican Women in Frontier Monterey, Alta California, 1770–1821." Ph.D. Diss., Stanford University, 1990.

Caughey, John Watson. *Hubert Howe Bancroft: Historian of the West*. Berkeley: University of California Press, 1946.

Chapman, Charles Edward. *The Founding of Spanish California: The Northward Expansion of New Spain, 1687–1783*. New York: Macmillan Co., 1916.

Coetzee, J. M. *White Writing: On the Culture of Letters in South Africa*. New Haven, CT: Yale University Press, 1988.

Cook, Sherburne F. *Expedition to the Interior of California, Central Valley: 1820–1840*. Berkeley: University of California Press, 1961.

Costo, Rupert and Jeanette Henry Costo, eds. *The Missions of California: A Legacy of Genocide*. San Francisco: Indian Historical Press, 1987.

Cowan, Robert G. *Ranchos of California: A List of Spanish Ranchos, 1775–1822, and Mexican Grants, 1882–1846*. San Bernardino, CA: The Borgo Press, 1985.

Cutter, Donald C. *Malespina in California*. San Francisco: John Howell Books, 1961.

———. *California in 1792: A Spanish Naval Visit*. Norman: University of Oklahoma Press, 1990.

Czarmosky, Lucille K. *Dances of Early California Days*. Palo Alto, CA: Pacific Books, 1950.

Dana, Richard Henry. *Two Years Before the Mast*. New York: New American Library, 1964.

Davis, William Heath. *Seventy-Five Years in California, 1831–1906*. Chicago: R.R. Donnelley & Sons Co., 1929.

Delgado. James P. *Witness to Empire: The Life of Antonio María Suñol*. San José: Sourisseau Academy for California State and Local History, 1977.

Deu Pree Nelson, Edna. *The California Dons*. New York: Apple-Century-Crofts, Inc. 1962.

Emparán, Madie Brown. *The Vallejos of California*. San Francisco: Gleeson Library Associates, University of San Francisco, 1968.

Eversole, Robert Wayne. "Towns in Mexican Alta California: A Social History of Monterey, San José, Santa Bárbara, and Los Angeles." Ph.D. Diss., University of California, San Diego, 1986.

Forbes, Alexander. *California: A History of Upper and Lower California from their Discovery to the Present Time*. London: Smith, Elder, and Co., 1839.

Francis, Jessie Davis. *An Economic and Social History of Mexican California, 1822–1846*. New York: Arno Press, 1976.

Figueroa, José. *Manifesto to the Mexican Republic*. Translated and edited by C. Alan Hutchinson. Berkeley: University of California Press, 1978.

Geiger, Maynard, O.F.M. *Franciscan Missionaries in Hispanic California, 1769–1848: A Bibliographical Dictionary*. San Marino, Calif.: Huntington Library, 1969.

Geiger, Maynard, O.F.M. Ed. and Trans. *As the Padres Saw Them: California Indian Life and Customs as Reported by the Franciscan Missionaries*. Santa Barbara: Santa Barbara Mission Archives Library, 1976.

Griswold del Castillo, Richard. *The Treaty of Guadalupe Hidalgo: A Legacy of Conflict*. Norman: University of Oklahoma Press, 1990.

Harlow, Neal. *California Conquered: War and Peace in the Pacific, 1846–1850*. Berkeley: University of California Press, 1982.

Hass, Lisbeth. *Conquest and Historical Identities in California, 1769–1936*. Berkeley: University of California Press, 1995.

Heizer, Robert F. and Alan J. Almquist. *The Other Californians: Prejudice and Discrimination Under Spain, Mexico and the United States to 1920*. Berkeley: University of California, 1971.

Hurtado, Albert L. *Indian Survival on the California Frontier*. New Haven, CT: Yale University Press, 1988.

————. *Intimate Frontiers: Sex, Gender, and Culture in Old California*. Albuquerque: University of New Mexico, 1999.

Hutchinson, C. Alan. *Frontier Settlement in Mexican California: The Híjar-Padrés Colony and Its Origins*. New Haven, CT: Yale University Press, 1969.

Jackson, Robert H. and Edward Castillo. *Indians, Franciscans and Spanish Colonization: The Impact of the Mission System on California Indians*. Albuquerque: University of New Mexico Press, 1995.

Janssens, Victor Eugene August. *The Life and Adventures in California of Don Agustín Janssens, 1834–1856*. Edited by William H. Ellison and Francis Price. San Marino, CA: Huntington Library, 1953.

Kotzebue, Otto von. *A New Voyage Round the World in the Years 1823, 1824, 1825, and 1826*. 2 vols. London: Henry Colburn and Richard Bentley, 1830.

Langum, David J. *Law and Community on the Mexican Frontier: Anglo American Expatriates and the Clash of Legal Traditions, 1821–1846*. London and Norman: University of Oklahoma, 1987.

Lockhart, Katharine Meyer. "A Demographic Profile of an Alta California Pueblo: San José de Guadalupe, 1777-1850." Ph.D. Diss. University of Colorado, 1986.

MacLachlan, Colin M. and Jaime E. Rodríguez O. *The Forging of the Cosmic Race: A Reinterpreation of Colonial Mexico*. Berkeley: University of California Press, 1980.

Margolin, Malcolm. *The Ohlone Way: Indian Life in the San Francisco-Monterey Bay Area*. Berkeley: Heyday Books, 1978.

Menchaca, Martha. *Recovering History, Constructing Race: The Indian, Black, and White Roots of Mexican Americans*. Austin: University of Texas Press, 2001.

Menchú, Rigoberta. *I, Rigoberta Menchú: An Indian Woman in Guatemala*. Edited and translated by Elisabeth Burgos-Debray. London: Verso, 1984.

Milliken, Randall. *A Time of Little Choice: The Disintegration of Tribal Culture in the San Francisco Bay Area*, 1760–1810. Menlo Park, CA: Ballena Press, 1995.

Mollins, Margaret and Virginia E. Thickens, eds. *Ramblings in California: The Adventures of Henry Cerruti*. Berkeley: Friends of the Bancroft Library, 1954.

Monroy, Douglas. *Thrown Among Strangers: The Making of Mexican Culture in Frontier California*. Berkeley and Los Angeles: University of California Press, 1990.

Moorhead, Max. *The Presidio: Bastion of the Spanish Borderlands*. Norman: University of Oklahoma Press, 1975.

Ord, Angustias de la Guerra. *Occurrences in Hispanic California*. Washington: Academy of American Franciscan History, 1956.

Osio, Antonio María. *The History of Alta California: A Memoir of Mexican California*. Madison: University of Wisconsin Press, 1996.

Padilla, Genaro M. *My History, Not Yours: the Formation of Mexican American Autobiography*. Madison: The University of Wisconsin Press, 1993.

Pérouse, Jean François de la. *Monterey in 1786: Life in a California Mission*. Berkeley: Heyday Books, 1989.

Pitt, Leonard. *The Decline of the Californios: A Social History of Spanish-Speaking Californians, 1846–1890*. Berkeley: University of California Press, 1966.

Pitti, Stephen J. *The Devil in Silicon Valley: Northern California, Race, and Mexican Americans*. Princeton and Oxford: Princeton University Press, 2003.

Poniatowska, Elena. *Here's to You, Jesusa*. Translated by Deanna Huikkinen. New York: Penguin Books, 2002.

Pratt, Mary Louise. *Imperial Eyes: Travel Writing and Transculturation*. New York: Routledge, 1992.

Priestly, Herbert. *A Historical, Political, and Natural Description of California by Pedro Fages, Soldier of Spain*. Berkeley: University of California, 1937.

Revere, Joseph Warren. *A Tour of Duty in California Including a Description of the Gold Region and an Account of the Voyage around Cape Horn*. New York: CCS Francis and Company, 1849.

Richman, Irving B. *California Under Spain and Mexico, 1535–1847.* Boston: Houghton Mifflin, 1911.

Robinson, Alfred. *Life in California: During a Residency of Several Years in that Territory.* Santa Barbara: Peregrine Publishers, 1970.

Robinson, Cecil. *Mexico and the Hispanic Southwest in American Literature.* Tucson: University of Arizona Press, 1977.

Rosenus, Alan. *General M. G. Vallejo and the Advent of the Americans.* Albuquerque: University of New Mexico Press, 1995.

Ruiz de Burton, María Amparo. *The Squatter and the Don.* Edited by Rosaura Sánchez and Beatrice Pita. Houston: Arte Público, 1993.

Taylor, Bayard. *El Dorado or Adventures in the Path of Empire.* New York: G.P. Putnam, 1859.

Tays, George. "Revolutionary California: The Political History of California During the Mexican Period, 1822–1846." Ph. D Diss., University of California, Berkeley, 1932.

Sawyer, Eugene Taylor. *History of Santa Clara County, California.* Los Angeles: Historical Record Co., 1922.

Saldívar, Ramón. *Chicano Narrative: The Dialectics of Difference.* Madison: University of Wisconsin Press, 1990.

Sánchez, Rosaura. *Telling Identities: The Californio Testimonios.* Minneapolis: University of Minnesota Press, 1995.

Weber, David J. *The Mexican Frontier, 1821–1846: The American Southwest under Mexico.* Albuquerque: University of New Mexico Press, 1982.

Weber, David J. *The Spanish Frontier in North America.* New Haven, CT: Yale University Press, 1992.

Wilbur, Margaret Eyer, ed. *Vancouver in California: The Original Account of George Vancouver.* Los Angeles: Dawson's Book Shop, 1954.

Articles

Archibald, Robert. "Indian Labor at the California Missions: Slavery or Salvation?" *Journal of San Diego History* 24 (Spring 1978):172–82.

Blackburn, Thomas. "The Chumash Revolt of 1824." *Journal of California Anthropology* 22 (1975): 223–24.

Bowman, J.N. "The Resident Neophytes of the California Missions, 1769–1834." *Historical Society of Southern California Quarterly* 40, No. 2 (1958): 138–48.

Brown, Madie E. "General M. G. Vallejo and H. H. Bancroft." *California Historical Society Quarterly* 29 (1950): 150–61.

Burgess, Sherwood. "Pirate or Patriot? Hypolite Bouchard and the Invasion of California." *American West* 11, No. 6 (1974): 40–47.

Burrus, Ernest J. "Rivera and Moncada, Explorer and Military Commander of Both Californias, in Light of his Diary and other Contemporary Documents." *Hispanic American Historical Review* 50 (November 1970): 682–92.

Campbell, Leon. "The First Californios: Presidial Society in Spanish California, 1769–1822." *Journal of the West* 11 (October 1972): 583–95.

―――. "The Spanish Presidio in Alta California during the Mission Period, 1769–1784." *Journal of the West* 16 (October 1977): 63–77.

Castillo, Edward D. "The Assassination of Padre Andrés Quintana by the Indians of Mission Santa Cruz in 1812: The Narrative of Lorenzo Asisara." *California History* 68, No. 3 (1989–90): 116–25.

Cook, Sherburne F. "Small Pox in Spanish and Mexican California, 1770–1845." *Bulletin of the History of Medicine* 12 (February 1939): 184–87.

Delgado, James P. "Juan Pablo Bernal: California Pioneer." *Pacific Historian* 23 (Fall 1979): 50–62.

Engstrand, Iris H. W. "Seekers of the 'Northern Mystery': European Exploration California and the Pacific." *California History* 78 (Summer–Fall 1997): 78–110.

Forbes, Jack D. "Hispano-Mexican Pioneers of the San Francisco Clara Bay Region: an Analysis of Racial Origins." *Aztlan* 14, No. 1 (1983): 175–89.

Galindo, Nazario. "Early Days at Mission Santa Clara: Recollections of Nazario Galindo." *California Historical Society Quarterly* 38 (June 1959): 101–11.

Garr, Daniel J. "A Frontier Agrarian Settlement: San José de Guadalupe, 1777–1850." *San José Studies* 2 (November 1976): 93–105.

Guest, Francis F. "Municipal Government in Spanish California." *California Historical Society Quarterly* 46 (1967): 307–335.

Guest, Francis F. "An Inquiry into the Role of the Discipline in California Misssion Life." *Southern California Quarterly* 62, No. 1 (1980): 1–68.

Guest, Francis F. "Cultural Perspective on California Mission Life." *Southern California Quarterly* 65, No. 1 (1983): 1–77.

Hackel, Steven W. "Land, Labor, and Production: The Colonial Economy of Spanish and Mexican California." *California History* 78 (Summer–Fall, 1997): 111–46.

Halpin, Joseph. "Musical Activities and Ceremonies at Mission Santa Clara de Asís." *California Historical Society Quarterly* 50 (1971): 35–42.

Hornbeck, Davis. "Land Tenure and Rancho Expansion in Alta California, 1784–1846." *Journal of Historical Geography* 4 (December 1978): 371–90.

Hutchinson, C. Alan. "An Official List of the Members of the Híjar-Padrés Colony for Mexican California, 1834." *Pacific Historical Review* 42 (1973): 407–18.

Messner, Elizabeth Eve. "California's First Civil Settlement: The Early Years of the Pueblo of San Jose." *Historias* (Local History Studies, California History Center) 20 (1976).

Monroy, Douglas. "The Creation and Recreation of Californio Society." *California History* (Summer/Fall 1997): 173–195.

Moorhead, Max. "The Private Contract System of Presidial Supply in Northern New Spain." *Hispanic American Historical Review* 91 (February 1961): 31–54.

Moorhead, Max. "The Soldado de Cuera: Stalwart of the Spanish Borderlands." *Journal of the West* 8 (January 1969): 38–55.

Neri, Michael C. "Narciso Durán and the Secularization of the California Missions." *The Americas* 33, No. 3 (1976–77): 411–29.

Padilla, Genaro. "The Recovery of Chicano Nineteenth Century Autobiography." *American Quarterly* 40, No. 3 (Fall 1988): 286–306.

Servín, Manuel Patricio. "The Secularization of the California Missions: A Reappraisal." *Southern California Quarterly* 47 (June 1965): 133–50.

Shipek, Florence C. "California Indian Reaction to the Franciscans." *The Americas* 45 (April 1985): 480–93.

Simmons, William S. "Indian Peoples of California." *California History* 78 (Summer–Fall 1997): 48–77.

Taylor, George. "Spanish-Russian Rivalry in the Pacific." *The Americas* 15 (October 1958): 109–28.

Whitehead, Richard S. "Alta California's Four Fortresses." *Southern California Quarterly* 65 (Spring 1983): 67–94.

Winther, Oscar. "The Story of San Jose, 1777–1869: California's First Pueblo." *California Historical Society Quarterly* 14 (1935): 2–27.

INDEX

Words in **boldface** are defined in Glossary.

Meza, Jesús, 95
Micheltorena, Manuel, 171, 173, 175, 177, 179, 181
migas, 143
Miller and Lux, 26
milpas, 219
Miranda, Hilario, 35
Miranda, Juan, 47
Missions (see California Missions)
Mollins, Margaret, 3
Montenegro, Eugenio, 131, 163
Monterey, 2 4 31 39 41 69 71 73 7S 91 113 115 119 131 137 139 147 159 161, 163, 167, 169, 173, 175, 177, 179, 181, 183, 185, 187, 201, 233, 235, 237
Montgomery, John, 1 87
Moquelemne Indians, 59, 63, 97
Moquelemnes, 45
Moraga, Gabriel, 43, 45, 49, 51, 71
Moraga, Guadalupe, 147
Moraga, Joaquín, 147
Moreno, Father Juan, 129, 129n8
Mormon Camp, 195, 197
Morris, Leo, 25
Mount Diablo, 193
Mount Gavilán, 185
mulatto, 11, 12, 14, 14n10
My History, Not Yours (Genaro Padilla), 6

N

Napa, California, 69
National Government, 165, 169
Navarrette, José, 47
Neve, Felipe de, 35
Noreña, Antonio, 205
Noriega, José, i 1
Noriega, María Ramona, 31

O

Olbes, Father Ramôn, 19, 93, 93n5, 95, 119, 121, 123, 125, 127

Oregon, 13, 141, 185
Ortega Ranch, 75

P

Pacheco, Bartolo, 63
Pacheco, Ignacio, 67
Pacheco, Lorenzo, 20, 67
Pacheco, Miguel, 63
Pacheco, Pablo, 43
Pacheco, Romualdo, 159, 159n18
Pacheco, Salvio, 237
Padilia, Genaro M., 6, 7, 22
Padres, José María, 161, 163, 165
Palancares, Jesusa, *S*
Palomares, Francisco, 57
panocha, 87, 91, 143
paño, 145
Pasión River, 45
Patria Chica, 8
pelado, 133, 135
Peña, Manuel, 67
peón (a game), 127
Peralta, Francisco, 3, 4
Peralta, Ignacio, 20
Peralta, Luis, *63,* 201, *203*
Permanent Fixed Battalion of the Californias, 173
Peru, 22
Pieo, Francisco, 20
Pico, Pío, 21, 181, 181n32, 183, 187, 189
pinole, 59, 143, 197
Pinto, Marcelo, 17
Pita de inmortal, 49
Pocahontas (frigate), 159
Poniatowska, Elena, 5
Portolá, Gaspar de, 14, 31
pozole, 205
Prado Meza, Jesús (Second Lieutenant), 53, 55, 59, 61, 63, 95
Pradon, Victor, 185
Pratt, Mary Louise, 2, 5, 6, 9, 10

CPSIA information can be obtained at www.ICGtesting.com
Printed in the USA
BVOW082236120713

325725BV00002B/5/P

9 781574 414387